SHAKESPEARE SURVEY

SHAKESPEARE SURVEY

AN ANNUAL SURVEY OF
SHAKESPEARIAN STUDY & PRODUCTION

20

EDITED BY
KENNETH MUIR

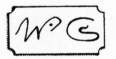

CAMBRIDGE
AT THE UNIVERSITY PRESS
1967

Published by the Syndics of the Cambridge University Press
Bentley House, 200 Euston Road, London, N.W. 1
American Branch: 32 East 57th Street, New York, N.Y. 10022

Shakespeare Survey was first published in 1948. For the
first eighteen volumes it was edited by Allardyce Nicoll
under the sponsorship of the University of Birmingham,
the University of Manchester, the Royal Shakespeare
Theatre and the Shakespeare Birthplace Trust.

Printed in Great Britain
at the University Printing House, Cambridge
(Brooke Crutchley, University Printer)

EDITOR'S NOTE

The first four articles in this volume were delivered as lectures at the Twelfth International Shakespeare Conference at Stratford-upon-Avon in September 1966. The theme of the conference was 'Shakespearian and Other Tragedy'.

As already announced, *Shakespeare Survey 21* will contain a number of articles on *Othello*. No. 22 will be a miscellaneous volume. Contributions, which should not normally exceed 5000 words, should reach the Editor (Department of English Literature, The University, Liverpool 3) by 1 September 1968.

K. M.

CONTRIBUTORS

NIGEL ALEXANDER, *Lecturer in English, University of Glasgow*

BARBARA HELIODORA C. DE M. F. DE ALMEIDA, *Brazil*

MARY BELL, *Lecturer in English, University of Lancaster*

RONALD BERMAN, *Professor of English, University of California, San Diego*

ALEXANDRU DUŢU, *Romania*

GARETH LLOYD EVANS, *Senior Lecturer and Staff Tutor in Literature, Extra-Mural Department, University of Birmingham*

ROBERT HAPGOOD, *Professor of English, University of New Hampshire*

G. R. HIBBARD, *Reader in English, University of Nottingham*

G. K. HUNTER, *Professor of English, University of Warwick*

MARCO MINCOFF, *Professor of English, University of Sofia*

SYBIL ROSENFELD, *Joint Editor of 'Theatre Notebook'*

NORMAN SANDERS, *Professor of English, University of Tennessee*

JOHN SHAW, *Professor of English, Hiram College, Ohio*

ARTHUR COLBY SPRAGUE, *Emeritus Professor of English, Bryn Mawr College*

OSCAR M. VILLAREJO, *Professor of Spanish, Georgetown University, Washington, D.C.*

J. K. WALTON, *Lecturer in English, Trinity College, Dublin*

ROBERT WEIMANN, *Professor of English, Humboldt University, Berlin*

STANLEY WELLS, *Lecturer in English and Fellow of the Shakespeare Institute, University of Birmingham*

CONTENTS

[Notes are placed at the end of each contribution, except in the Reviews section]

LIST OF PLATES

LIST OF PLATES

SHAKESPEARE, FLETCHER AND BAROQUE TRAGEDY

BY

MARCO MINCOFF

The supremacy of Shakespearian tragedy is no doubt unchallenged and unchallengeable, though it may be that its superiority to other types lies more in the man than in the actual type, and that if the type had been represented only by Marlowe, Chapman and the rest its position would be less assured. The purpose of this paper, however, is not to discuss questions of value, though I believe that the later seventeenth-century type of tragedy, which begins with Fletcher and in England reaches its fullest growth with Dryden, suffers rather unfairly in critical opinion from being regarded, especially in its earlier stages, too much as a degenerate descendant of a great model rather than an attempt to evolve something answering to the needs of a different age, with a different vision and climate of opinion. The paper is much more an attempt to point out some of the more essential differences between the two types which may help us to see better where Shakespeare's strength does chiefly lie.[1] It may seem strange that I should choose to demonstrate the later type mainly on Fletcher, who after all has only two not very outstanding tragedies to his name—for I do not believe that he had much to do with the planning of the Beaumont tragedies. But most of what I say applies to his tragi-comedies too. And for me the peculiar interest of Fletcher lies in the fact that he does represent the gateway to seventeenth-century tragedy, or what I should call the Baroque type in its essentials and without the neo-classical accidentals that loom so large with Dryden and his fellows, as also with the French classicists.

Perhaps the most obvious difference between the two types lies in the kind of conflict at the centre. The Shakespearian conflict is, I should say, essentially individual, a war within the state of man himself, in which the hero's personality is torn apart and may even disintegrate before our very eyes. Hamlet is racked between an intense desire for revenge—it is with him desire, not mere obedience to a distasteful duty—and the inhibiting 'vicious mole of nature', the melancholy in the Elizabethan sense, induced by disillusionment, not originally a part of him but the 'O'ergrowth of some complexion' that has become second nature. Othello in the same way is rent asunder between his love and a jealousy which again is not a part of his true nature but implanted in him by what I think we must accept as overwhelming proof of his wife's unfaithfulness. Lear's anger differs from the disintegrating force of the other two in that it has always existed in him as a germ capable of growth, which had no cause to spread and break down the pales and forts of reason as long as there was no one to thwart his will. And perhaps it is for that reason, because the disintegrating force really is a part of his nature from the first, that Lear is the one Shakespearian hero who does not merely win back to himself but undergoes a regeneration. While Macbeth on the contrary is slowly but inexorably swallowed up by the disintegrating sense of his crime. In this point Shakespearian tragedy actually seems to be unique, and differs from Elizabethan or Jacobean. For with his contemporaries it is only the last kind of disintegration through progressive moral blindness that is sometimes shown, above all with Middleton. And that is the least dramatic kind, for except with Macbeth at the first, and only at the first, there is no real struggle; and also it is the least completely tragic, for it is lacking in the sense of exaltation, or at least relief, that the reassertion of the true man brings us. Shakespeare, it is true, gives us something of that effect even with Macbeth, though he accords him no such final eulogy as he does his other heroes. Middleton's figures die in a huddle without even such a partial reassertion of their better selves as Macbeth achieves.

This intensely personal conflict is practically timeless, and that no doubt is a large part of the reason for Shakespeare's perennial appeal. We do not, with him, need to adjust ourselves so sharply to other ways of thought and other moral assumptions as we do with other tragedians. But though its appeal is universal, I believe that the conflict itself could only be conceived at a very peculiar juncture in the development of human culture. A stronger religious pull, and the concept of man's independence becomes impossible; a further slackening of that pull, and man is revealed as bound by social ties instead. Not that I wish to suggest that with Shakespeare man is free from either of these ties, rather that the two pulls are so equally adjusted that they cancel out, and the stress can fall on man himself as at no other time.

Scarcely a generation after Shakespeare, tragedy all over Europe, and not only in England, is dominated by what is mostly summed up as the love-and-honour conflict. It too is an internal conflict, and in so far one might say it shows an increase in psychological depth on the greater part of Elizabethan tragedy outside Shakespeare, where, although internal conflict is not entirely lacking, the main dramatic tension is more often external. To us this new conflict seems frigid and conventional—partly because the peculiar concept of honour leaves us cold, partly too because by constant repetition it has lost its savour. Actually neither of Fletcher's tragedies centres on a real love-and-honour conflict; but that conflict is only the most typical expression of the more general conflict of passion with a social code, or even two opposing codes, which does lie at the bottom of *Valentinian*. Maximus, like Hamlet, is eager for revenge. And like Hamlet he is held back by something within himself. But that something lies very much more on the surface of his being—it is in part the political code of loyalty to the sovereign, which, however, in his case presents no very serious obstacle so that it can be debated externally between him and his friend Aëcius; on the other hand it is the necessity to get rid of that friend as a preliminary to the vengeance itself—an unpleasant task and involving a secondary conflict, but again not two parts of his very being. Thus he can, and he does, debate the question within himself. And the soliloquy in which he does so is in its way a fine piece of work, as he sways this way and that, and first one consideration brings a decision, which is at once revoked by another. And that tremulous line, in which the slightest motion of the mind may tip the balance, was to become extremely characteristic of the seventeenth century. Racine, in *Bérénice* in particular, was to extend it throughout the whole length of his play; and so also Dryden, rather more crudely, in *All for Love*. Here, no less than in the type of conflict, Fletcher was heralding the new type of tragedy. Indeed at this point the two things may seem almost identical. But the precarious balance makes itself felt as a structural principle in other ways, not only in internal debate.

Hamlet has nothing that he can debate. One part of him cries for revenge at any price, another refuses to convert will into action; he cannot even come to grips with his problem, let alone debate it with reason as the arbiter. Actually Maximus in his indecision is closer to Mac-

2

beth than to Hamlet, and here too the contrast is instructive. Macbeth also does not debate—he piles up all the reasons against his act, but the impulse towards it is too great to need statement at all, and we feel that the more he brings against it the more he commits himself. One can hardly say that either method of presentation is intrinsically better. Undoubtedly Shakespeare captures our imagination and Fletcher does not, but that is presumably a question of poetic power, not of the dramatic concept. Probably Fletcher's method, even though the form is somewhat simplified, does come closer to the way we actually reach our decisions—at least it is a serious attempt to present a psychological process.

The chief reason for the popularity of the new type of conflict was, however, moral rather than psychological, one would say. As religion began to lose its hold more and more, as the new scientific discoveries of Kepler and Copernicus began to push through into the general consciousness of the educated—and that was a very slow process—as the spirit of rationalism asserted itself, the necessity for new moral sanctions was beginning to make itself felt. Religion had probably never had a very strong hold on the upper crust, though it was perhaps stronger in England than in many parts of the continent. But even in England, and under Elizabeth, there were already men like Raleigh and his circle, suspected of downright atheism, and who, even if their own ideas perhaps went no further than a mild form of deism, tolerated an actual atheist among them. At least the idea of a God directly concerned in every private sin and peccadillo was becoming less and less easy to accept imaginatively, and for the aristocracy the sense of noblesse oblige was probably, and long had been, especially on the continent, quite as important a moral deterrent as the fear of offending God. As the theatre became more and more a form of upper-class entertainment, the concept of morality as a social rather than a religious obligation imposed itself. One can see the attitude drawing nourishment from the most various roots. Chapman and Jonson with their stress on Roman virtue contributed something. So did Italian tragi-comedy. And the *Astrée* with its ineffable codes of behaviour even more. Fletcher himself was saturated in D'Urfé's work, which had taken western Europe by storm. The story of *Valentinian* was taken from there, though Fletcher had recourse to a French translation of Procopius as well; so was the sub-plot of *Monsieur Thomas*, while *The Mad Lover* is a tissue of motifs and situations from the *Astrée*. And the conflict between honour and loyalty that looms so large in Fletcher's treatment of *Valentinian* was already developed by D'Urfé, though less centrally. Equally, when his Lucina dies because she cannot bear the thought of what people may say of her should she survive, she dies differently from D'Urfé's heroine, but quite in accord with the general tenor of his work. To us the morality may seem narrow and pusillanimous; but after all, the duty of setting an example to others, which is at the back of Lucina's misgivings, and which also tips the scales for Maximus, though it is out of fashion now and seems to smack of spiritual arrogance, is not a contemptible ideal. It is what moved Cinthio's Epitia to plead for her husband's life, it is still very much a concern of Clarissa's in the eighteenth century. It may be that in abandoning that ideal society has lost something of value to its structure. At least it smacks no less of spiritual arrogance to condemn it out of hand.

Thus it may well be that Fletcher had something to say of more immediate importance for his time than Shakespeare, and that the prestige of his name during most of the seventeenth century was not merely due to a frivolous pleasure in slick sensationalism; that the complimentary poems of the Folio were not entirely beside the mark in praising his works as a school of morality. It is the sad fate of authors that the more they are of an age the less likely they are to be for all time. And above all the spirit of rationalism to which Fletcher and Dryden were trying to adapt tragedy has in fact proved destructive of tragedy altogether. For one of the most important effects of tragedy, which Aristotle did not and could not mention, is a strong sense of the mystery of life, indeed it is probably all the stronger for not imposing itself too clearly, but it remains as a background. And since for Aristotle it was the normal background of most thought, he obviously could not conceive it as a specific ingredient of tragedy. For Shakespeare too it was probably part of the normal background, or at least we presume that it was. It is true that with him a great deal of the sense of supernatural forces participating in the life of man, while yet leaving him a free agent, is due to what are at bottom theatrical tricks and conventions. We cannot say whether he actually believed in the ghosts, witches, omens and other manifestations of the supernatural that appear in most of his tragedies; and tragic irony, which he also used effectively, was definitely a Senecan trick. But except perhaps in *Richard III*, where they are piled a little too thick, we accept the tricks, and not merely as a part of our willing suspension of disbelief, but as something that adds a further depth to the tragedy. I do not know whether it is only a kind of intellectual snobbery that makes the same effects appear insincere and irritating in the *Schicksalsdramen* of the German Romantics; that we feel, whether the Romantics believed in a supernatural order governing the world or not, they certainly did not believe that it manifested itself in such ways, and had no right to exploit them for theatrical effects. Why it is we accept and are stirred by the idea of fate in *Oedipus*, without believing in it ourselves, but not in Grillparzer's *Ahnfrau*, it would be hard to say—I do not believe the difference lies only in the quality of the work, and I very much suspect that if we were to learn that *Oedipus* had been written in 1860 it would cease to impress us. Be that as it may, however, and believing in it ourselves or not, the sense of some supernatural order in Shakespeare's tragedies does contribute very much to their power. And perhaps not so much through these more overt expressions as by a general all-pervading sense of belief which it might be difficult to pin down exactly, but which one feels to be there.

In Fletcher, however, this sense of mystery is lacking. He has no ghosts except in *The Triumph of Death*. He has a rather ironical apotheosis in the near-comedy of *The Mad Lover*, and an omen or two in *Valentinian*. But he is on the whole honest in eschewing the outer signs of the supernatural, as Dryden does after him. He has, like Shakespeare, allusions to heaven and providence that might provide the same background sense of mystery, but somehow do not. I do not think we can say they fail because Fletcher did not believe in religion himself—there is nothing to suggest that either he or Dryden had actually broken with it. Nor can we balk the whole question by the simple and obvious declaration that Fletcher was not a great poet. Neither was, say, Heywood, yet he suggests more of the mystery of life. Probably the real answer lies once more in the type of conflict and the difference between a moral law and a social code, a difference which is at bottom emotional rather than logical, but dramatically none the less essential for that. For the code is obviously artificial. Its infringement may lead as inexorably to disaster as that of the moral law, but its operation is more obviously mechanical, and less emotionally satisfying. Maximus in his desire for revenge raises his hand against the divinely appointed ruler and so brings destruction on himself and his country. There are all the elements of tragedy there. And probably even, for a generation that really believed in the divine right of kings, it would be easy to see God's hand in the logical working out of that situation, and to feel a sense of mystery. But for us the feeling is rather that Maximus has infringed not a divine law but a code of expediency. The state needs a head; to cut that head off is bound to weaken the state and lead to disaster without any intervention from above. And the revenge itself is not condemned. We are told again and again that if the offender had been anyone but the emperor the code of honour could only be satisfied by bloodshed, and are not predisposed to believe in a moral order that distinguishes so nicely between ranks. In fact we are caught up in a system of conflicting and palpably artificial codes whose operation, though it may be inevitable, brings no sense of mystery, nothing beyond our logical comprehension. And also in practice a large part of these conflicts do have something exaggerated, artificial, or, as Waith has put it, hypothetical about them,[2] even when the hypothesis is not ultimately destroyed, as it so often is in tragi-comedy. For the loss of tragic elevation through awe and a sense of mystery demanded compensation, and it was sought for in the ineffable heroic gestures that these strained situations called forth.

There is also another way in which the conflict of reason and passion less perfectly answers our expectations of tragedy and of a sense of mystery. The man who can debate in himself, who can weigh in his mind his expectations of satisfaction, seems to be a completely free agent, and the choice he makes, where a single straw tips the balance, seems to be almost a matter of chance, yet at the same time his sole responsibility—his tragic error is his own entirely, and the disaster that it brings, the price of his own folly. I lay the stress on *seems*, for actually Maximus is no freer in his choice than Macbeth; but the mechanism of that choice, as it is presented to us, gives the effect of complete freedom. Macbeth is obviously not free to choose. He foresees all the results of his choice—much more clearly indeed than Maximus—yet under a dull compulsion he goes his way. We do not know, as we are supposed to know with Maximus, just what it was that tipped the balance; the outcome, we feel, has been decided before even he has begun to struggle with himself, and he shares the responsibility for his choice with whatever it is that has made him what he is. Thus the pattern of events unrolls itself much more inexorably from first to last, and aesthetically that is a more satisfactory pattern. Which is actually truer to our concept of existence, however—whether we see man as part of a wider scheme, or dependent on himself alone—one may hesitate to say. Probably Fletcher's way is truer to what we feel about ourselves, Shakespeare's to what we feel about other people. And that brings us to another very essential difference between the two types—the subjectivity of the approach.

Wölfflin in his famous analysis of Renaissance and Baroque art[3] gave as one of his definitions of the pair, the art of things as they are, and as they seem. The Renaissance artist's vision was turned outward on things as they are in themselves, he tries to present them in their most ideally perfect and typical aspect and complete in all their details, while the Baroque artist tries to capture the fleeting impression they produce on him at a given moment. And that is an opposition that applies not only to the visual arts. In narrative the Renaissance writer presents things from the bird's eye view of omniscience—we are aware of the situation in its completeness and of the motives, intentions and plans of all concerned.[4] The seventeenth-century writer tends rather to narrate from the perspective of one of the participants; and in the typical heroic romances of La Calprenède and his school, just as in the Alexandrian romances out of which they grew, we know no more of what is really happening, and why, than does the hero himself.[5] We move in a world, not of deep, all-embracing mysteries, but of riddles—bewildering, but not mysterious—that are gradually explained away through layer after layer of inserted narrative. And that is already, and well before La Calprenède, the world of Beaumont and Fletcher, a disconcerting world of ever-shifting circumstances and sudden reversals in which we must constantly re-orientate ourselves, typically a world from which all sense of stability has disappeared, and one must cling to appearance for, deceptive though it is, there is nothing else to cling to. It is true this applies more to the tragi-comedies than the true tragedies, for in tragedy the hero still tends to be the active shaper of his world, and seeing through the eyes of the hero we still see more or less objectively. And one might indeed say that the subjective view and the sense of instability naturally led to tragi-comedy. But even in tragedy the subjective or introspective view did lead to very definite changes. Already in *The Maid's Tragedy* Beaumont, who departed from the Renaissance view much less markedly than his friend, had shown a new sort of approach and a new sort of situation; the revelations of the wedding-night represent for hero and for audience alike a reversal as sudden and unexpected as the final reversals of tragi-comedy, and serve to trigger off an almost paradoxical shift of emotions with their juxtaposition of happy sexual expectation and the horrified realization of blasted honour. And nevertheless here, though we are absorbed in that emotional flux, we are probably even more absorbed in the realization of Evadne as a personality—portrait and emotional evocation are at least held in balance. In the other key scene of Evadne's reclamation, written mainly by Fletcher, though probably heavily overwritten by Beaumont, this balance has been largely destroyed, and the stress lies almost exclusively on a scintillating play of the emotions as they pass through puzzlement, alarm, indignation, fear, shame, contrition, horror, grief. Evadne here is, practically speaking, Everywoman, or at least every woman in such a situation—it is the situation alone that defines the personality. And in *Valentinian* too it is effects such as these that form the substance of the play. The quarrel scene between Valentinian and Aëcius, like that between Melantius and Amintor in *The Maid's Tragedy*, passes through a whole gamut of various emotions and pulsating tensions to end in reconciliation. Both scenes no doubt owe a great deal to the quarrel in *Julius Caesar*, but they employ the situation very differently, and while with Shakespeare we are aware above all of a contrast of personalities, here again it is much more with the fluctuations of the emotional barometer that we are concerned. As in the later and even more famous quarrel scenes of Dryden—Antony and Ventidius, Sebastian and Dorax—the opponents differ in position, to some extent in outlook or even in temper, but as individuals they seem all but identical in manner of speech, ways of thought, interests, in everything that goes to make up personality.

Personality is in fact something that one is aware of only in others, something that one can only grasp through objective observation of external behaviour. Of one's own one has but the vaguest concept, except perhaps as a sort of norm, as impersonal as a yardstick, by which to measure what we observe. In ourselves, what we are aware of, and all that the introspective view can give, is a succession of constantly changing emotions, reactions, judgments, which it is impossible for us to build up into any sort of system, because they seem to us the natural and inevitable response of human nature. Other people's idiosyncrasies may form systems, but on the levels on which we know ourselves human nature does seem ultimately to be very much the same—as Hobbes maintained, and as in fact the various attempts in recent times to represent the stream of consciousness seem to have demonstrated with devastating effectiveness. The streams may differ in the actual debris they sweep along with them, but in the patterns they make of it they are distressingly alike. And so it is not surprising that Fletcher's heroes, and the Baroque heroes in general, should all appear essentially the same. Shirley in his preface to the Beaumont and Fletcher Folio singled out as the central virtue of these plays the treatment of the passions; and 'the passions' were to remain a focus of critical attention for over a century to come. It is to the passions and their interplay that one naturally turns if one's view is turned in on oneself. And the writer's interest will centre on human nature in the abstract, he will seek the universal rather than the individual, the type rather than the personality. From Boileau down to Johnson this was in fact the accepted attitude. And to Rymer an Evadne or an Iago were equally an offence against art because they were too strongly individualized and broke away from what he regarded as their essential types.

How far Fletcher in reducing his characters to standardized types was consciously following a theory of art, and how far he was instinctively submitting to a trend that was to bring such a theory with it, it would be hard to say. But one can say fairly definitely that the paring away of the individual touches that build up the effect of a personality was deliberate, or at least not due to inability. Fletcher's comic heroes are somewhat more highly individualized than those of his serious plays, but in general only slightly so. However, with two figures he does quite astonishingly, without even disrupting the framework of his highly mannered style, give the effect of a very distinct personality: with the unctuous demureness of Monsieur Thomas and the slow, gentle naivety of Leon in *Rule a Wife*—and in both cases the men are playing a part and pretending to be what they are not. But these assumed personalities are put across so vividly that it is obvious that, had he wanted to, Fletcher could have rivalled the very greatest masters of comic portraiture. And equally obviously he regarded such a high degree of individualization as a form of caricature that should be used only very sparingly.

By paring away the details of personality one is able to concentrate on what one regards as essentials. Maximus and Aëcius are practically indistinguishable in everything except in their attitude on loyalty, and in that they are contrasted from the first and before Maximus has any reason to rebel. In a way one might say that within the dramatic structure they are contrasted much as Brutus and Cassius are contrasted. With Shakespeare, however, the contrast is worked out in such detail and on such various levels that one cannot reduce it to a single principle. In the final summing up we are told that Brutus alone of the conspirators acted from purely disinterested motives. But though one will have felt that a personal dislike and irritation at being ruled over by someone whom he feels to be no better than he, does enter into Cassius's motives, to say that he acted merely 'in envy of great Caesar' seems unjust. Ultimately Brutus has no better reason for his fear of tyranny than Cassius—a general suspicion of human nature when left without control, but which with both of them is formulated more as a general and unreasoned loyalty to a republican tradition. In fact one would have to say that if Shakespeare had really intended the contrast suggested by Antony's summing up, he had muffed it rather badly. What he gives, however, is the contrast not between two different attitudes towards authoritarian rule, but between the expression of similar if not identical attitudes in contrasting personalities. And in that way one is made acutely aware of the complexity of the motivation in general. But it is not the 'problem' of tyrannicide that stands at the centre of Shakespeare's play. Indeed it is very hard to say what does stand at the centre, or what the play is 'about'.

2-2

One can if one likes read any amount of so-called meanings into it, as one can into any series of events, actual or fictitious, and all the more easily the more details one has to hand; but one has no guarantee that any of these meanings is really Shakespeare's, or at least was at all central for him. In fact the play seems to be about the murder of Caesar and its results—simply that. *Valentinian* however is clearly not merely about the murder of Valentinian and its results, though like *Julius Caesar* it gives a tolerably accurate account of historical events. But it uses those events to discuss the question of loyalty, and through the historical main plot, and the invented sub-plot of Pontius, it presents various attitudes towards this question and demonstrates the disastrous results of opposing the divine right of kings.

That is, of course, an important point in most of Shakespeare's history plays too; yet there it is so little stressed that it is only within the present generation that its importance has been realized. It is an important point in *Macbeth* too, and probably determined Shakespeare's choice of that particular plot at that particular time. But having once chosen the plot, Shakespeare, one would say, left the political message to take care of itself, and what really interested him was working out the character of Macbeth and the interactions of character and situation. In *Hamlet* the theme of a son's revenge is taken up in three different ways—some would even include the rugged Pyrrhus in the count and say four—as the theme of loyalty is taken up in *Valentinian*. But though the most varied meanings have been propounded for the tragedy, no one has really suggested that it is 'about' the problem of revenge. And in fact the attitude of all four sons towards revenge itself is basically the same—they are all eager for it, though they differ in the ways they set about it. Revenge is no more the theme of *Hamlet* than filial ingratitude is that of *Lear*. In *Bonduca*, however, where the various attitudes towards a code of military honour are worked out in every conceivable way among a large group of characters who basically, all but the women, answer perfectly to what Rymer would have Iago to be—the typical soldier—the result is to raise that code to the subject of the play. And in the same way in *Aureng-Zebe* Dryden takes up the conflict of love and duty in no less than five sets of relations.

Thus Fletcher, and Baroque tragedy in general, tend to subordinate everything to a dominant concept, a concept which, with Fletcher especially, is not even inherent in the plot. It is by expanding the figure of Aëcius, actually a secondary figure, a minor obstacle in the path of Maximus's revenge, and making of him the real hero of the play, that he imposes the theme of loyalty on it. In treating the defeat of Bonduca and the suicide of Penius after he has severed himself from participation in a glorious victory, he imposed a unity of theme by making Bonduca's defeat appear as the result of her imperviousness to the ideal of true military glory, and above all by introducing the figure of Caratach—who historically had nothing to do with Bonduca—as the true hero and mouthpiece of the play's idea. Here it would be well to remember Rymer's stricture on *The Maid's Tragedy*—that it lacks a centre and seems to be pulling in different directions. Fletcher at least was careful to provide a centre.

By that I do not mean to suggest that Shakespearian tragedy lacks a centre. But it is a centre of another kind—the light concentrated on the central figure and, so to say, spreading out from there to illumine every nook and cranny. And that is a kind of centre that Rymer could have found in *The Maid's Tragedy* if he had been ready to look for it. For the figure of Evadne is outstanding enough to dominate the play, even though by Shakespearian standards her part is small. But Rymer, as is obvious from his analysis, was looking for his centre in plot and meaning, in a clearly stated theme, not in personality or the complex relations of a group of people to an event, which is what gives *The Maid's Tragedy* its unity and relates it, in spite of certain approaches to the Baroque type, with Shakespearian tragedy. Personality was not for Rymer a subject for art at all, he was looking for generalized, typical human nature. Evadne, by offending against typical feminine modesty, was automatically excluded from his mental horizon as a centre.

This Baroque insistence on the typical, the paring away of all but the essentials of character, plot, and setting, is of course clearly related to what we regard as classicism. And naturally it drew most of its authority from classical practice. But after all the Renaissance no less than the age of Baroque had accepted imitation of the classics as the essential literary method without being able to grasp this principle of concentration. And if there was a change in the manner of imitation it must have been that the new period found certain aspects of classicism more congenial to its outlook, not that it changed its outlook through studying the classics, or the Senecan *Controversiae*. Classical literature as a whole was not subjective or introspective in its approach—except for the Alexandrian novel of post-classical times. And the tremendous influence of Heliodorus and his compeers on the heroic novel of the Baroque age, and the tremendous difference between Sidney's acceptance of the *Aethiopica* and La Calprenède's, is a fascinating illustration of the point for which there is no space here. But the classical concentration on essentials, though it had its roots in something very different from Baroque subjectivity, did coincide with and help to nourish the Baroque concentration on the universal passions. Equally it helped to overcome the essential multiplicity of the Renaissance view with its roots in an intense delight and interest in the objective world about us. We get the same sort of opposition as between the Victorian novel and the more introspective approach of today—the sense of teeming, many-coloured life, embracing a large section of society, and the modern concentration on the inner man and the narrower range of his most intimate contacts. Fletcher does not give us the intense concentration of a Racine, or even of a Dryden, but he is very obviously moving in their direction. His backgrounds as compared with Shakespeare's are very sketchily suggested. He has few atmospheric scenes or introductions to scenes, he is not interested in bringing out aspects of character that have no immediate bearing on events. He has his subservient courtiers like Shakespeare, but he is not prepared to spend time on showing how, like Rosencrantz and Guildenstern, they are sucked into the whirlpool of events—they are simply there as part of the plot mechanism. However, the English Baroque dramatists were hampered by a tradition from which they had not the strength to break away completely, and even Dryden, with the example of the French before him, still tried to maintain a compromise between the intense concentration of classical tragedy and the varied action of Shakespearian; and to some extent they fell between two stools, unable to give the full satisfaction of either type.

As a final point of contrast one may take the structural pattern, for here there is a reversal that might seem odd if it was merely a question of Renaissance (or native, or medieval) versus classical; for in structure it is Shakespeare who seems closer to the classical line than either Fletcher, or Dryden, or Racine. In spite of his multiplicity, in spite of the combination of what may seem very heterogeneous elements, in spite of the tendency to treat each scene as a separate, self-contained unit, and the sharp breaks and contrasts between them, Shakespeare's tragedies clearly follow what is generally known as the classical pyramid. Whether it actually is classical and not rather Shakespearian I am not at all sure, but at least one feels it to be 'classical' in its simplicity, harmony and balance—rising to a climax of tension about the middle, and then ebbing away unhurriedly to the catastrophe. With Shakespeare the rise is not a steady swell, but rather an ascending series of minor peaks. Yet there is nothing abrupt or unexpected about it; we survey the whole course of the action from its first inception, and every turn of events is well prepared in advance. Generally the opening scene is purely atmospherical, and even the separate scenes, especially in the earlier parts, tend to follow the same pyramidal line as the whole. It is a structure that seems to reflect a stable, balanced view of the world, and to correspond to the sense of inevitability that is brought out in other ways too. And it is, I believe, a native development, independent of classical models, for it is characteristic of the more complex Renaissance lyrics too, though in epic forms it is generally obscured by the more dominant multiplicity.

The Baroque line of Fletcher and Dryden is far more hectic. We are pitchforked as a rule straight into the middle of an already created field of tension, often into the middle of a conversation. And the tension tends to shoot up and drop down with the giddy effect of a switchback. In *Valentinian* there is not a central climax but a whole series of climaxes, no one of which can be said to out-top the others—the rape of Lucina, the death of Aëcius, the murder of the emperor, the sudden reversal by which Maximus is thrown down from the throne he has won. And each of these points tends to centre on a different person or permutation of the persons. Not a confrontation of Hamlet with each in turn, but of each with each. For the stress on the variety of unindividualized emotions demands a greater variety of unindividualized, or at least only very slightly individualized, persons to embody them. And so the precarious balance of the emotions is paralleled by the precarious balance of the situation. With Dryden in *The Conquest of Granada* or *Aureng-Zebe* the prince who is in favour at the beginning of the act may find himself in chains at the end, restored to fortune again, and again cast down, at the whim of a tyrant, through a palace revolt, or by the fortune of war. And if the Shakespearian structure reflects a sense of a stable universe, the Baroque structure would seem equally to express the insecurity of an age marked by its hysterical witch trials, by the poignant cries of its religious lyrics, by the overwrought emotionalism of its statuary.

This fever-chart line of action is of interest too because it came to be adapted to the five-act structure. Indeed it was through it that a real act structure came to be evolved, for the first time in history I should say. There has been much talk lately of Shakespeare's five-act structure and its classical origins. To me at least it seems like a tremendous red herring.[6] A mere division into acts is not in itself an act structure, and Roman comedy with its acts of indeterminate and incommensurable length, even if we accept the idea of a specific function for each act, which seems to me mainly a doctrinaire construction of the critics, does not have a structure dependent on the acts, but rather the distribution of the acts must depend on the individual structure of the comedy. Whether Shakespeare regularly divided his plays into acts or not is an open question still; but in any case the essential structural unit for him was the scene. And though he appears not infrequently to have set out with the intention of a structural division into acts, the intention seldom seems to have been carried out beyond the first one, which does quite often form a distinct unit, as in *Hamlet* or *Othello*. But the example of *Romeo and Juliet*, where the act choruses are dropped after the first pause, seems entirely characteristic of his attitude. The first act covers the protasis (and not the first two as in the classical prescription, followed by Jonson—and how slow his plays are to get under way!), after that the complications become too involved, the impetus of the action too strong, for any clear articulation into sections, except sometimes the last one. But Fletcher already in *Valentinian* was beginning to make use of the act pause to mark a turn in the events, to bridge a gap in the action, to raise the tension: Act I closes with Valentinian preparing to see Maximus for a purpose that we cannot altogether fathom, though we know it to be directed against Lucina; Act II opens in the middle of the fatal game of dice that will deliver her into his hands at its close; and though it ends with him promising to spare her, we know that his intentions have not altered, and are left to wonder what the next step will be. Actually it is the rape, which takes place during the pause, and the third Act opens with the abrupt anouncement: 'It is done!'—to finish with Maximus committed to the act of vengeance and the destruction of his friend, but with the question of How? (to maintain the tension). Act IV brings the death of Aëcius, and closes with Maximus instigating others to deal with the emperor, but again no plan decided on. The actual poisoning, however, is done, like the rape, during the pause, and the last Act opens with the announcement that the poisoners have themselves taken poison and Valentinian's death is imminent. Yet this use of the pause—and that it was a real pause can be seen from the licence Fletcher allows himself in reintroducing characters from the last scene—appears almost tentative compared with the crashing act curtains of, say, *The Island Princess*, where each of the pauses seems to be filled out with a huge question-mark—what is to happen now? That is a real act structure, where the act pauses are functional and serve not only to mark the definite stages of the story but to raise the tension by whetting one's appetite for the next lap. It is a structure characteristic of Dryden too, and also of Corneille and Racine—there is nothing comparable to it in Shakespearian tragedy, except the first act of *Hamlet*.

There are further contrasts between the two types, like interruption and flow for instance: Shakespeare is anxious to secure a maximum of contrast between each scene, while Fletcher tries to link his scenes together by pointing forward to the next one, and even carries the flow of the action, as we have seen, through the break of the act pause; and Dryden, like the French tragedians, links his scenes together within the act by liaison. But these further points are at bottom corollaries of those mentioned—Shakespeare's interruptions are concomitants of his multiplicity, the delight in explicit detail, while the Baroque flow, even though its final expression in the liaison of the scenes links up with classical practice, is no less bound up with the centring and concentration of the action. I have discussed such points at greater length in my study of *Baroque Literature in England*, and it will be of greater interest to show here how much of this analysis of Fletcher's methods applies to later seventeenth-century tragedy also, and not only to the English tradition culminating in Dryden, but even to a writer like Racine. I shall take as my text *Bajazet*, not one of his greatest plays, but a very typical one, and completely independent, owing nothing to ancient legend or to Euripides. The conflict here is a variant of the love-and-honour theme in which love and honour are for once on the same side, and Bajazet must choose between his love and his life. It is a situation as hypothetical in its way as anything in Fletcher; it may have some historical or ethnographical justification, but it is as remote from Western mores as it well could be. Bajazet is expecting to be murdered at the order of his brother, the newly crowned Sultan, in the good old Ottoman tradition; and it is the Sultana to whom the execution has been delegated while Amurat is away on a campaign that may well end in his defeat. But Roxane has been delaying the execution, for she is in love with Bajazet, who however loves Atalide, and the first Act ends with the crash of her announcement that she intends to spare his life if he will head a revolt against his brother and take her as his official wife—something that Amurat, again in obedience to Ottoman traditions, has omitted to do. The situation is in fact basically the same as in Fletcher's *Wife for a Month*, but with a woman in the tyrant's place. And Bajazet himself behaves in the same way as the passive heroes of Fletcher's tragi-comedies (but not his tragedies proper): he does not waver for an instant in his choice between Atalide and Roxane, so that there is no real conflict within him, and he remains true to his code of heroic love. But, unlike Fletcher's heroes, he is willing to temporize. Act II brings the confrontation between hero and temptress in a typical scene of precarious emotional balance: a certain lack of enthusiasm, the plea that marriage is against the established custom, turns the tide of Roxane's advances—indignation, reproaches, a melting mood, and a final burst of indignation, and Bajazet's fortunes sink almost to zero—he is to die. That would be a possible point for the second act pause. But Racine prefers a stronger flow and ends with a more definite question, for now Atalide, by threatening to draw Roxane's wrath down on herself, forces Bajazet to attempt a reconciliation. And this reconciliation, in true Baroque fashion, takes place during the pause, so that the new Act begins with a complete reversal—Bajazet's fortunes have shot up to the height again, and—paradoxically—Atalide is plagued by jealousy. It is a misunderstanding, however; Bajazet has not actually promised marriage after all, or anything else than unspecified gratitude, and the quarrel ends with the typical reversal of mood. But the desire to clear himself more fully in Atalide's eyes makes Bajazet cooler towards Roxane, who in her turn sways over again to doubts, suspicions, recriminations. And the Act ends with the arrival of the Sultan's emissary, expectations of new developments, and Bajazet's fortunes again sinking fast. Just such an emotional chain-reaction does not occur in Fletcher, though the triangle of *A Wife for a Month* brings something rather similar; but Fletcher is already a master of emotional interactions of considerable subtlety and complexity, as in the bedroom scene of the same play when the hero is finally forced to pretend impotence to save his wife's life—actually a fine and delicate piece of work if you can once get over the artificiality of the situation. But after all Racine is no less artificial.

The fourth Act continues the downward trend of the hero's fortune, down to zero once more. The Sultan's emissary has brought news that he is returning victorious from his campaign, and Roxane declares her intention of abandoning Bajazet to his fate—chiefly in order to watch the effect on Atalide, whom she has begun to suspect—one may note Racine's use of the permutation of the various confrontations, as with Fletcher and Dryden.[7] The effect of the ruse is devastating, the lovers' secret is exposed, and Roxane is now bent on vengeance to the uttermost. Nevertheless the Act ends with a ray of hope—Bajazet has friends in the palace who are preparing a coup, and so the last act opens on a situation that may turn either to tragedy or tragi-comedy. And really there is nothing in all that has gone before to make the tragedy that follows seem inevitable. No more than in Fletcher—even less so indeed—is there any sense of an external force compelling the course of events. The whole impasse has really hung on a ridiculous question of precedence—is Atalide to be the acknowledged first wife of Bajazet, or the favourite of his harem?—a possibility which she has rejected in advance, but which in view of the mores on which the play is supposed to be built seems eminently reasonable. Or alternatively, should Bajazet give his promise and retract it once he has the power in his hands?—a possibility which is scarcely envisaged, so high-minded is the young man, but which one feels would be no more than Roxane has been asking for. The ultimate motive behind all the actions has been a foolish pride, or at best a sense of noblesse oblige, a pride that can turn love to hate in a single moment—hell has no fury like a woman scorned. If one reads the play in a crib one may well feel that it is quite as silly as anything of Fletcher's, though even so the stark concentration of it has a certain power. If you read it with Racine's verse to carry it, you are overwhelmed by the delicacy and subtlety with which the fluctuations of the emotions are conveyed, and the tremendous energy behind the extraordinarily restrained language. Compared with that, Fletcher's characters seem to be screaming at the tops of their voices and yet only achieving a fraction of the force. But basically both men are striving after the same sort of effects, and achieving them in much the same way. Fletcher's peaks of tension are more sensational, more external and more varied. But the chief difference, if we set aside the force of the actual writing, lies in the greater clarity and simplicity of Racine's line, the reduction of the minor figures, the completer balance between the three or four major ones. Fletcher's tyrant is decidedly a secondary figure, whose emotions are taken for granted; Roxane is emotionally the most complex figure of Racine's play. Yet even in these points Fletcher has moved a long way from the Shakespearian type and in the direction of Racine. And they, and even more the points of positive resemblance—the codes of behaviour, the switchback line, the precarious balance, the paradoxical play of the emotions—seem to me much more important than the adherence to the neo-classical rules that loom so large on the surface of French and Restoration tragedy.

Many of these resemblances can be explained by the *Astrée* and what it stands for. Fletcher was certainly well abreast of the French literature of his day, and working so to say with much of the same background as the later French tragedians. A great deal too can be explained by the spirit of the age working independently. But there are points of dramatic technique like the act structure and the permutations of the dramatic conflicts that seem to suggest a more direct connexion, and remain an enigma. For an English influence working across the Channel appears out of the question, yet there is no French dramatist from whom Fletcher could have learned anything. Hardy, whose works were only beginning to be published at the time of Fletcher's death, shows, as far as I can see, no traces of the precarious balance of the Baroque, or any other Baroque feature.

In conclusion, to return to Shakespeare, the lodestone of our gathering, I should like to say that this necessarily rather sketchy comparison does bring out one thing very clearly: that among the many and very essential differences between the two types of tragedy, what stands out most markedly is the different approach to the presentation of man himself—man seen in the round as an individual, differentiated in his reactions and behaviour, in the aura of imagery that he carries with him, in his very speech rhythms, as with Othello and Iago, and man at most rather superficially differentiated into a few basic types, as a conductor of various currents of emotion, reacting seismographically to every little impulse. Roxane and Atalide do differ in character, the one bold, resolute, cruel, the other gentle and timid, but both are dominated by their pride, both speak with the same voice, and it is at bottom their part in the plot that differentiates them more than anything else. Much the same might be said of Maximus and Aëcius, or Aureng-Zebe and Morat. What interests their creators is not the sort of people they are, not all the myriad ways in which they do differ, but the way in which the human mind in general works, the paradoxical cross-currents of emotions that sway their decisions from one moment to the next, which with Racine becomes the almost microscopical analysis of motivation. Motivation and the mechanics of the mind do not seem to interest Shakespeare, he does not try to explain them or present them in detail. And thus it is largely on such points that critical opinion is most sharply divided—why does Hamlet delay?—what is Iago's motive?—is it jealousy that moves Othello? He sees people not, like Fletcher and Racine, as we see ourselves, but as we see those about us. He provides motives, fairly obvious motives—and subtly belies them, suggesting rather that we do not know the whole story. He gives us all the data, as they would be accessible to an intimate friend, and rather more even, but he does not try to penetrate to the ultimate mechanism, to identify all the cogwheels and demonstrate their interactions. We do not know whether it is ambition, or his wife's taunts, or a feeling that his path has been marked out for him anyhow, that is the deepest-lying factor in Macbeth's decision. It is enough that we should feel that there are such various cogwheels. The mystery of Cleopatra's death must have fascinated Shakespeare—he gives us all the conflicting data as Plutarch did. He does not attempt a solution. But he creates a character of such variety, of so many moods and caprices, that the ultimate mystery fits into it perfectly. And that, I believe, is the real centre of the creative process for him. He chose his plots for various reasons, mainly practical, sometimes political, never, I should say, philosophical or moral. And having made his choice, the main question for him was, what were the people like to whom such things happened, and how would they appear to us? As to the meaning, he left it to take care of itself—that is why it appears so deep, as deep as life itself, and capable of as many interpretations, all of them the critics', and none of them, probably, Shakespeare's. In other words, I should like to end up with a plea for the good old Bradleian approach, which, though it does not, and never pretended to, give a complete account, does at least put first things first, and incidentally was neither Bradleian, nor Victorian, nor Romantic, but the natural centre of Shakespeare criticism since Shakespeare criticism has existed. The real problem, of course, is not what Shakespeare's characters are like, but why they affect us as they do. Still the answer to this does inevitably pass through the other, and Bradley gives a substantial part of that answer. The greater part probably lies in the poetry, but not poetry *qua* poetry, still less as an esoteric system of semi-philosophical hints and references, but as a means of dramatic expression; in the difference between 'O girl, O gold!' and 'My daughter, O my ducats!'.

© MARCO MINCOFF 1967

NOTES

1. The comparison will be confined to Shakespeare, leaving aside the question of his appurtenance to the Renaissance or, possibly, Mannerism. This point I have discussed at greater length in 'Baroque Literature in England', *Annuaire de L'Université de Sofia, Faculté Historico-Philologique*, XLIII (1946–7), 1–71, which, although published 20 years ago, still seems to me the only attempt to discuss the question of literary style from the point of view of literature in the first place, and not merely as a vague parallel to that of the other arts. The question of Mannerism had not yet arisen then, and I feel that it is scarcely ripe for discussion even now, until more agreement has been reached about the more basic concepts of Renaissance and Baroque in literature. For the present I should say that if there is a Mannerist period in English literature it would be that transitional period *c.* 1598–1612 which I have termed the Revolt and claimed as essentially a sub-division of the Renaissance.

2. Eugene Waith, *The Pattern of Tragicomedy in Beaumont and Fletcher* (New Haven, 1952), p. 37.

3. Heinrich Wölfflin, *Kunstgeschichtliche Grundbegriffe* (München, 1915).

4. The point is worked out more fully in *Baroque Literature*, pp. 31 ff.

5. See *Baroque Literature*, pp. 29 ff.

6. For further details see my 'Shakespeare's Comedies and the Five-Act Structure', *Hommage à Shakespeare, Bulletin de la Faculté des Lettres de Strasbourg, 1965*, pp. 131–46. Unfortunately this was written without knowledge of W. T. Jewkes, *Act-Division in Elizabethan and Jacobean Plays* (Hamden, Conn., 1958).

7. *Bajazet*, with only three main characters, is not a very good example of this, however. *Phèdre* with five of the six possible confrontations of four characters illustrates the point better.

SENECA AND THE ELIZABETHANS:
A CASE-STUDY IN 'INFLUENCE'

BY

G. K. HUNTER

Once-upon-a-simple-time, while the modern languages were seeking to make their way as serious studies, the subject of 'The Influence of Seneca on Elizabethan Tragedy' was quite self-evidently an example of what serious study could provide in modern literature. The scholar who set out to study an author ('B') learned that the scientific way of doing this was to discover, embedded in B, the echoes or reminiscences of an earlier author or work (which we may call 'A'). It was the business of the Ph.D. student, charged with the investigation of B, to discover his 'A'; then he could list the echoes and reminiscences, enlarge these into a discussion of 'influence'— and his dissertation was made. Of such a kind, in the field under discussion here, the most notable example is John W. Cunliffe's 1893 D.Litt. dissertation 'The Influence of Seneca on Elizabethan Tragedy'—a book which has occupied its field with apparent adequacy since 1893, and which was reissued as recently as 1965. Professor Peter Ure could remark (in his *Durham University Journal* article of 1948, 'On some differences between Senecan and Elizabethan tragedy') that the day of Cunliffe 'is now apparently past'; but this cannot be allowed to be entirely true in 1966. The central attack on Cunliffe, in Howard Baker's *Induction to Tragedy* (1939), seems to have disappeared into the sands of time, and Cunliffe's assumptions remain the common assumptions. I notice a bland restatement of them, as if of undisputed truth, in the preface to the excellent new Penguin translation of five Senecan plays (1966).

Cunliffe's book is, at its kernel, a list of parallel passages, and it takes the influence of Seneca on Elizabethan Tragedy to be 'proved', or demonstrated in detail, by the existence of these parallel passages; but it is not clear that the conclusion follows from the premiss. Certainly we must ask what are the Elizabethan tragedies involved in Cunliffe's book, and to what extent his parallels are continuously persuasive. The central play for the thesis is, obviously, Thomas Hughes's *The Misfortunes of Arthur* (1587), whose 'imitations of Seneca' occupy twenty-five pages—the whole of 'Appendix II' in the book. The case that *The Misfortunes of Arthur* is a cento of Senecan imitations is a brilliant example of what this kind of study can do: it is proved beyond doubt.[1] If Thomas Hughes had been the central figure of English Renaissance tragedy, or if *The Misfortunes of Arthur* were the great seminal play of the period, then 'the Influence of Seneca on Elizabethan Tragedy' would be as categorical as Cunliffe and other early investigators[2] supposed it to be. Fair-minded literary history cannot, however, make either of these assumptions.

Not only is Cunliffe's book centred on a minor play; but the thesis becomes less convincing as the works he treats get more interesting and more important aesthetically. The thesis works very well for *The Misfortunes of Arthur*, well for *Gismond of Salerne* (and not badly for Dr Legge's *Richardus Tertius*) but it is on very shaky ground with *The Spanish Tragedy* (where Baker's strictures are especially important) and works not at all for Marlowe's plays or for Shakespeare's. Even more telling is the objection that it fails to take account of an alternative line of tragic writing, running through *Damon and Pithias*, *Horestes* and *Cambyses*. This would seem to show, at the very least, that something else was going on in English tragedy of the period beside the influence of Seneca. Nor would I regard this progressive thinning-out of Cunliffe's thesis as an accident; indeed I suggest that it points to something basic in *Quellenforschung*. The process involved in this type of study is, as I have said, that the scholar looks at work B for evidence that it derived elements from work A, which then may be inflated to the status of '*an influence*'. But if work B is more than a passive and parasitic object—that is, if it is any good—it will make new whatever it borrows, it will render what it treats into organic substance, into substance whose principal relationship is to context, not to source. The danger of *Quellenforschung* is that it tends to treat as *passive* a situation in which good work is essentially active, creative and to this extent unique. And this is why a book like Thorndike's *Influence of Beaumont and Fletcher on Shakspere* can never command simple assent; for the Last Plays of Shakespeare (the 'B' of Thorndike's thesis) are too rich, various and difficult to place to be put under the influence. They refuse to stay etherized upon the table.

It is interesting and important, of course, to know where plots come from, and I do not seek to deny this. But 'the influence of Painter (or Brooke or Sidney) on Shakespeare' obviously fails to emerge as a possible thesis subject, even though plots are taken from these authors; unless, that is, we are content to derive 'influence' from the most tenuous of links. John Webster's tragedies raise this problem in an acute form. We know that Webster's plays are mosaics of borrowings. Should we therefore discuss 'the influence of Sir William Alexander, Sidney, Montaigne, Guazzo, Guevara, Matthieu, etc., on Webster'? Surely not, unless we have evidence of a more general relationship than is provided by the lists of parallels. One must return here to the important point already made (*vis-à-vis* Seneca and Renaissance tragedy) by Professor Jacquot: 'Un dénombrement des emprunts directs ne suffit donc pas à rendre compte de l'influence du poète latin' (*Sénèque et le Théâtre de la Renaissance*, 1964, p. 307).

But if the 'scientific' definiteness provided by parallel passages disappears from literary theses dealing with 'influence', what then is left? It might seem that the concept of influence then becomes too vague to be tenable. But we should take comfort by remembering that the etymology of *influence* suggests no single link, but rather a stream of tendency raining down upon its object. The complexity of the situation in which B is subject to the influence of A need not prevent us from trying to describe it. Certainly the point must be made that we cannot talk effectively about the influence of A on B unless we are prepared to see A (as B saw him) as part of a whole intellectual climate. We should not discuss 'the influence of Seneca on Elizabethan tragedy' except in the context of the other competing influences that were raining down at the same time. Ideally, indeed, we should know the whole nature of the air breathed by English writers between the 1560s and the 1590s, the literary, historical, artistic scenery of these years, before we discuss 'the development of English tragedy'. Such knowledge would, inevitably, produce complex views; but it does not follow that it would rule out of court the present vulgate supposition that classical literature played a vital part in the development of English tragedy; indeed I do not suppose it. I do not suggest that such knowledge would cause the name of Seneca to die away from Shakespeare conferences. But I do assume that the limpid simplicities of the person-to-person type of influence-study would have to be broken up by the cross-currents and complexities of a larger view. And it is to these complicating factors that I wish to devote the rest of this study.

I have used Cunliffe's 1893 thesis as my paradigm of a scientific study of 'influence'. The thesis itself contains no direct statement of its simplest assumptions, no plan of the intellectual model that is being used; but an admirably economical statement of this kind occurs in the opening paragraph of Cunliffe's *Cambridge History of English Literature* article on 'Early Tragedy' (Vol. v, p. 61), published in 1910, some 17 years after the thesis, but sharing with it, I think, the same basic attitudes:

The history of renascence tragedy may be divided into three stages, not definitely limited, and not following in strict chronological succession, but distinct in the main: the study, imitation and production of Senecan tragedy; translation; the imitation of Greek and Latin tragedy in the vernacular.

I am not concerned to dispute how far this is, or is not, true of continental tragedy; but as far as English tragedy is concerned the lucidity of the pattern of development described depends on a rejection of competing relevant factors. Two simplifying assumptions may be noted in particular: first, that the vernacular tradition need not be mentioned, because it had nothing positive to offer; and that, in the main, the Renaissance served up classical tragedy on a *tabula rasa*. This might *resist* influence, it is allowed, but it could hardly exercise it. The second assumption is that one can talk about tragedy as a simple watertight genre, open to influence by other tragedy in the first place, and only secondarily and subordinately influenced by other genres.

I wish to discuss the second of these assumptions first. Most of us nowadays have learned to go behind the Chinese wall of the theory of genres and to apply in detail our general knowledge that the Renaissance was an age of syncretism and eclecticism. Farnham[3] and Baker[4] have laid great stress on the continuity of tragic narrative and what we tend to call 'tragedy proper'; and there is no need to reiterate the point that Seneca's 'non-theatrical' or narrative qualities helped to make him assimilable;[5] but at the same time as we say this we should see that his assimilability helped to submerge *his* qualities among the apparently similar qualities of the Gothic tradition,[6] his ghosts melting away among the throng of their ghosts, his horrors rendered barely visible against the background of their horrors.[7]

The Gothic willingness to juxtapose things historically distinct, preferring flat anachronism to the perspective of history, made such assimilations both inevitable and easy. If we wish to see how visual anachronism can alter the whole tone of a work impeccably classical in origin, we may look at the plates drawn from the only illuminated manuscript of Seneca known to me[8] (Plates I–II). We may see the same principle operating in the 1581 translation where Studley translates

> Cruentis paelicem poenis premat
> Regalis ira, vinculis oneret manus   (*Medea*, 462 f.)

by

> Let Creon *in his princely ruffe* lay to his heavy handes
> To whip an whore in torments sharp with iron gives and bands.   (my italics)

What we cannot know for certain is how far this anachronistic principle operated in the Elizabethan reading of the Latin text. But it would surely be wrong, in the light of what we know about Elizabethan anachronism, to suppose that stories from the classics were received in a distinctly 'classical' frame of mind, which caused them to appear potentially classical in manner. This is the assumption of H. B. Charlton, who tells us that plays like *Cambyses*, *Horestes* and *Apius and Virginia* were, because 'classical in story,...potentially classical in dramatic motive and incident, and thus competent to create in due season a taste for certain elements of classical tragedy'.[9] The assimilative powers of the Renaissance would in fact have been impossible if separate contributions to the age had remained as distinct as this implies; it is only in the compost-heap of history that new literatures breed. Panofsky's *Renaissance and Renascences in Western Art* (1960) is, indeed, devoted to just this discontinuity between subject matter of the classical past (seen clearly but in terms of a modern—usually Christian—meaning)[10] and a feeling for classical form (applied to a close imitation of contemporary reality). The discontinuity is one that does not seem to be resolved at any point in Elizabethan literature.

Moreover, the lack of a clear division between tragedy and other genres meant that a greater proportion of the classical inheritance was relevant to Elizabethan tragedy than Cunliffe seemed to allow. The *tabula rasa* theory of tragic origins implies that the only relevant question is 'Greek or Latin?'; we should note in passing the extent to which H. B. Charlton's essay is based on this; but the relevant questions stretch in fact far more widely. The great importance of Ovid in this respect should never be underestimated. Scaliger's typical tragedy (Bk. III, chap. xcvii of the *Poetices libri septem*) came from Ovid's story of Ceyx and Alcyone, at the end of Bk. XI of the *Metamorphoses*—the same tragedy as Chaucer had used in *The Book of the Duchess*, and which W. Hubbard, the 1569 translator, called 'the tragicall and lamentable historie of Ceyx, Kynge of Trachine and Alcione his wife'—and a glance at this will show the extent to which the ingredients of 'Senecan' tragedy were present in Ovid. I would point to the brilliantly horrific description of the storm in which Ceyx died (a description imitated, I believe, in the *Antonio and Mellida* of Marston), the effective scene where the ghost of Ceyx comes to Alcyone to announce his own death, the tragic irony of Alcyone's weaving a garment for the husband who is already dead, the supernatural brilliance of the descent of Iris to the Underworld and to the Cave of Morpheus (imitated by Spenser), the effective rhetoric of the divided mind in the scene with Alcyone at the seashore, torn between despair of the future and memories of the past; finally the horrific climax of the recovery of Ceyx's body and the strange metamorphosis of the lovers into birds. All that is lacking is moralization, and this Scaliger finds easy enough to supply in the Choruses he invents:

(1) 'detestans navigationes';
(2) 'vota approbans';
(3) 'exempla adducens naufragiorum';
(4) '[naufragium] deplorans'.

The cardinal tragedies of the popular tradition—Kyd's *Spanish Tragedy* and Shakespeare's *Titus Andronicus*—draw heavily on Ovid for both matter and manner. *Titus Andronicus* (like *Lucrece* and *Venus and Adonis*) is a mainly Ovidian piece; as Baker has pointed out, only a determination to find Seneca in every woodpile could have suppressed the Philomela story in order to reveal *Thyestes* as the source. Tenderness in the midst of horror is a characteristic of both *Spanish Tragedy* and *Titus*; it is a characteristic of Ovid; it is not a characteristic of Seneca. In fact, take down the artificial barriers between tragedy and narrative, and Seneca all but disappears into the engulfing sea of Ovidian and quasi-Ovidian imitation. Modes of rhetoric and subject matter are often so similar in the two poets that it is difficult to separate them as models; but there can be no doubt where we must place the preference if a single name has to be adduced. For Ovid is everywhere in Elizabethan England, in schooling, in Art and in endless quotations, translations, paraphrases, imitations. But Seneca (in spite of Cunliffe's confident assertion) seems to have played little or no part in the Tudor scheme of grammar school education;[11] we should also notice that there was only one translation of each tragedy in the period 1540–1640, and that the one complete edition of 1581 enjoyed only one printing. Where Seneca *does* differ from Ovid—as in his gloomy devotion to horror as the only real truth about humanity—the Elizabethans seem to have avoided noticing the fact. As Christians they could hardly endorse his resolute sense of divine malevolence, and in their adherence to the idea of 'the Christian Ethnicke Seneca' as Studley, the first translator of the *Medea*, learned from Erasmus to call him, they probably did not observe it. Studley's well-known mistranslation of the last line of the *Medea*

> testare nullos esse, qua veheris, deos

into

> Bear witness, grace of God is none in place of thy repayre

may serve as a paradigm of this easy distortion.[12]

Even the formal aspects of tragedy, such as its five-act structure, once confidently attributed to Seneca, the massive researches of T. W. Baldwin have shown to be more likely to come from Terence. Terence, not Seneca, was at the centre of school instruction in drama, and therefore of formal adult practice. The chorus, which Seneca has and Terence lacks, is a dead letter. We are left with a few well-worn anthology passages and a few isolated tricks like stichomythia (and even that occurs outside tragedy)[13] as relics of the once extensive empire of Seneca's undisputed influence.

Mention of these formal characteristics brings me back to the first part of Cunliffe's simplified diagram of English tragic origins. He took it for granted that the vernacular tradition was a passive or dying body waiting for replacement, ripe only for modernization. Memory of the process by which classical influence affected other arts in the period, and the extent to which a broad survey like Panofsky's *Renaissance and Renascences* is able to find similarities of process, should, however, make us pause. In general it would seem that the Gothic style only gradually admitted modifications, and those superficial ones. It continued to exercise its powers with ease and authority, not as a senile creature waiting for the end and the take-over-bid of the new generation, but as a master well able to command such new-fangled servants as it chose to employ. Hampton Court (1515–36), Henry VII's chapel at Westminster (1502–12), Christ Church, Oxford (1525 *et seq.*) are not obviously the products of decay or degeneracy. Wolsey might place medallions with the heads of the Roman Emperors on the gateways of Hampton Court, but this is as far as his interest in classical models seems to take him. As Sir John Summerson has remarked:

...although foreign fashions in ornament, and sometimes in plan, were excitedly adopted, they were adopted for the intrinsic pleasure they gave rather than from any sense of apprenticeship to foreign achievements greater than [Tudor Englishmen's] own. If ancient Rome and modern Italy received their homage, it was homage to a legend...it is only by insisting falsely on the importance of accurate grammatical interpretation of classical elements that we are tempted to see them as groping preliminaries to the Italian classicism of Inigo Jones...Classical architecture made its way in England not as a method of building but as a mode of decorative design...of columns and entablatures, pediments and consoles.[14]

The Latin quotations which abound in Elizabethan drama form an obvious example of literary parallel to Wolsey's medallions. As found in florilegia, polyanthea, thesauruses, books of quotations and commonplaces these *sententiae* bear an obvious relation to the 'classical' designs found in pattern-books. The Senecan quotations which appear in Elizabethan plays, even when the quantity is as great as that which decorates Marston's *Antonio and Mellida*, bear little or no relation to the contexts of the plays in which they originally appeared. This was indeed one of the rules of imitation, as Ralph Johnson noted in his *Scholars Guide from the Accidence to the University* (1665), under the heading 'Rules of Allusion':

We may allude to Sentences of Authors, applying them to another matter...We may say of drunkenness as the Poet did of love, *raptam tollit de cardine mentem.*   (p. 9)

Seneca's name appears frequently in such florilegia as list authors, but the quotations often do not come from Seneca at all (the whole set of Publilius Syrus' *Sententiae* gets attached to Seneca's name).[15] Seneca as a name for a collection of grave moral and near-Christian sentiments is one thing; Seneca as an instructor in tragedy is quite another; and we should beware of subsuming the first into the second. We should not forget that the first works of Seneca to make their way into English in the Tudor period are the *De Quattuor Virtutibus* and the *De Moribus*, not by Seneca at all, but by St Martin of Braga, writing in the sixth century. Indeed, throughout the Renaissance, Seneca the moral sage is much more widely acclaimed than Seneca the tragic exemplar. The name of Seneca gave a classical gloss to moral collections; it did not give either a classical form or a classical substance. Indeed, even where the tragedies were read, the practice of digesting reading-matter into private commonplace books placed an effective barrier between the original (as a literary structure) and the 'imitation'. I would direct attention back again to the interesting case of John Webster.[16]

The tendency to pile up examples, to enrich by amassing materials from a wide variety of sources, to treasure the curious detail—these are, from a formal point of view, signs of the Gothic rather than the classic, even when the materials so collected have classical origins. The idea that tragedy as a classical structure would be 'spoiled' by over-repetition, by addition of side-chapels, secondary plots, new episodes (especially if these had Greco-Roman origins), would not, I suspect, have made a great deal of sense in the period; for the equation of 'classicism' with 'purity' had not yet been made. The Gothic minds of the Elizabethan audience exercised a natural sovereignty over the classical past. They looked at the Classics out of their own eyes, seeing as most central those Greco-Roman authors whose styles were close enough to their own preferences to be intelligible. And the landscape of classical literature that their minds allowed them to see was different in many respects from that which has prevailed in Western Europe since Winckelmann. Not Sophocles or Horace,[17] but Ovid and Plutarch were at the centre of their vision of classicism. We should remember that English Greek studies begin with a translation not of Homer or Plato, but of Synesius on baldness,[18] that More and Erasmus concentrated their literary attention on Lucian and the Anthology, and that Lucretius had to wait until 1656 before his work was translated into English.

Tragedy, though seen as a classical genre, was not exempted from this general sense that the road to improvement lay through the multiplication of instances. We may find this equation of intensity with horrific repetitiveness in as popular an area as the Induction to *A Warning for Fair Women* (before 1599), where the materials of tragedy are thus described:

> How some damn'd tyrant to obtain a crown
> Stabs, hangs, impoisons, smothers, cutteth throats;
> And then a Chorus too comes howling in
> And tells us of the worrying of a cat:
> Then [too] a filthy whining ghost
> Lapt in some foul sheet, or a leather pilch
> Comes screaming like a pig half-stick'd,
> And cries Vindicta!—Revenge, Revenge!
> With that a little rosin flasheth forth
> Like smoke out of a tobacco pipe, or a boy's squib.
> Then comes in two or three like to drovers,
> With tailors' bodkins stabbing one another—

We may also find it in no less a classicist than Julius Caesar Scaliger; he defines the materials of tragedy as follows:

Res tragicae grandes, atroces, jussa Regum, caedes, desperationes, suspendia, exilia, orbitates, parricidia, incestus, incendia, pugnae, occaecationes, fletus, ululatus, conquestiones, funera, epitaphia, epicedia.

The searcher for classical purity would find little comfort here: he might, indeed, seem to be little beyond Dante's definition:

dicitur propter hoc a *tragos*, quod est *hircus*, et oda, quasi *cantus hircinus*, id est foetidus ad modum hirci, ut patet per Senecam in suis tragoediis.

A strange confirmation of Scaliger's 'Gothic' view of tragedy as centred on its horrors appears in an English work very remote from Scaliger, in John Greene's perfervid diatribe against acting, called *A Refutation of the Apology for Actors* (1615). Greene is concerned to make the point that tragedy is concerned exclusively with wickednesses, and that therefore it corrupts its spectators. The resultant description reads almost like a translation of Scaliger. To the seventeenth-century Puritan (writing, we should note, at the end of Shakespeare's career), as to the neo-classical critic, tragedy is characterized by its trail of horrors:

The matter of tragedies is haughtinesse, arrogancy, ambition, pride, iniury, anger, wrath, envy, hatred, contention, warre, murther, cruelty, rapine, incest, rovings, depradations, piracyes, spoyles, roberies, rebellions, treasons, killing, hewing, stabbing, dagger-drawing, fighting, butchery, trechery, villany, etc. and all kind of heroyick evils whatsoever. (p. 56)

While we are thinking of tragedy in these terms, we ought to remember that a vernacular acting tradition already existed, to encourage a repetitive, aggregative dramatic structure. The tradition of the vernacular drama, unlike that of the neo-classical drama, was already a theatrical tradition. It sometimes seems to be assumed that, because the Middle Ages defined Tragedy in terms of literary rather than a theatrical experience, the Renaissance drama had to await the recovery of the classics before it could recover the art of acting. But this, of course, must be nonsense. Bevington[19] has shown very clearly how the exigencies of acting in late medieval England shaped the kinds of plays that were produced, and how this repetitive structure was carried forward by the acting profession into the art of Marlowe. The arts of spectacle, of emblematic presentation, of dumb show, of multi-level statement, of pictorial metaphor—these go forward from the miracle plays and the interludes as a continuous tradition, and something like a guild structure of actors exists to preserve them and keep innovation at bay. The texts of Seneca, especially given their avoidance of stage-direction, could contribute nothing more than occasional *sententiae* to this stage-tradition; and we should remember that it was in this tradition that all the major plays of the Elizabethan age were produced. It is not classical tragedy, but *The Famous Victories of Henry V*, *The Chronicle History of King Leir*, *The Troublesome Raigne of King John*, that Shakespeare can use for his foundations. The diagram of development that sees Elizabethan tragedy beginning from the Senecan translations of the 1560s, going on to Academic drama in the late sixties or seventies (*Misfortunes of Arthur*, *Gismond of Salerne*, *Richardus Tertius*), and so, without a glance left or right, to similar and therefore 'Senecan' plays like *The Spanish Tragedy*, *Locrine* and *Selimus*, omits too much to be convincing.

If we look more closely at the tradition of repertory drama, of *Apius and Virginia*, *Horestes*, *Damon and Pithias*, *Cambyses* and *Patient Grissil*, I think we can see, inside a single acting tradition, a gradual but continuous adaptation of the discursive and moralizing drama of the late Middle Ages into the polydimensional story-drama of mature theatre. This is a movement that could not have taken the course it did without the criticism of vernacular methods that the classics imply. But the exact composition of that classical front does not seem to be so vital. If Seneca's tragedies had not survived, some details would have had to be changed—but the overall picture would not have been altered.

© G. K. HUNTER 1967

NOTES

1. I do not wish to be taken to mean that Cunliffe says all that can be said about *The Misfortunes of Arthur*. See W. A. Armstrong, 'Elizabethan themes in *The Misfortunes of Arthur*', *R.E.S.* VII (1956), 238–49.

2. For example, J. A. Symonds, *Shakespeare's Predecessors in the English Drama* (1884); A. H. Thorndike, *Tragedy* (Boston, 1908); H. E. Fansler, *The Evolution of Technic in Elizabethan Tragedy* (Chicago, 1914); F. E. Schelling, *Elizabethan Drama*, 2 vols. (Boston, 1908).

3. Willard Farnham, *The Medieval Heritage of Elizabethan Tragedy* (Berkeley, Cal., 1936).

4. Howard Baker, *Induction to Tragedy* (Louisiana S.U.P., 1939).

5. One may be permitted to add, however, to the testimony adduced by Baker an interesting passage from Thomas Storer's *The Life and Death of Thomas Wolsey* (1599), where Seneca is invoked as patron of the narrative form of tragedy:

> Now write, Melpomene, my tragicke mone,
> Call Neroes learned maister, he will ayd
> Thy failing quill with what himself once sayd:
> Never did Fortune greater instance give
> In what fraile state prowd Magistrates do live.

6. The use of the word 'Gothic' in such a context may seem barbarous. I use it deliberately in order to suggest that pre-classical literary practice in the Tudor period is not to be explained by ignorance, is not necessarily haphazard, but may often belong to a recognizable *system* of art.

7. The horrors of the 'Senecan' plays of the Elizabethan period are often very close to those in the medieval plays concerned with the lives (and deaths) of the saints. Long before Hieronimo bit out his tongue to defy his interrogators, St Catherine did the same. St James the dismembered, moralizing each limb as it is severed, reminds us of the horrific grotesquerie of Theseus (at the end of the *Phaedra*) reassembling the jig-saw portions of Hippolytus. Indeed, even the most horrific of the 'tragedies of blood' have nothing to rival the disembowelling of St Erasmus, to take only one example in the catalogue of horrors that the *Golden Legend* bequeathed to the medieval imagination.

8. The manuscript ('L. A. Senecae comoediae') is of North French or Flemish provenance, and is probably to be dated in the first quarter of the fifteenth century. It may have been made for Charles VII of France. It is

described in the *Bulletin de la Société française de reproduction des MSS*, XXI (1938) and (more fully) in H. J. Herrmann, *Verzeichnis der Illuminierten Handschriften in Osterreich*, Band VII, 3 (1938), pp. 86–100.

9. H. B. Charlton, Introduction to the *Works of Sir William Alexander*, ed. Kastner and Charlton, I (S.T.S. n.s. xi, 1921), p. cxlii.

10. An interesting example of the recovery of classical stories in terms of modern (Christian) meanings appears in Dean Nowell's draft preface to a performance of the *Phaedra*, presumably at Westminster School and probably in 1546 (preserved in Brasenose College MS 31, fols. 25 ff.):

Senecae tragici poetae hypolitum, spectatores candidissimi, apud vos acturi, non formidamus haec praefari, ut inter tragicos omnes latinos non tantum primus, sed propemodum etiam solus—vel fabii iudicio—dignus [est] quod legatur est hic Seneca; ita inter omnes huius tragedias longe primas obtinet, haec quam sumus representaturi hyppolitus fabula. ad eius, tum apud alios omnes, tum apud vos praecippue, utpote sacrarum literarum Audiosos, commendationem etiam hoc accedit, quod a iosephi et pitipharis uxoris historia in sacris genesios libris prodita haec hypoliti fabula non procul alludit: et quod illic citra omnem controversiam revera gestum legitur.

11. See T. W. Baldwin, *William Shakespere's Five-Act Structure* (Urbana, 1947), p. 741.

12. I should perhaps enter a caveat here, and make the point that I am not seeking to deny the influence of Seneca in order to sell the influence of Ovid. I wish rather to suggest the danger of extracting any *one* name from the generalized mass of classical example, splayed out by the methods of imitation in terms of topics rather than authors.

13. If by stichomythia we mean 'dialogue in alternate lines, employed in sharp disputation' (as *O.E.D.* seems to imply) there seems to be a largely comic tradition of this in English drama, quite independent of classical models. The earliest English example known to me (missed by J. L. Hancock, *Studies in Stichomythia*, Chicago, 1917) occurs in the *Mactatio Abel* of the Wakefield Cycle (first half of the fifteenth century) in the concluding dialogue between Cain and his comic servant Garcio:

Caym: I commaund you in the kyngys nayme,
Garcio: And in my masteres, fals Cayme,
Caym: That no man at thame fynd fawt ne blame,
Garcio: Yey, cold rost is at my masteres hame.
Caym: Nowther with hym nor with his knafe,
Garcio: What! I hope my master rafe.

Caym: For thay ar trew full manyfold.
Garcio: My master suppys no coyle bot cold.
Caym: The kyng wrytys you vntill.
Garcio: Yit ete I neuer half my fill.
Caym: The kyng will that thay be safe.
Garcio: Yey, a draght of drynke fayne wold I hayfe.
Caym: At thare awne will let tham wafe.
Garcio: My stomak is redy to receyfe.
Caym: Loke no man say to theym, on nor other—
Garcio: This same is he that slo his brother.
Caym: Byd euery man thaym luf and lowt.
Garcio: Yey, ill-spon weft ay comes foule out.
Caym: Long or thou get thi hoyse, and thou go thus aboute!

Similar passages occur among early Tudor plays, and, again, Classical influence seems not to be the determining factor. Indeed, in plays written in couplets, the witty division of the couplet between two speakers is so obvious a device that it needs no messenger from Argos to make the point. In Bale's *King Johan* (1534) the stichomythia of divided couplets fits in well enough with the polemical purpose of the play. The anonymous *Jacob and Esau* (1554) uses quite an amount of comic stichomythia—as between Esau and his servant Rogan (*MSR*, 105–18) and between Isaac and Rebecca, husband and wife (381–413). *July and Julian* (1570) shows it between the two servants Fenell and Wilkin. In *The Marriage of Wit and Science* (?1567), Wit and his servant Will have many short dialogues in line-by-line exchange.

On the other hand, plays as 'Senecan' as *Gorboduc* and *Cambyses* show no traces of stichomythia. *Damon and Pithias* has one passage (861–91) clearly modelled on that between Seneca and Nero in the *Octavia*; but this is the only one, out of the many passages of stichomythia in the play, that has a clearly classical origin.

14. *Architecture in Britain 1530–1830* (Pelican History of Art) (1953), p. 20. The process here described may remind some of the transformations that appear in Lebègue's account of *La Tragédie religieuse en France...* *1514–1573* (Paris, 1929); as, for example, the process which turns the scene of Judas' repentance, in Nicholas Barthelemy's classical passion-play, *Christus Xylonicus* (1529), into a dialogue (in good hexameters) with *Alecto* rather than with *Desespoir*. The substance remains but a classical 'finish' has been applied to it.

15. For the so-called 'Collectanea Senecae' MSS of Publilius Syrus see J. Wight Duff, *Minor Latin Poets* (Loeb Classical Library) (1934), pp. 6–12. The general role played by Seneca in the florilegia of the Renaissance can only be sketched here in respect of a few of the

most popular books. The *Fiore di Virti*, which had a European circulation under sundry titles—*Le Livre des Vices & des Vertus, La Fleur de Vertu* (Brunet, II, 1286), *Le Livre de Saigesse* (Brunet, III, 1123), *Armonia coi Soavi accenti, The Book of Virtues and Vices* (?1485) (E.E.T.S. o.s. 217), *The Boke of Wisdome* (?1575)—devotes some of its space to Seneca (as well as to Boethius, Solomon, David, Socrates, Tully, etc.), usually through the medium of the *Compendium moralium notabilium* of Geremia da Montagnone; but of the 38 'Seneca dice...' paragraphs noted by Carlo Frati (*Ricerche sul 'Fiore di Virtu'*, Studii di filologia romanza, VI, 1893) only three seem to derive from authentic works of Seneca, and these are prose works. As Frati remarks: 'per Seneca in fine, delle cui sentenze troviamo riscontro, sia in opere autentiche di Seneca...sia nel *De forma honestae vitae*... o nel *De moribus*... o in alcuni *Proverbi volgari di Seneca*...che ci attestano quanto consentita fosse nei tempi, in che fu scritto il *Fior di Virtu* l'attribuzione di essi a Seneca' (p. 272).

The *Manipulus Florum* or *Flores omnium pene doctorum* of Thomas Hibernicus—often reprinted, and much used by such a popular Elizabethan writer as Dekker—draws on Seneca as the most notable pagan author in a company of scholastics, saints and fathers—Augustine, Bernard, Bede, Jerome, Cassiodorus, Alanus, Innocent, etc.—but, again, the references are largely to the supposititious works, the *proverbia* and the *de moribus*, though the *epistulae* and *de remediis fortuitorum* are also heavily drawn on. The tragedies do not seem to be mentioned. Of the English florilegia of the Elizabethan period the *Treatise of Moral Philosophy* by William Baldwin (1547 and numerous later editions) is probably the most popular early example. It is in the same tradition as the two works already mentioned, of heavily

moral paragraphs conveying at undue length the tritest of sentiments. To Seneca are attributed such statements as 'Marry a young maid that thou mayest teach her good manners', 'order thy wife as thou wouldest thy kinsfolk', etc., etc. If any of the sharp sayings of the tragedies lie buried in Baldwin's massy prose, it is difficult to disinter them.

The *Politeuphuia* or *Wits Commonwealth* (which STC lists under Nicholas Ling) had numerous editions from 1597 onwards and was obviously much used. L. B. Wright has said that 'of all the handbooks of wisdom, the one having the greatest popular acceptance was *Politeuphuia*' and the Jacobean schoolmaster, Hoole, tells us that 'it is generally imposed upon young scholars to translate out of English into Latin'. *Politeuphuia* did not list authors in the early editions, but later included Seneca's name with those of Guevara, Socrates, Gregory, Olaus Magnus, Augustine, Aristotle, Solon, Hermes, etc., etc. But no image of Seneca as different from these almost professional purveyors of wisdom emerges. *Seneca Moralis* emerges only as a mouthpiece for standard wisdom.

16. It is Seneca in this anthology sense, I suspect, that Nashe is referring to in the famous passage of the preface to *Menaphon* where 'English Seneca read by Candlelight yields many good sentences, as *Bloud is a begger* and so forth'.

17. I mean 'not the Horace of the *Odes*'. *Orazio Satiro* was, of course, well known, and had been translated by several hands.

18. The translation, made before 1461, was by John Free. See Robert Weiss, *Humanism in England during the Fifteenth Century* (1941).

19. D. M. Bevington, *From 'Mankind' to Marlowe* (Cambridge, Mass., 1962).

GEORGE CHAPMAN: TRAGEDY AND THE PROVIDENTIAL VIEW OF HISTORY

BY

G. R. HIBBARD

In the comparatively short passage that he devotes to the subject of poetry in *The Advancement of Learning*, Bacon, who has just been discussing at some length the state of historical knowledge and enquiry, defines poetry as 'nothing else but feigned history'. He then proceeds in characteristic fashion to examine its utility, saying of it:

The use of this feigned history hath been to give some shadow of satisfaction to the mind of man in those points wherein the nature of things doth deny it, the world being in proportion inferior to the soul; by reason whereof there is, agreeable to the spirit of man, a more ample greatness, a more exact goodness, and a more absolute variety, than can be found in the nature of things. Therefore, because the acts or events of true history have not that magnitude which satisfieth the mind of man, poesy feigneth acts and events greater and more heroical. Because true history propoundeth the successes and issues of actions not so agreeable to the merits of virtue and vice, therefore poesy feigns them more just in retribution, and more according to revealed providence.

(Bk. II, IV, 2)

Whether there is or is not a touch of irony in these remarks—the Neoplatonist Henry Reynolds was emphatically of the opinion that Bacon's whole attitude to poetry was a slighting one[1]—that last sentence describes not only the way in which the poets, to Bacon's mind, handled the material of history, but also the way in which most historians handled it at the time when he was writing. The dominant tradition in historical works was still what R. G. Collingwood has called 'the providential idea';[2] and, some nine years later, in 1614, this approach to the past received its most impressive formulation in English with the publication of Sir Walter Raleigh's *History of the World*. In the Preface to it Raleigh leaves his readers in no doubt about the assumptions that underlie his conception of causation in history. Proclaiming that 'the judgements of GOD are for ever unchangeable' (ed. 1677, B2r), he goes on to demonstrate—by some judicious selection of evidence—that both English and European history are nothing but a record of human crime and divine punishment. As he does so, he resorts repeatedly to images drawn from the theatre to enforce his meaning, employing them to such an extent that it is almost impossible to avoid the conclusion that, for the author of the poem which begins 'What is our life? a play of passion', history and tragedy were practically interchangeable terms. Indeed, when he comes to write of the reign of Edward IV, he does so in such a manner that it is not easy to say whether his historical sources, or Shakespeare's version of them in *Richard III*, were uppermost in his mind, for he writes:

this *Edward* the King...beheld and allowed the slaughter which *Gloucester, Dorset, Hastings*, and others, made of *Edward* the Prince in his own presence; of which tragical Actors, there was not one that escaped the Judgement of GOD in the same kind.

(B2v)

And, while the historians tended to think of history as a series of tragedies, the playwrights, using history as the main source for their tragedies, tended to think of tragedy as history, seeing it as the re-enactment on the stage of 'tragic facts' from the past, rather than as a purely dramatic form. In these circumstances interaction between the two kinds of writing was bound to occur.

But *The History of the World*, enormous though its popularity was in the first half of the seventeenth century, was already a bit old-fashioned as history at the time when it was being composed. The climate was changing. Bacon himself had no use for history of this sort. The historian's task, as he saw it, was to get on with the essential work that was within his powers and that would be of practical value to others—that of narrating the facts historically with as little admixture of private judgment as possible, instead of indulging in vain speculations about those 'first causes' which were beyond the reach of human wisdom. Nor was Bacon alone in taking this view. Less assured than he about the way they were going, but also less theoretical in their approach, men like Camden, Stow, and Selden were, nonetheless, moving in the same direction towards the secularization of historical studies. So much so, in fact, that according to a recent historiographer the period 1580–1640 was the time of 'The Historical Revolution'.[3]

Now, it will not have escaped the attention of an audience such as this that precisely these same years were also the time when the theatre too enjoyed its great flourishing. 'The Historical Revolution' and 'The Dramatic Revolution' went on side by side; and one is almost driven to ask whether there was not a connexion between them. Needless to say, I think there was; and part of the evidence for it lies in those remarks of Bacon's about the subject of poetry with which I began. Far-sighted though he was in many things, Bacon was, so far as some of the poets writing tragedy were concerned, badly out of date and out of touch in 1605. Far from showing 'the issues of actions...more just in retribution, and more according to revealed providence', the tragic dramatists tended to do the opposite. Shakespeare's *Richard III*, where the action is presided over by the 'upright, just, and true-disposing God' that Queen Margaret invokes in IV, iv, fits in perfectly with Bacon's view of the relationship between poetry and true history; but *King Lear* does not, for its ending is of a very different kind from the 'fortunate' outcome of *The True Chronicle History of King Leir*, and poses questions about the nature of divine justice that the restoration of Lear to the throne, followed by the irrelevant suicide of Cordelia several years later, which is what Shakespeare found in Holinshed and his other possible sources, does not and cannot do. Bacon need not have looked so far afield as to Machiavelli in order to find an example of the writers who 'write what men do, and not what they ought to do' (*The Advancement of Learning*, Bk. II, XXI, 9), for by the time these words were published the tragic dramatists—or at least some of them—had been doing just this for years. In the Prologue to *Antonio's Revenge* John Marston had announced his intention to show 'what men were, and are'; and Ben Jonson's *Sejanus* is as bleak and unconsolatory a piece of history as anyone could wish for. But then, Jonson had gone for his material to Tacitus, who was still being reprehended by Edmund Bolton in his *Hypercritica* (1618?), which is a fairly enlightened work on the theory of history, for completely ignoring 'The Part of heavenly Providence in the Actions of Men'.[4]

The peculiar interest of Chapman in this connexion lies in two things: first, all his tragedies are historical, in the sense that they are set in a definite time—four out of the five in very recent time—and deal mainly with characters and situations that had actually existed, and about which a good deal was known; and, secondly, the experience they embody and explore seems to me to spring in no small measure from the tension that is created in them by conflicting attitudes to historical material and to history itself. At a first glance, Chapman appears to be decidedly of the old world, sharing the outlook of his friend and contemporary Raleigh—exactly the kind of poet that Bacon was thinking of. Not at all averse from theorizing, he rebuts, in the Dedication to *The Revenge of Bussy d'Ambois*, the criticisms of those who had objected to the cavalier manner in which he treats historical fact in that play, by asserting the poet's right to do as he will with historical matter in the interests of morality. The fact that criticisms on this score had been made is, incidentally, evidence of the extent to which new ideas about history were gaining ground; and I have often wondered whether Ben Jonson, who placed such a high value on 'truth of Argument', can have been one of the critics. Here are Chapman's words:

And for the authentical truth of either person or actions, who (worth the respecting) will expect it in a poem, whose subject is not truth, but things like truth? Poor envious souls they are that cavil at truth's want in these natural fictions; material instruction, elegant and sententious excitation to virtue, and deflection from her contrary, being the soul, limbs, and limits of an authentical tragedy.[5]

The self-defence needed to be made, for Chapman had exercised his freedom as a poet to the limit. Not content with reading God's judgments into history, like Raleigh, he had showed no hesitation in supplementing and anticipating them. In order that the assassination of the historical Bussy should no longer go unpunished, as it had done for over thirty years when the play was written, Chapman had invented a brother, Clermont d'Ambois, for him, and had shown Clermont killing Montsurry in a duel, though the real Montsurry was still alive in France at the time when he was dying daily on the stage at the Whitefriars'. And it was not only for the moral edification of his audience that Chapman altered the data of history, but also, if I read him aright, in order to sustain and support his own faith and convictions. The argument with which that most rational and dialectically skilled of Elizabethan spectres, the Ghost of Bussy, eventually persuades Clermont of the rightness of revenge, is that the continuance of religion and of civilized living is dependent on the execution of justice in this world. Accusing Clermont of putting off the duty of revenge for selfish personal motives that defy the will of God, the Ghost continues:

> To live to Him, is to do all things fitting
> His image, in which, like Himself, we live;
> To be His image is to do those things
> That make us deathless, which by death is only
> Doing those deeds that fit eternity;
> And those deeds are the perfecting that justice
> That makes the world last, which proportion is
> Of punishment and wreak for every wrong,
> As well as for right a reward as strong.   (v, i, 87–95)

Few poets can ever have gone further than Chapman does in this play towards correcting the errors of time, and subjecting the brute facts of history to the demands of the moral order.

Caesar and Pompey, however, runs it a close second. Here, having chosen Cato as the right historical figure to exemplify the thesis that 'only a just man is a free man', Chapman makes the Roman stoic the mouthpiece for his own beliefs about the immortality of the soul and the resurrection of the body. In his other tragedies he remains closer to the facts of history, but affirms in each of them, usually at the outset, as in the Prologue to *Byron* and in that long opening speech by Bussy which is virtually a prologue, that his main concern is with moral instruction.

Yet, despite these statements of intention, only one of Chapman's tragedies, *Chabot*, comes anywhere near to meeting the demands of poetic justice, which is what the theorizing leads one to expect that they should all do, and, in so far as it does so, it seems to me to stand apart from the rest of the tragic *œuvre*, and to be less characteristic of its author and less truly tragic. The strength of the other tragedies comes, at least in part, I would suggest, from the fact that they embody other attitudes to history and to human life which cut across the providential one. The first— and it is, I think, something that Chapman, more than any other dramatist of the time, shares with the Shakespeare of *Richard II*, of *Antony and Cleopatra*, and of *Coriolanus*—is his perception that many of the great conflicts of history arise, not out of the clash of right with wrong, but of right with right. He may well have been helped towards it by the *Antigone* of Sophocles, which he refers to and quotes from in *The Revenge of Bussy d'Ambois* (II, i, 113–38), but it is undoubtedly something of which he was acutely aware. It is presented as a problem for the individual at the end of *Bussy d'Ambois*, where, after the hero's death, Tamyra finds herself faced with a moral dilemma which she defines thus:

> O wretched piety, that art so distract
> In thine own constancy, and in thy right
> Must be unrighteous: if I right my friend
> I wrong my husband; if his wrong I shun,
> The duty of my friend I leave undone. (v, iv, 167–71)

In the form of the larger general issue of the individual, with his desire for self-realization, coming into collision with the state, this conflict of right with right informs all the tragedies, finding its most complete statement in *Byron*, where Chapman's sympathies are equally engaged for, and equally divided between, the turbulent noble who has lived by strife, and the King seeking to bring peace and order to a torn and distracted country. And, because he has this awareness of conflicting principles, Chapman writes tragedies that can fairly be read as penetrating insights into the history of his own times, looking not only back but also forwards. If *Byron* is about the struggle between the new monarchy and the over-mighty subject, which was substantially over by the time he wrote it, *Chabot* is about the conflict between the Common Law and the Royal Prerogative, which was soon to assume far larger proportions in real life than it has in the play. Indeed, is it going too far to say that Bussy putting the case for 'man in his native noblesse' is, much as Chapman would have disliked the idea, not so far removed from figures like John Lilburne? Chapman had insights into what was really happening in the England he lived in; and there is, I think, a connexion between his understanding of right versus right as a factor in history and such different works as Marvell's *Horatian Ode* and Clarendon's *History of the Great Rebellion*.

Crossing the two lines of thinking I have described, there is another, which seems to me to have nothing to do with historical processes, except in so far as it is really anti-historical. I mean, of course, Chapman's Neoplatonism, which is fundamental to his whole view of life, and which gives his tragedies their unique quality. I call it anti-historical because it sees the human condition as being essentially the same in all places and in all times. Erwin Panofsky writes of Michelangelo that under the influence of Neoplatonism he saw human life on earth as 'an unreal, derivative and tormenting form of existence comparable to a life in Hades'.[6] Something of the same kind is true of Chapman. The real tragedy his heroes experience is that of their descent into this mode of being. Condemned to the 'earthly prison' of the body, they suffer frustration of their hopes for justice and for freedom, until they eventually escape from it and recover their lost liberty through 'the eternal victory of death', as Byron calls it. For Michelangelo, the symbol of the soul deprived of freedom by being tied to the body is the slave.[7] So it is for Chapman. Feeling that his soul is about to leave its prison, Byron says, in the last scene of his play, that his body is 'A slave bound face to face to Death till death' (v, iv, 38).

It was, above all else, this apprehension of the nature of human existence that enabled Chapman to transcend the limitations that his adoption of the providential view of history would otherwise have set to his tragic writings, and to present figures who have that 'more ample greatness...than can be found in the nature of things' which was, for Bacon, one of the things that distinguished poetry from 'true history'.

© G. R. HIBBARD 1967

NOTES

1. See *Critical Essays of the Seventeenth Century*, ed. J. E. Spingarn (Oxford, 1908), I, 177.

2. R. G. Collingwood, *The Idea of History* (Oxford, 1946), p. 51.

3. F. Smith Fussner, *The Historical Revolution* (1962).

4. Spingarn, *op. cit.* I, 84.

5. All quotations from Chapman are taken from T. M. Parrott's edition of *The Tragedies* (1910).

6. *Studies in Iconology* (Harper Torchbooks ed. New York, 1962), p. 180.

7. See Panofsky, *op. cit.* pp. 194-7.

CRITICAL DISAGREEMENT ABOUT
OEDIPUS AND HAMLET

BY

NIGEL ALEXANDER

'The art of representation', says Henry James in the Preface to *Roderick Hudson*, 'bristles with questions the very terms of which are difficult to apply and appreciate.'[1] Questions of dramatic representation almost invariably involve the critic in attempts to apply and appreciate terms first used by Aristotle in the *Poetics*. Critical controversy about Aristotle's exact meaning has tended to distract attention from the fact that, although his terms may not always be satisfactory, the questions that he asked are still important. In re-opening two old controversies I should like to try to demonstrate that there is a tradition of disagreement about certain passages in the *Oedipus Tyrannus* and in *Hamlet*. These disagreements are not simply an occupational hazard of criticism or further evidence of what Aldous Huxley has eloquently described as 'the prevalence of folly, its monumental unchanging permanence, and its almost unvariable triumph over the forces of intelligence'. So far from belonging to the *Dunciad Variorum* these disagreements are relevant to our own concerns and are part of the evidence for believing, with Sir John Myres, that:

Criticism, in spite of popular misapprehension, is a progressive and constructive study, tending not only to the discipline of a liberal education, but in the strictest sense to the advancement of science.[2]

As an example I should like to turn to the work of Henry James Pye, who is a poet laureate entirely without honour in his own country. Few Englishmen, apart from professional scholars, would recognize him as the man who succeeded Thomas Warton as poet laureate in 1790 and few, even among professional scholars, will have read his epic poem *Alfred* published, three years after *Lyrical Ballads*, in 1801. He claims my attention because he was involved in critical controversy about both Oedipus and Hamlet. In 1788 he produced the first respectable translation of Aristotle's *Poetics* in English, a translation which he revised and re-published with an extensive commentary in 1792, and in 1807 he published a small volume called *Comments on the Commentators of Shakespear. With preliminary Observations on his Genius and Writings*. There he warns the reader that:

After so much that has been written on this subject in the prolegomena to the various editions of Shakespear, and after the two luminous Essays of Mrs Montague and Mr Morgan, it is difficult to say anything new upon the subject,[3]

and continues to inform him that:

The chief faults of his commentators, besides this, arise from a desire to say everything they can say, not only on the passage commented on, but on everything that has been said in the comment, as well as from a too great display of black-letter reading.[4]

This last attribute of scholarship, he remarks, may be necessary, but only as dung is necessary to fertility, no one should want to make an ostentatious display of it. These formidable strictures do not, of course, inhibit Pye himself in any way when he feels that scholarship or comment are called for and so they need not prevent us from considering Oedipus's speech to Jocasta at line 771 of Jebb's edition, the forged commission which sends Rosencrantz and Guildenstern to their deaths in England, and the dumb show.

Pye comments on the first passage when he is dealing, in his *Commentary Illustrating the Poetic of Aristotle*, with Aristotle's remarks about the nature of the tragic hero in chapter 13 (1452 b–1453 a). Pye makes as reasonable an attempt as many of his more scholarly successors to explain Aristotle's meaning. But he is also a more thorough commentator than many of his successors and feels compelled to deal with the troublesome point, which they often pass over in simple silence, that Aristotle's two examples of the 'intermediate' kind of person who falls, not through vice or depravity but through some ἁμαρτία, are Oedipus and Thyestes. And, however we translate ἁμαρτία, and whatever we think of Oedipus, Thyestes appears to be the model of exceptional depravity. Pye reflects the disagreement about this point by quoting two most interesting and instructive opinions:

Metastasio is much dissatisfied with both these examples. He maintains that Thyestes is a character entirely vicious and that Oedipus, to use his own words, 'is a man of so sublime and pure a virtue that to avoid the risk of becoming, as the oracle had menaced, incestuous and a parricide he quits what he believes to be his parental house, hazards the succession of a crown, and goes alone and voluntarily into exile. He is a man of such exalted courage that, being attacked and insulted by a multitude of persons, instead of flying he valiantly defends himself though alone, kills one, wounds another, and disperses the rest'.

To this eulogy on Oedipus we may oppose the reasoning of Batteux: 'It was in his power to avoid his crime and his misfortune, although foretold by an oracle. This was the common belief of all Greece. Laius believed that by destroying his son he should avoid his destiny, Oedipus believed that by flying from Corinth, where he thought his father and mother then lived, he should avoid the fatal disaster with which he was threatened. Admonished as he was by the Oracle, should he have thought it sufficient to fly from Corinth? Should not he have respected the age of every man who was of a time in life to be his father? Should not he have been afraid of marrying any woman of an age to be his mother? So far from taking this precaution he no sooner leaves Delphi than he kills the first man he meets, which happens to be his father Laius: he arrives at Thebes, he triumphs over the Sphynx; elated with his victory and the offer of a crown he marries a woman who evidently might be his mother, since she actually was so. His unhappiness therefore was obviously the fruit of his imprudence and his passions and might serve for an example to all the Greeks.'[5]

More recent critical approaches to the play attempt to bypass this kind of disagreement by drawing attention to the fact that the play is a process of self-discovery which saves the city as well as revealing that the oracle has been fulfilled and that questions of moral guilt or innocence are not raised by Sophocles until the *Oedipus Coloneus*. The past history of Oedipus is, however, a vital part of the action and Metastasio and Batteux are clearly basing their opposed views on Oedipus's partial account of his past history to Jocasta at line 771. Sophocles is here engaged in one of the most necessary and difficult tasks that face any dramatist: the task that Henry James calls 'Harking back to make up'[6] and Arthur Miller 'the biggest single dramatic problem, namely, how to dramatize what has gone before'.[7] The account that Oedipus gives to Jocasta is designed to explain to her why the killing of an old man and his retinue at a place where three roads met, an event which had previously not been near his conscience because he had felt himself the injured party, should now, in the light of the evidence he has just uncovered, begin to trouble his mind. The speech looks before and after. It informs the audience of events that had occurred before the action began and it indicates or warns them of the future course of the action. Given the information in this speech the audience can now take an ironic or doubting view of Jocasta's statement that the actual murder of Laius, at least, can never be made to agree with the oracle which foretold that he should be killed by his son. This sense of irony or doom is then intensified by the following ode in which the Chorus virtually pray that the oracles may be fulfilled. The whole action of the play is then swung into its new, final and fatal direction by the arrival of the Corinthian messenger. The speech, then, is a point of balance in the play which sums up the action that is past and predicts, more or less, the action that is to come.

Disagreement about this speech, therefore, indicates a genuine disagreement about the entire structure of the play. And if the exact question of moral guilt or innocence is not directly raised, the question of responsibility surely is. Guilty or not, Oedipus accepts responsibility for his actions and, at the end of the play, demands the sentence of exile which will clear the city of pollution. The real disagreement between Metastasio and the Abbé Batteux is a disagreement about the degree and nature of that responsibility. The difficulty arises from the fact that, as Oedipus tells the story to Jocasta, it is an account of actions which are determined by his free will; as a speech within the context of the play it is part of a pattern which, if not pre-determined, has at least been predicted. Metastasio emphasizes the first of these elements and admires the driving will and courage of Oedipus; the Abbé Batteux stresses the second, respects the divine guidance of the Gods, and gives advice which is practically equivalent to the opinion of the Chorus: it would have been better for Oedipus never to have been born. This difference of opinion and emphasis continues to run through criticism of the play. For Cedric H. Whitman:

The action of the play itself, therefore, is motivated by the free will of the hero, which culminates in the act of self-blinding;[8]

while for Bernard M. W. Knox:

The play, in the simplest analysis, is a reassertion of the religious view of a divinely ordered universe, a view which depends on the concept of divine omniscience, represented in the play by Apollo's prophecy.[9]

The problem is that either view can, with a bit of scraping and shoving, be made to fit the case but that the play, as Sophocles wrote it, does not really contain enough definite information to allow us to say unequivocally that one view is correct and the other mistaken. Nor should we find this uncertainty entirely surprising. Anton Chekhov once wrote to I. L. Shcheglov:

As regards the ending of my *Lights* I take the liberty of disagreeing with you. A psychologist should not pretend to understand what he does not understand. Moreover, a psychologist should not convey the impression that he understands what no one understands. We shall not play the charlatan, and we will declare frankly that nothing is clear in this world. Only fools and charlatans know and understand everything.[10]

It would, I think, be unreasonable to expect Sophocles to have solved the question of determinism and free-will in his play since it still seems to come into the category of questions that no one understands. His critics can only do him disservice if they attempt to show that he unquestionably favoured the solution that they find most appealing. Sophocles treated the question of free-will and determinism in the only way that a dramatist can—he dramatized it. Such a dramatization will not solve the problem for the audience but will leave them facing some difficult questions whose significance they had perhaps previously only half realized. Critical opinion is, therefore, so divided about the structure of this play because the structure of the play is designed to divide critical opinion at precisely this point. Whether or not we accept a Freudian interpretation we can hardly deny that the play is most delicately balanced at a critical point for the human psyche. And this is why, in my opinion, it is so important to listen to the views of those who are engaged with us in the common pursuit of true judgment and to listen with more attention the more violently their judgments conflict with our own. In the dramatic equation presented by the poet they may have guessed the value of certain terms undreamt of in our philosophy.

Hamlet, like *Oedipus Tyrannus*, is an extremely finely balanced dramatic structure. Both plays provide us with what Henry James has called the soul of drama, 'a catastrophe determined in spite of oppositions'.[11] In both cases the chief opponent of catastrophe is the protagonist who brings about the determined end in unpredictable fashion. These actions compel us to ask for answers and seek emotional resolutions of problems which have remained difficult and intractable. Here, too, I believe that an examination of the traditional disagreements allows us to consider the problem in a more critical spirit.

One of the traditional disagreements about Hamlet has always been his method of transposing the commission given to Rosencrantz and Guildenstern and sending them to execution in England. In *Comments on the Commentators of Shakespear* Henry James Pye deals with the matter in this way:

Steevens's note on Malone's observation on this passage is insolent and impudent, and he is, as usual, positive in the wrong; there is not one word uttered by Rosencrantz and Guildenstern throughout the play that does not proclaim them to the most superficial observer as creatures of the king, purposely employed to betray Hamlet, their friend and fellow-student.[12]

The comments of George Steevens on the character of Hamlet had first appeared in his edition of Shakespeare of 1773 as a note to Horatio's 'Good-night, sweet prince'. Malone had attempted a refutation on historical principles in his edition of 1790 and Steevens had replied by asserting that the critic must judge by what he found in the text in front of his eyes not by what he could deduce from the 'black-letter history'. In 1963 Patrick Cruttwell[13] joined issue with L. C. Knights[14] over the same question. Knights has written of the 'murder' of Rosencrantz and Guildenstern but Cruttwell appeals to the military imagery as a guide to response. Hamlet is at war and the language is a clear indication of this state of affairs to the audience. If Knights ignores these indications it must be because, for him, war and murder are synonymous terms.

It is perhaps worth while to have a closer look at two of the passages involved. The first occurs at III, iv, 205. At the end of the closet scene Hamlet mentions to his mother the scheme of sending him to England, suspects that Rosencrantz and Guildenstern are involved in the plot, and predicts that he will circumvent it:

> Let it work;
> For 'tis the sport to have the engineer
> Hoist with his own petar; and 't shall go hard
> But I will delve one yard below their mines
> And blow them at the moon. O, 'tis most sweet
> When in one line two crafts directly meet.

The imagery here certainly refers to a military operation. The operation is siege warfare and the mine and counter-mine which Hamlet describes were last used in Europe in 1917 under Messines ridge. The delving below an opponent's mine to blow him at the moon with the force of his own explosive charge implies secrecy in operation and terrible suddenness in execution. It is an apt metaphor for Rosencrantz and Guildenstern sent to execution, 'not shriving time allowed', by the forged commission. When Horatio challenges Hamlet's account of their deaths at v, ii, 56 with the quiet comment,

> So Guildenstern and Rosencrantz go to 't,

Hamlet changes his metaphor and provides a rather different defence:

> Why, man, they did make love to this employment;
> They are not near my conscience; their defeat
> Does by their own insinuation grow:
> 'Tis dangerous when the baser nature comes
> Between the pass and fell incensed points
> Of mighty opposites.

Rosencrantz and Guildenstern are not now caught in the tunnels under the hill and blown up with their own charge. They have openly intervened in a duel. In both cases the language used, the 'two crafts' which meet and the 'mighty opposites', implies that a war is being fought between two persons or parties but Rosencrantz and Guildenstern participate in significantly different ways. In the first they are servants of the King overwhelmed in the course of their muddy but necessary duty, in the second they are men aware that they have intervened in a deadly and desperate business. Their exact role depends on whether or not they knew the nature of their employment in England. Hamlet's words suggest that they did, but when the King finally reveals the journey-to-England plot to the audience Rosencrantz and Guildenstern are not on the stage. This is another occasion when we are simply not given enough information to be able to make up our minds. Disagreement between those who find Hamlet's actions culpable and those who find them excusable at this point is, therefore, inevitable. But this disagreement is again one which is forced on the audience by the entire structure of the play. Hamlet's references to the secret working of the counter-mine and the duel between mighty opposites fit into a recognizable pattern in the play. The mining image had already been used at I, v, 162:

> Well said, old mole! Canst work i' th' earth so fast?
> A worthy pioneer!

and he talks to his mother of 'rank corruption, mining all within'. I am not suggesting that these linked images could have even a subliminal effect on an audience across three-quarters of the play.

What I wish to emphasize is that the double description of the deaths of Rosencrantz and Guildenstern, as an unexpected secret explosion and as an incident in a duel, is part of a whole series of double descriptions and contrasted effects.

Hamlet's words, 'the fell incensed points of mighty opposites', are the only direct reference in the play to a duel with the King. Yet the image of the duel between Hamlet and Claudius is referred to by many commentators. Such an image depends not simply on the words but upon the whole stage action of the play. The play ends, and the final catastrophe is brought about, during the duel scene between Hamlet and Laertes. This is a duel scene, but it is also a play scene since the bout with foils is frequently referred to as 'play' and Hamlet himself has the significant line, 'And will this brother's wager frankly play'. It is also a poisoning scene, the poison of the anointed rapier and the poisoned union in the cup from which the Queen, the King and finally perhaps Hamlet himself all drink. These elements have all been in the play from the beginning. The play begins with the appearance of the Ghost, and the Ghost is first referred to as the majesty of buried Denmark who had fought the famous duel with Fortinbras of Norway. The Ghost reveals the secret of his murder, by poison, to Hamlet who has already, in the hearing of the audience, defended himself against the charge of playing one part, the over-intense mourner, and now deliberately announces that he will adopt another, the antic disposition. The use of the antic disposition leads on naturally to the presentation of *The Murder of Gonzago* or *The Mousetrap*. This is certainly a 'play' scene. It is also a poisoning scene since we twice see the murderer pouring poison into the ear of his victim. This is performed the first time in dumb show but on the second occasion the character is identified as one Lucianus, nephew to the King. This poisoning is performed because the play scene is also a duel scene— an attack by Hamlet on the King to catch his conscience and force him to unkennel his guilt. This attack is at least partly successful. It does force the King into the open and puts him, literally and metaphorically, on his guard. It also appears to have caught his conscience since Hamlet finds him on his knees at prayer and, because conscience is at work, rejects that opportunity for secret murder. If Hamlet here means what he says, and if the King had actually repented, then the opportunity for secret murder would have passed for ever. The attempt at repentance, however, merely starts the King upon his second secret murder, a murder which will eventually require the use of poison.

Hamlet had first attacked the King by using words as weapons under the cover of the antic disposition. He has now used the *Murder of Gonzago* under cover of the entertainment provided by the players. Claudius, in his attempts to penetrate the antic disposition, had used Polonius as a spy and Ophelia and Gertrude as bait for the trap. Now that Hamlet has put him on his guard he employs Rosencrantz and Guildenstern, formerly used as spies, as secret and perhaps unwitting murderers. When they, too, fail, Laertes is used as open duellist and conscious murderer and turns out to be a conscious murderer who chooses poison as his method.

The play scene, therefore, in *Hamlet* fulfils a dramatic function similar to Oedipus's speech to Jocasta. It harks back to make up and dramatizes what has gone before. In dumb show it dramatizes the original murder. In the Play, with its attack on the Queen and careful identification of the murderer, it predicts the poisoning of the King by his nephew. Claudius does, in the end, die by his own poison but the play is not an exact prediction of the manner of his death. Throughout *Hamlet* the audience are waiting for the Prince to fulfil prediction and obey the command of the Ghost. He does so, but obeys it in his own fashion, and not by committing the predicted secret revenge murder. The killing of Rosencrantz and Guildenstern is the closest that Hamlet comes in the play to deliberate secret murder. It can be justified or it can be condemned but, in the context of the play, it is the action of Hamlet's that most resembles secret murder by poison, the choice of Claudius, and that is farthest from trial by combat, the choice of King Hamlet. Yet, as Hamlet's words make clear, even it can be regarded as an incident in a deadly duel since the entire action of the play shows us a player poised between duel scenes and scenes of poison and invites our judgment. The actions of the chief player, Hamlet, bring about the predicted end of the play, the killing of Claudius, but in unexpected fashion. The determined end of the *Oedipus Tyrannus* is similarly brought about by the unexpected action of Oedipus in determinedly pressing forward to solve the problem which he had previously tried to escape and from which all others now draw back in horror. This double function of the play as summing up and prediction, the vision of the murder that is past and the vision of the murder that is yet to come, accounts for the double use of dumb show and play that troubled Henry James Pye as it was later to trouble Professor Dover Wilson.

The tension in *Oedipus Tyrannus* between prediction and free will is not solved intellectually, merely resolved dramatically. Similarly the tensions in *Hamlet* between the revenge murder called for by the Ghost, the secret poisonings so exactly practised by Claudius, and Hamlet's own vision of the struggle as similar to the task of the actor and the soldier engaged in a duty which is finally a duel, cannot be concluded by neat moral sententiae. The murderous and aggressive instincts of humanity remain one of the problems that no one can solve. Shakespeare does not offer us moral prescriptions but shows us Hamlet finely balanced between the open duel of the soldier and the secret murder of the poisoner and leaves us with the question, What, then, must we do?

Hamlet, like Oedipus, is called to perform a task. To set right a time which is out of joint. Like Oedipus he succeeds. Both Thebes and Denmark appear clear of pollution as these plays end. But, like Oedipus, he succeeds in such a fashion and about such a task that those who look pale and tremble at this chance, those of us who are but the audience to these acts, are left attempting to answer a number of difficult questions which appear to have no settled or received solutions but which each individual may yet be called upon to solve for himself as best he can. The audience has not remained mute. Instead it has indulged in a vigorous critical debate which, I believe, testifies to the importance of the questions asked and the skill and artistry of those who asked them. They hold a mirror up to nature and show us a reflexion that may be the head of the Gorgon and that may, also, bear an uncomfortable likeness to our own faces.

NOTES

1. Henry James, *The Art of the Novel*, ed. R. P. Blackmur (New York, 1934), p. 3.

2. J. L. Myres, *Homer and his critics* (1958), p. 9.

3. H. J. Pye, *Comments on the Commentators of Shakespear* (1807), p. ix.

4. *Ibid.* p. xiv.

5. H. J. Pye, *A Commentary Illustrating the Poetic of Aristotle* (1792), pp. 254 ff.

6. *The Art of the Novel*, p. 121.

7. Arthur Miller, Preface to *Collected Plays* (1958), p. 21.

8. Cedric H. Whitman, *Sophocles* (Cambridge, Mass., 1951), p. 141.

9. Bernard M. W. Knox, *Oedipus at Thebes* (New Haven, 1957), p. 47.

10. Anton Chekhov, letter to I. L. Shcheglov, 9 June 1888. *Letters on Literary Topics*, ed. Louis S. Freidland (New York, 1924), p. 8.

11. *The Art of the Novel*, p. 290.

12. H. J. Pye, *Comments on the Commentators of Shakespear*, p. 326.

13. Patrick Cruttwell, 'The Morality of Hamlet', in *Hamlet: Stratford-upon-Avon Studies 5*, ed. J. R. Brown and B. Harris (1963), p. 119.

14. L. C. Knights, *An Approach to Hamlet* (1960), p. 32.

SHAKESPEARE'S THEMATIC MODES OF SPEECH: 'RICHARD II' TO 'HENRY V'

BY

ROBERT HAPGOOD

Just as Shakespeare's characters in a given play tend to use the same words and images, they also tend to use the same 'modes' of speech. For instance, *Hamlet*, one of the few plays in which this characteristic has been noted,[1] is full of questions. Not all of its speeches take the form of questions, of course, or even most of them; nor is questioning the play's only recurring mode of speech, many of the characters being equally inclined toward lengthy admonition. Yet the 'interrogative mood' the questions create does make a contribution of thematic importance to the tone and meaning of the play. The same can be said, I believe, of comparable modes of speech in many—perhaps all—of Shakespeare's plays. As a start toward testing this belief, I should like to look at *Richard II*, *1 Henry IV*, *2 Henry IV*, and *Henry V*.

I

The central mode of speech in *Richard II* is that of denunciation. Of the four plays, this is the only one which draws its modes to a large extent from its sources. For the most part, Shakespeare intensifies the denunciations he finds in Hall and Holinshed. Where, for instance, in Holinshed York simply 'delivered the indenture' to the king which exposed his son's plot, in the play he inveighs repeatedly against the 'villain' and 'traitor' (v, ii and iii).[2] Only the formal accusations and grievous crimes that Northumberland tries to make Richard read at his deposition (IV, i, 223–7) receive less emphasis in the play than in the *Chronicles*.

Shakespeare has also added a large number of denunciations, chiefly by Richard. An inspired name-caller, Richard variously denounces Gaunt ('lunatic, lean-witted fool'), Bolingbroke ('this thief...who all this while hath revell'd in the night'), Northumberland ('thou haught insulting man'), his followers ('snakes in my heart-blood warm'd, that sting my heart'), parliament ('conveyers are you all'), and himself ('I find myself a traitor with the rest'). So strong is the prevailing mode that speeches which begin as something else tend to become denunciatory. Gaunt intends to give sage dying counsel to his king; yet before he is through he is accusing Richard of deposing himself (II, i, 93–115). The Duchess of Gloucester's exhortation to Gaunt (I, ii, 9–36) leads her finally to call his 'patience', 'pale cold cowardice'. An analogous, though calculated, progression comes at the end of II, i, where Bolingbroke's supporters after at first sounding one another out make increasingly vituperative attacks on the king.

It is not surprising that a play about civil war should be filled with vehement denunciation. What is surprising is that the two main antagonists never denounce one another face-to-face.[3] The nearest they come to doing so is when Bolingbroke like Mowbray refuses the king's suit to 'throw up his gage' (I, i). Why isn't there an all-out confrontation? It is easy to see why Bolingbroke wants to avoid one since by a show of verbal 'fair duty' to Richard he hopes to convert deposition to 'resignation'. The mystery is Richard's acquiescence, the play's chief 'anti-mode' of speech.[4]

Like York when he capitulates to Bolingbroke (II, iii), Richard often begins with a strong denunciation only then to weaken and give in altogether. That is the pattern of the scenes at Barkloughly (III, ii), Flint (III, iii), and parliament (IV, i). Doubtless these acquiescences result in part from Richard's love of the 'sweet way to despair'; in part, perhaps, from a prescient bowing to the inevitable. But they also reveal specifically verbal weaknesses, not often noted in the poet-king. As extraordinary as Richard's verbal powers are, they are ironically not those required by his situation. When strong words are called for, he starts brilliantly but lacks the nerve and will to sustain them effectively. On the other hand, when strategic retreat is called for, he is unable to 'fight with gentle words', as Aumerle counsels, 'Till time lend friends and friends their helpful swords' (III, iii, 131–2). A further irony is that the very proclivity for acquiescence that contributes to Richard's defeat does much in the deposition episode to keep Bolingbroke's victory from being complete. For Richard's self-protracted humiliation converts what Bolingbroke meant to be a scene of 'resignation' by 'tired majesty' into a 'woeful pageant'.

Acquiescence is not by any means forgiveness. Richard does not achieve anything like that until shortly before his death. He at first 'rails' against roan Barbary as of old: 'That jade hath eat bread from my royal hand.' But he ends—in the new vein begun in his soliloquy just before— by crying 'Forgiveness, horse!' and turning his condemnation upon himself. Ironically, it is only then that Richard finds the valour to sustain his denunciations and carry them into action, resisting his murderers. When Exton finally strikes him down, Richard dies on a note of malediction and self-assertion:

> That hand shall burn in never-quenching fire
> That staggers thus my person. Exton, thy fierce hand
> Hath with the King's blood stain'd the King's own land.
> Mount, mount, my soul! thy seat is up on high;
> Whilst my gross flesh sinks downward, here to die.   (v, v, 109–13)

II

The central mode of speech in *1 Henry IV* is retrospection, chiefly concerning the deposition and death of Richard. The play opens with the king recalling the recent 'civil butchery', as do Worcester and Northumberland a scene later. Such speeches might be regarded as no more than necessary dramatic exposition if they did not continue throughout. Thus for his son's benefit the king reviews Richard's mistakes (III, ii); Hotspur, in a long inopportune speech (IV, iii, 52–105), recalls how

> My father and my uncle and myself
> Did give him [the king] that same royalty he wears;

in his parley with the king, Worcester makes an extensive survey of their past relationship (v, i, 30–71).

This preoccupation with the past extends to other events as well, every man being his own historian and constructing the past—whether he realizes it or not—to his own way of thinking.

The king in I, iii, for example, sees Hotspur's denial of the prisoners as a piece of defiance; Hotspur represents it as merely a warrior's impatience with a popinjay messenger. They then go on to offer contradictory versions of Mortimer's capture. Hotspur similarly puts his own humorous interpretation on Glendower's account of his birth (III, i). No one, however, rewrites history more drastically than Falstaff. His tall tales about the Gadshill robbery, the pocket-picking, and the death of Hotspur put a characteristic twist on the general impulse to recall and interpret the past. For his distortions are deliberate, exaggerated, and meant to be shown up as false—all to regale the prince.

Amid the constant remembrance of things past, the speeches which look ahead stand out as the play's chief anti-mode. *1 Henry IV* has no prophets, like Carlisle and Richard in *Richard II*; its characters regard the future pragmatically, for the sake of controlling it. Hotspur often talks about the future, but he never looks beyond an immediate goal; to him, even 'Doomsday is near'. It is Worcester who does the long-range planning for the rebels. The king and Falstaff are very much alike in their views of the future, the difference of course being that the king fears and tries to avoid the extension of Hal's 'degenerate' tavern-past (III, ii) that Falstaff hopes for and tries to promote (I, ii). The Prince himself sees further ahead than anyone else in the play, and his is the dominant voice of the future. All of his most important speeches are cast in the future tense, particularly his soliloquy (I, ii, 218–40) and his assurances to his father (III, ii, 129–59). Even his eulogies over Hotspur and Falstaff (V, iv, 87–110) move from the past-tense through the present to the future.

In a world largely given to looking backward, the young prince's confident and discerning talk of the future does much to assure us that he is after all 'the hope and expectation of his time'. For where everyone else sees the future as an extension of the past, only he sees its opportunities for radical change.

III

The central mode of speech in *2 Henry IV* is that of true and—almost as frequently—false report. Of course, Shakespeare's plays often include messages and messengers, as they often include liars. Yet in *2 Henry IV* indirect and/or corrupt speech is much more than usually emphasized. 'What news?' is a constant question; numerous messengers bring word from battle-areas; emissaries and letters ply among the main characters; 'I hear' and 'they say' are frequent comments. Comic vices of speech are exploited—Pistol's swaggering, Mrs Quickly's mala-propism, Shallow's repetitiousness. Everyone is acutely aware that report and fact may not correspond. It is not for nothing that Rumour, 'painted full of tongues', is prologue to this play, nor that in its first scene two accurate reports are required in order to correct a single false one.

False report is part of the general corruption of communication that marks *2 Henry IV*,[5] an aspect, in turn, of the play's general concern with physical and moral decay. At times, communication breaks down altogether. That is one of the causes of the rebellion. The Archbishop complains of the king that we 'might by no suit gain our audience' (IV, i, 76); yet when in the same scene the rebels are offered such an audience, the Archbishop can accept it only over the protests of Mowbray. Even when communication is held, it is likely to be misleading. These people are quite prepared to break their words, Northumberland being of course a prime offender. The rebels are alert to this hazard with him (I, iii, 17–30), but they are taken in by

Prince John's equivocation about their grievances (IV, ii), the success of which turns significantly on the refusal of his men to accept a second-hand order.

Since language and fact are so far apart, mere reputation is an obsessive concern. Mrs Quickly is intent on remaining 'in good name and fame with the very best'; Poins avows that he is 'well spoke on'; Justice Shallow fears backbiting. His elaborate lies glorifying the wildness of his youth are a sophistication of this same concern. Nor is it absent from the nobility. The Archbishop is careful to 'publish the occasion of our arms', and his leadership is welcomed because

<blockquote>
the bishop,
Turns insurrection to religion.   (I, i, 200–1)
</blockquote>

The king assures Hal that the crown will descend to him with 'Better opinion, better confirmation'.

The decay of language extends to unexpected places. In what other play would a newly-bereaved father play on his dead son's name ('Hotspur Coldspur?')? a widow recall with pride how the valiant turned 'their own perfection to abuse' in order to 'speak thick' like her husband? a king attempt to make his own death in Jerusalem Chamber fulfil the prophecy that he 'should not die but in Jerusalem'? an Epilogue apologize for his poor speech? Even silence in this play is corrupt, being the product of dread (I, i, 95–6), mercenary obsequiousness (II, ii, 179), or sheer vacuity (it is right that the few words Silence says should be inconsequential). Most alarming of all, Shakespeare himself seems in his nameplay to be caught up into this same mode. Not only do we see characters with names like Fang, Snare, Shallow, Feeble, Bullcalf: but we hear about Master Smooth the silk-man, Jane Nightwork, Master Dumbe, William Visor, and others—all denizens of a world where a person's name is likely to be a true or false report of his character.

Falstaff is of course the chief master of false report and general abuser of language. Hardly a character escapes his incidental slander or abuse. He has a taste for hearsay and indirect communication, especially about awkward matters. He is preoccupied with names, especially his own (II, ii, 143–5). As the scenes with Coleville (IV, iii) and Shallow demonstrate, he exploits brilliantly the whole school of tongues in his belly. He twists words every which way, not mistakenly like the Hostess and Pistol but knowingly; indeed, he parodies Pistol's helplessly stagey bombast to his face: 'O base Assyrian knight, what is thy news?' (V, iii, 105). Having broken his word to Mrs Quickly, he pacifies her with new 'smooth comforts false' (II, i).

Falstaff's verbal vices momentarily infect even the Lord Chief Justice. At the end of their first exchange (I, ii), the Justice for the first time uses an expression which Falstaff has used repeatedly: '*I hear* you are going with the Lord John of Lancaster.' (This is third-hand information, in fact, reported as hearsay by his servant at the beginning of this scene.) For the first time, he uses repetition for emphasis, Falstaff's 'gravy, gravy, gravy' being echoed in the Justice's 'fie, fie, fie' and 'be honest, be honest'. Still worse, his last speech includes not only another repetition but a Falstaffian pun! To Falstaff's impudent request for a thousand pound, he replies: 'not a penny, not a penny: you are too impatient to bear crosses'.

Prince Hal knows the mode of indirect and corrupt speech that prevails in his world and how to operate within it. He understands that if he grieved openly about his father's illness, every man would, like Poins, think him a most princely hypocrite (II, ii, 51–65); he plans as king to

> raze out
> Rotten opinion, who hath writ me down
> After my seeming.   (v, ii, 127–9)

Yet he ultimately transcends this mode, I believe, and succeeds in speaking truly and directly, the play's chief anti-mode.

Even in *Part One*, Hal could talk straight, except where Falstaff was concerned. Even his exposures of Falstaff's prevarications were playful and indulgent; and on Falstaff's behalf he himself lied to the Sheriff ('The man, I do assure you, is not here') and promised to back up Falstaff's fiction about killing Hotspur. Only when he spoke in his father's voice in the tavern-playlet could the prince warn Falstaff of his eventual banishment: 'I do, I will.'

Part Two shows Hal in the process of acquiring the kingly manner of speech in which he finally does make a direct rejection of Falstaff. His lessons in straight-talk come not only from another long interview with his father (IV, v) but also from an important exchange with the Lord Chief Justice, in which the new king first anticipates a time when he shall live to echo his dead father's words to the Justice (v, ii, 107) and then adopts the Justice as a new father:

> You shall be as a father to my youth:
> My voice shall sound as you do prompt mine ear.   (v, ii, 119–20)

Regarded unsympathetically, as the cold-blooded and long-premeditated dismissal of a tool who has outlived his usefulness, the young king's speech of rejection (v, v, 51–77) might seem a supreme denial of true communication, as he silences Falstaff ('I know thee not old man... Reply not to me with a fool-born jest') and speaks with the self-righteousness and end-stopped formality of someone twice his years. But if—as I believe—Hal genuinely had a taste for small beer and truly is here renouncing his old self as well as his old companions, then the weaknesses of his speech can be seen as the poignant ones of a beginner. If he sounds too much like the Lord Chief Justice that is because he has so recently vowed that his voice shall sound as the Justice prompts his ear.

Predictably, not only Falstaff—once the first shock is over—but also Prince John misconstrues the king's words, each interpreting them in his own sick idiom. Falstaff assures Shallow: 'this that you heard was but a colour...I shall be sent for soon at night'. Prince John is nearer the truth but still immersed in verbal appearances:

> He hath intent his wonted followers
> Shall all be very well provided for;
> But all are banish'd till their conversations
> Appear more wise and modest to the world.   (v, v, 104–7)

IV

The central mode of speech in *Henry V* is that of dispute. Unlike the other three Lancastrian plays, each of which announces its central mode at the outset, *Henry V* begins with its main anti-mode, concert and agreement: the Prologue invokes a Muse of fire, appeals to English national feeling, and apologetically seeks the cooperation of spectator with performer; and the first scenes show the church and the crown working out the terms of their mutual assistance.

Not until the end of the second scene, when the Ambassadors of France arrive with their tennis balls, is the dominant mode sounded. Disputes between the two enemies were of course to be expected in this play, and we are not disappointed; shamelessly weighted to favour the English, they continue until the agreements of the finale. What might not have been expected is the extent to which the two sides quarrel among themselves. Such disputes are even more frequent than those between the two sides.

The French mode of dispute is that of mocking insult. This is emphatically the manner of the Dauphin's gift of tennis-balls and of the Constable's advice that the English repent before they die (IV, iii, 83–7). Among themselves, it marks the Constable's barbed raillery with the Dauphin and Orleans (III, vii) and seems even to be the mode of French women; the Dauphin protests:

> Our madams mock at us, and plainly say
> Our mettle is bred out and they will give
> Their bodies to the lust of English youth... (III, v, 28–30)

The French are much given, also, to bragging, both to the English and among themselves. As King Henry jokes to Montjoy:

> forgive me, God,
> That I do brag thus! This your air of France
> Hath blown that vice in me; I must repent. (III, vi, 159–61)

Yet they are quickly reduced to unconditional surrender, most abjectly in Monsieur le Fer's cries: 'O, je vous supplie, pour l'amour de Dieu, me pardonner!' (IV, iv, 42).

Like the top levels of the French court, the lower orders of the English army are constantly in dispute; yet unlike the French, whose disagreements are often left hanging in the air, theirs are always resolved, as in the quarrel (II, i) between Nym and Pistol over Nell Quickly. Captain Fluellen, the very embodiment of disputatiousness, is at the centre of these disputes. His 'prawls, and prabbles, and quarrels, and dissensions' are what he lives for, and he is too prone to equate love of dispute with valour in battle. He grossly underestimates Captain Macmorris, who is all fight and no talk; while he at first grossly overestimates Pistol, who—as the Boy puts it—'hath a killing tongue and a quiet sword'. Fluellen is so disputatious that he can even provoke a slight tiff with the otherwise ever-agreeable Gower (IV, i, 76), but his main disputes are of course with Pistol. Their contention echoes the international dispute, as the braggart's mocking insults give way to easy and total submission: 'Must I bite?' King Henry's magnanimity to a conquered foe is reflected in the groat Fluellen gives Pistol to 'heal your pate'.

Apart from his international exchanges, King Henry's chief disputes come when he is in disguise—first, as Harry le Roi, with Pistol (IV, i, 35–63); then, later in the scene, with Williams. The latter is easily the most searching of the play's disputes, the disguised king and his men debating the highest issues of duty and rule before descending to embroilments about the king's 'foolish saying' and Williams's 'something too round' reproof.

The king's most characteristic mode of speech, however, is the play's chief anti-mode: concert and agreement. Among the English nobility, especially in contrast to the French, there is notable amity among themselves and loyalty to the king. If the three traitors pervert this solidarity in their false expressions of fidelity (II, ii, 18–51), the king is not deceived; and their exception is more than counter-balanced by Exeter's account of the deaths of Suffolk and York

(IV, vi, 7–32), which is the most extreme expression of amity in the play, perhaps in Shakespeare. Henry knows how to knit his band of brothers. Of course there are those who do not respond to his appeals. Among the stragglers, Bardolph can only parody the king's battle-cry: 'On, on, on, on, on! to the breach, to the breach!' (III, ii). The king is prepared to sacrifice their friendship. In their place, he welcomes Fluellen, who does respond to his cry and echoes it, if very much in his own idiom: 'Up to the breach, you dogs! avaunt, you cullions!'

With France, Henry's is again the voice of unity: not as a mediator—he is not a Bardolph or a Bates or, at the international level, a Burgundy—but as a magnanimous conqueror. Typically, his victory with Kate is on his own terms—she goes much further than he in an attempt to 'talk the same language'—yet he has the magnanimity to attempt a little French.

V

There are many more modal resemblances among these four plays than I have brought out in the preceding sections. For instance, the last scenes of *1 Henry IV* (V, i, 126 to the end) anticipate *Part Two*'s indirect and corrupt speech, while *Part Two* has a heavily retrospective portion (III, i, 56 through IV, i, 139) which is very much like *Part One*. As I have defined them, moreover, the 'modes' often overlap; for they are obviously not part of a system of exclusive categories. Thus, many of the denunciations in *Richard II* are retrospective; many of the retrospections in *1 Henry IV* are in the form of reports; many of the reports in *2 Henry IV* are disputed; many of the disputes in *Henry V* are denunciatory. Yet the plays do differ in their treatment of these various modes of speech; and furthermore these differences fit together into a coherent sequence when seen as part of the whole use of speech in the four plays.

The dialogue of these successive plays—like their politics—moves from initial disorder through virtual chaos to a final restoration of order. The first verbal disorder is the gap between word and deed which Richard II creates by his exaggerated notion of the power of words. By trying to substitute words for deeds, however, he only separates the two, a gap which Bolingbroke of course exploits. In *1 Henry IV* the general validity of speech continues to diminish, reaching an extreme in the utter nominalism of Falstaff's catechism on honour (V, i, 126–44). His talk throughout registers the first boom of possibilities in an inflated verbal economy where speech is scarcely hampered by fact. In *2 Henry IV* the debasement of speech has become still further widespread. The dying king now seems ironically remote from a world which his own verbal techniques have helped to create. He must rely on intermediaries, especially his son John, who understands fully the way the Archbishop seeks to turn 'the word to the sword' and in the grievance-trick (IV, ii) beats him at his own word-game. Prince Hal has already begun to break out of this descending verbal spiral. As Henry V, he is much concerned with true speech, cautioning the churchmen to be sure that

> what you speak is in your conscience wash'd
> As pure as sin with baptism.   (I, ii, 31–2)

Since he knows their stake in endorsing his claims to France, this 'conjuration' might seem hypocritical. To my ear, however, it seems an eleventh-hour bid for candour, all politics aside. For the king makes the same kind of request of the French ambassadors:

> with frank and with uncurbed plainness
> Tell us the Dauphin's mind, (I, ii, 244–5)

and himself practises such speech with Montjoy:

> to say the sooth,
> Though 'tis no wisdom to confess so much
> Unto an enemy of craft and vantage
> My people are with sickness much enfeebled,
> My numbers lessen'd... (III, vi, 151–5)

It is upon such speech that Henry V seeks to found a new order. He ends the play by telling Kate and the others:

> Prepare we for our marriage: on which day,
> My Lord of Burgundy, we'll take your oath,
> And all the peers', for surety of our leagues,
> Then shall I swear to Kate, and you to me;
> And may our oaths well kept and prosperous be!

Sketchy as it is, this outline may serve to suggest a rationale for the successive thematic modes.[6] The denunciations of *Richard II* are obviously manifestations of an exaggerated sense of word-power: in this world of discourse, to denounce a traitor is tantamount to a curse! As the gap between word and deed widens in *1 Henry IV*, it is natural that many of the characters should look back—in sorrow as well as anger—to a time when unkept promises were first made and when in other ways their words and lives began to lose their meaning; hence the obsessive retrospection. When this loss of meaning continues, it is not surprising to hear the characters in *2 Henry IV* trying to find it not only in the past but in current opinion—what other people are saying. *Henry V* then redeems this corrupt speech by restoring its bond with action. One might wish for a less truculent mode of settling differences than its constant disputes, but at least a genuine dialogue takes place in which speech is truly meant and leads directly to action.

Certain of the individual modes, when followed through the four plays, also reflect this overall progression. The grandiose denunciations of Richard II, for example, give way to the tavern jocularities of Hal and Falstaff (who make a sport of base comparisons) and then to the gutter invective of Doll Tearsheet. Henry V, in contrast, is notably unwilling to call names (he orders that none of the French should be 'upbraided or abused in disdainful language'), although he can call treachery by its right name when necessary (II, ii).

What stands out most of all is the sequence of anti-modes which Shakespeare gives Harry Monmouth: in a world of retrospection, his is the voice of the future; in a world of false report, his speech is direct and true; in a world of dispute, his call is to concord. Whatever the prevailing mode, and however advanced the general decay of language, Shakespeare always lets us hear in his voice its heroic opposite.

NOTES

1. Maynard Mack, 'The World of *Hamlet*', *YR*, XLI (1952), 502–23 and Harry Levin, *The Question of Hamlet* (New York, 1959). Other related studies include: Maynard Mack, 'The Jacobean Shakespeare', in *Jacobean Theatre: Stratford-upon-Avon Studies 1*, ed. J. R. Brown and B. Harris (1960), particularly pp. 13–24; Francis Berry, *Poets' Grammar* (1958), particularly ch. III: 'Pronoun and Verb in Shakespeare'; Winifred M. T. Nowottny, 'Lear's Questions', *Shakespeare Survey 10* (1957), 90–7; Judith M. Karr, 'The Pleas in *Tit.*', *SQ*, XIV (1963), 278–9. In 'The Life of Shame: Parolles and *All's W.*', *EIC*, XV (1965), 269–78, I discuss the thematic interplay of lying and 'telling true'; in *The Explicator*, XXIV (1966), item 60, I analyse *As You Like It*'s shift in modes from sympathy and encouragement to mockery and *flytings*. The prehistory of these modes is to be found in the set-speech, studied by Wolfgang Clemen in *English Tragedy Before Shakespeare*, trans. T. S. Dorsch (New York, 1961). The modes relax the strict forms of the set-speech, immensely widen its range of types, and extend its functions.

2. References are to *The Complete Works of William Shakespeare*, ed. H. Craig (Chicago, 1951).

3. This is the more surprising in view of the frequency of comparable confrontation scenes in Shakespeare's predecessors and in his own *Henry VI* plays. See Robert Y. Turner, 'Shakespeare and the Public Confrontation Scene', *MP*, LXII (1964), 1–12.

4. There are other contrasting modes. The denunciations often occasion or are accompanied by speeches of passionate self-assertion or self-defence, the most extreme of these being King Richard's rhapsodies of self-glorification. The few expressions of genuine sympathy also stand out, especially York's account of Richard's humiliation in London (v, ii, 6–40). So, too, does flattery. Ironically, although we hear a good deal about Richard's flatterers, the most obvious flattery is directed, unsuccessfully, to Bolingbroke; Northumberland lays it on with a trowel: 'your fair discourse hath been as sugar...' (II, iii, 2–18).

5. Particularly in the Quarto text. For a discussion of the profanity, 'colloquialisms, vulgarisms, and other improprieties of expression which give the Q text some of its racy flavour', see the New Variorum *2 H IV*, ed. M. A. Shaaber (Philadelphia, 1940), p. 503.

6. For a fuller survey along these lines (published after my article had gone to press), cf. Eric La Guardia, 'Ceremony and History: The Problem of Symbol from *R. II* to *H.V*', in *Pacific Coast Studies in Shakespeare*, ed. W. F. McNeir and T. N. Greenfield (Eugene, Oregon, 1966), pp. 68–88.

ANARCHY AND ORDER IN 'RICHARD III' AND 'KING JOHN'

BY

RONALD BERMAN

The Tragedy of King Richard III has been called a Senecan tragedy, Tudor propaganda, a development of Marlovian drama, and a historical Morality. Any or all of this may be true, although it seems that at some point these ideas are mutually exclusive. It may be best simply to note how this play and *King John* differ from other Shakespearian histories. These two among the history plays are distinguished by tough, cynical and realistic wit on the part of those whose business it is to maintain the idealized image of monarchy. Their 'heroes' have a sceptical and ironical attitude toward themes which are taken with great seriousness in the other histories—among them legitimacy, honour, and the sacredness of blood relationships. They prepare for the great encounter of individuals and institutions in the Henry IV plays.

Richard III is psychologically and philosophically complex. When he speaks of his brother Clarence it is with a blend of feelings and meanings:

> Simple, plain Clarence! I do love thee so,
> That I will shortly send thy soul to heaven,
> If heaven will take the present at our hands.[1]

It is the voice of a certain kind of intellect, which can take neither Clarence nor heaven seriously. Richard's remark, 'I will deliver you, or else lie for you', is a complex blend of double meanings addressed as much to his own perception of his wit as it is to the unfortunate Clarence, or to the appreciative audience. All three parties concerned are expected to interpret this in varying ways.

The emancipation of Richard's morality is like that of the Bastard in *King John*. In a less sophisticated but more virile way the Bastard makes the relationships of the world of moral order seem equivocally comical. It is arguable whether or not he is the dominant figure of the play, but it is evident that he represents a dominant attitude of self-interest. In a play much concerned with the rights of legitimacy he allows us to see this and other ethical institutions through his own pragmatic eyes. He glories in the name of bastard. He feels liberated, as Richard III does, and as Edmund in *King Lear* does, by being naturally outside of the normal course of human development. He has a clear idea of the antithetical relationship between his role and his inner being.

These three characters form a homogeneous group in Shakespeare. They are intensely concerned with dissimulation, and domination of their milieu. They have an exaggerated consciousness of their *difference*. The low comedy of the first scene of *King John* is full of references to the joys and consequences of cuckoldry: one summation is that this fault is a hazard

> of all husbands
> That marry wives.

51

But it is another summation which changes the tone of the scene and relates it to the scenes which are to follow. This is the speech of the Bastard which connects his identity and his beliefs:

> But this is worshipful society
> And fits the mounting spirit like myself,
> For he is but a bastard to the time
> That doth not smack of observation;
> And so am I, whether I smack or no;
> And not alone in habit and device,
> Exterior form, outward accoutrement,
> But from the inward motion to deliver
> Sweet, sweet, sweet poison for the age's tooth:
> Which, though I will not practise to deceive,
> Yet, to avoid deceit, I mean to learn;
> For it shall strew the footsteps of my rising.

The rejection of old beliefs and a new faith in the self will be the basis of his success. This kind of attitude would have been impossible for the protagonists of the first trilogy, with their simple and often honourable faith in descent, and in the meaning of their past. It is symbolic of a new kind of attitude in England, which began with Marlowe in art and Bacon in philosophy, and permeated the Jacobean drama. Its political philosopher, needless to say, was Machiavelli. In his Sermon LXXX Donne writes of the man who rejects his religious and ethical past. He is the 'natural man' as opposed to the Christian man. The natural man has no universal belief; he rejects all that is not demonstrably of the world of the material and the present. In the story of Richard III Shakespeare found ready to hand the equivalent of a workable myth in which the 'natural' and the traditional engage in what is quite literally a death struggle. He writes in these two plays actually of far more than the involvement of political ideologies. He writes of a world of order attacked by the anarchy of the self.

Richard III is a dramatic success because we are made to feel a certain empathy with both morality and wit, with both traditional order and the will that attacks it. There are many declamations in this play which serve a double purpose. The following registers what evidently is simple truth:

> Foul devil, for God's sake, hence, and trouble us not;
> For thou hast made the happy earth thy hell,
> Fill'd it with cursing cries and deep exclaims.
> If thou delight to view thy heinous deeds,
> Behold this pattern of thy butcheries...

Thus Anne to Richard in their first encounter. According to Tudor history and in the manner of the earliest histories of Shakespeare the wickedness of Richard is fully expressed. He is a 'lump of foul deformity', 'inhuman', and 'unnatural'. Yet this speech is hyperbolical where Richard is rational, hysterical where he is dispassionate. Because of this it is readily apparent that the speech reveals intellectual inadequacy. It is all feeling, and the purpose of the entire scene around it is to show the mastery of feeling by intellect. It is farcical in the sense that (Eliot remarks) *The Jew of Malta* is a farce.

However monstrous Richard may be, it is his mind which engages us, and which turns the creaking drama of declamation into what he calls the 'keen encounter' of wits and wills. In so doing he makes the chronicle more rich and infinitely more true to life. Richard III has the empirical temper; he understands nothing by its reference or relationship to things universal, nor does he give Anne credit for doing so. For him there is no universal truth. His witty dialogue with Anne is a triumph not only of strength over weakness but of mind over ideal. It is impossible to reproduce here the full extent of the scene, and the nuances of its movement. Yet lines like the following can indicate the daring of Richard's rhetoric, which forces Anne to vitiate her hatred in reasoning:

> O, he was gentle, mild and virtuous!
>
> *Glou.:* The fitter for the King of Heaven, that hath him.
>
> *Anne:* He is in heaven, where thou shalt never come.
>
> *Glou.:* Let him thank me, that holp to send him thither;
> For he was fitter for that place than earth.
>
> *Anne:* And thou unfit for any place but hell.
>
> *Glou.:* Yes, one place else, if you will hear me name it.
>
> *Anne:* Some dungeon.
>
> *Glou.:*   Your bed-chamber.

His fluidity is the manifestation of a new kind of mind. The high place that Richard occupies among Shakespeare's sophists (and he leads to the two greatest, Falstaff and Iago) is due to his amoral freedom. For him there are no boundaries between a sinful will and a dreaded moral law. Faulconbridge, the Bastard, should be included in the periphery of this group because of his profane but logical mind. What is a matter of considerable seriousness, the chastity of his mother, is for him merely a gambit:

> Now, by this light, were I to get again,
> Madam, I would not wish a better father.
> Some sins do bear their privilege on earth,
> And so doth yours.

This is to be interpreted in the light of Spenserian and Miltonic morality, which defined the vision of the age, or at least its official version.

If Faulconbridge, like Richard, exists to obscure moral questions, and, like Edmund, to balance iniquity with heroic energy, he serves also to illuminate the nature of the world about him. The point of his speech on 'tickling Commodity' is that this is what might be called an amoral awakening. He begins to see that the affairs of the world are themselves based on materialistic realism. Like Edmund and Richard III he comes to the conclusion that the natural world constitutes the whole of reality. So far as it is possible to get final answers from a naturalistic interpretation of the order of things, these characters supply such answers. They fail ultimately because naturalistic truth is not enough. It is the business of such characters—and to them we might add the later figures of Iago and Wolsey—to manifest an interpretation of the world which complements their intentions. The intentions fail and the interpretations prove inadequate. The nature of man proves to be less bestial than Iago conceives, the nature of Fortune less arbitrary than Wolsey conceives. Edmund fails to understand loyalty, Richard III fails to understand that hatred cannot be contained by fear. These characters are all great reasoners, but the kind of reason they stand for never elicited the respect of the Elizabethans. The saving grace for Faulconbridge consists in his being assimilated in the *mystery* of love for his nation.

Before he reveals this love he becomes the spokesman for a particular position of 'realism'. If we think of the well-known speech of Ulysses in *Troilus and Cressida* which establishes the principle of order, we can see that the speech of the Bastard on 'Commodity' and the entire complex of Richard's beliefs point to a principle which is the polar opposite. The universe, in their eyes, is a 'mad world', and its principle 'all-changing'. Whereas Ulysses speaks for 'course, proportion, season, form', the Bastard holds for 'indifferency' in 'all direction, purpose, course, intent'. The Bastard uses the language of Renaissance Epicureanism when he describes the universal principle as a 'sway of motion', an 'all-changing word'. Richard is able to act as he does because he sees far enough into things to be *confident* that 'every thing includes itself in power'.

It is a mixture of philosophical materialism and Machiavellian politics which animates the minds of these characters. They have the wit to perceive that 'the old is always thrust aside to make way for the new', but they do not have perception enough to see that 'one thing must be built out of the wreck of another'.[2] The wit of Richard is only possible because certain moral ties have been cut. It is predominantly the wit of the new man, who finds in himself resources which would be unrecognized in the older world of order. Machiavelli wrote of this new man in politics, Jonson and Middleton wrote of him in the world of social and financial mores. He is essentially a destructive figure, yet within his limitations he can make the moral order of civilization seem ineffectual. Marlowe's new man was not only Faustus but the Jew of Malta, a perfect individualist.

Buckingham, Richard's first counsellor of *Realpolitik*, has also been liberated from conscience and the moral law. Like Richard he sees politics *qua* politics. This was a freedom widely feared in the Christian Renaissance. When the Cardinal invokes 'mild entreaties' and 'God in heaven' (III, i) he is taking precisely the position taken by Henry VI in the preceding history cycle. He is, so far as Richard and Buckingham can see, confusing politics and morality. He speaks of guilt and sin, two concepts which the dry wit of Machiavelli makes very little of. The speech of Buckingham in response is quite explicit. He makes plain the irrevocable conflict between that which is 'ceremonious and traditional' and that which has 'the wit to claim the place'. He does this in a rather impressive way:

> You are too senseless-obstinate, my lord,
> Too ceremonious and traditional:
> Weigh it but with the grossness of this age,
> You break not sanctuary in seizing him.
> The benefit thereof is always granted
> To those whose dealings have deserved the place,
> And those who have the wit to claim the place:
> This prince hath neither claim'd it nor deserv'd it;
> And therefore, in mine opinion, cannot have it:
> Then, taking him from thence that is not there,
> You break no privilege nor charter there.

54

He claims the relevance of the present necessity. Like Machiavelli's Prince he is 'able by astuteness to confuse men's brains'.[3] And like the 'new prince' of whom Machiavelli speaks so often, he sees that tradition is the enemy of that necessity. Tradition is persistently defined in terms of 'virtue' but the Machiavellian definition of virtue is *power*. It persists in defining by regulation and precedent, but Machiavelli says 'I know of no better precepts for a new prince to follow *than may be found in his actions*'.[4] The Cardinal is an honorable but ineffectual relic of the older age alluded to by Ben Jonson in his poem on Penshurst as that of the 'mysteries' of order. The encounter is itself symbolic: secular statesman against churchman, young against old, strong intellect against helpless faith.

The prevailing uncertainty of *King John* is a consequence of the relativism which informs it. This, more than any other of the histories, speaks of politics as the art of the possible. In so doing it attacks the vast structure of Christian politics grounded on the *jus divinum*. This may be seen in the tirades of Constance. She looks back to the stable world of 'Nature', but the new prince and his abettors belong to the changing world of 'Fortune'. She says to Arthur:

> ...at thy birth, dear boy,
> Nature and Fortune join'd to make thee great:
> Of Nature's gifts thou mayst with lilies boast
> And with the half-blown rose. But Fortune, O,
> She is corrupted, changed and won from thee;
> She adulterates hourly with thine uncle John,
> And with her golden hand hath pluck'd on France
> To tread down fair respect of sovereignty.

The idea of time, which the Bastard contemptuously calls 'old Time the clock-setter, that bald sexton Time', is central to both plays. In them, as in *Macbeth*, it is the point of leverage for devastating irony. If at first time is the servant of 'mad composition' it has a way of enforcing retribution. Time present inexorably turns into time future, to mock the expectations of those who see only the relevance of the present necessity. King Philip, in his pride, speaks of his ability to turn time into his own memorial:

> ...this blessed day
> Ever in France shall be kept festival:
> To solemnize this day the glorious sun
> Stays in his course and plays the alchemist,
> Turning with splendour of his precious eye
> The meagre cloddy earth to glittering gold:
> The yearly course that brings this day about
> Shall never see it but a holiday.

But it is a day of reckoning, and will be one of atonement. Constance, the frenzied Cassandra of this drama, knows that

> This day, all things begun come to ill end,
> Yea, faith itself to hollow falsehood change!

It is typical of the histories that those who prophesy are ignored. The time to come will in fact be the time of nemesis: the first sin against good faith will become an 'original' sin and a world will arise in which 'all form is formless, order orderless'.

This great theme of disorder is expressed by more than the structural pattern of intrigue and betrayal. The chaotic violence of *King John* exists also in terms of ethical confusion. Religion and legitimacy are invoked ceaselessly by those who are indifferent to both. Rites and ceremonies like treaties and marriage sacraments are used simply as counters; they indicate neither friendship nor love. There are two realities: money and power. Yet throughout the play there is a constant appeal to justification. The words that crop up again and again are 'hearts', 'heaven' and 'law'. God, the saints, royalty, the state and the family appear almost as frequently, and with as little meaning.

The central mode of the play is paradox. Law is coupled frequently with right, and as frequently with power. Constance sees that while it 'can do no right' it can 'bar no wrong'. In fact, 'law itself is perfect wrong'. A tremendous sense of strain is generated when violently different ideas of the same thing are juxtaposed. What King Philip calls a conjunction of

> inward souls
> Married in league, coupled and link'd together,

is for Constance simply 'false blood to false blood join'd'. The glowing imagery of 'deep-sworn faith, peace, amity, true love' has followed a definition of faith as simply 'need'. Indeed the possibilities of the phrase 'play fast and loose with faith' are those of paradox alone: what is intimated is that even truth is subject to necessity. Pandulph's statement to Philip comprises one of the morals of the play. Faith must be made 'an enemy to faith'. The paradoxical tone of such utterance indicates that there is no central truth capable of holding the world of this play together. The most important speech tending to demonstrate this is that of Pandulph:

> For that which thou hast sworn to do amiss
> Is not amiss when it is truly done,
> And being not done, where doing tends to ill,
> The truth is then most done not doing it:
> The better act of purposes mistook
> Is to mistake again...

Men as well as beliefs are caught between the anvil of sophistry and the hammer of interest. 'They whirl asunder', cries Blanch, and our total impression of the drama is of 'inconstancy', 'Fortune', and 'need' dominating men while they cry, as Philip does to Pandulph, 'devise, ordain, impose/Some gentle order'.

In *Richard III* paradox is manifested especially where the protagonist is involved. Time in this play has been the servant of the unnatural—from beginning to end the 'accursed womb' becomes the 'bed of death'. Gloucester has distorted the laws of being:

> Marry, they say my uncle grew so fast
> That he could gnaw a crust at two hours old.

He was born to renew the 'ancient sorrow' of usurpation, although his own vision is both freed and limited by the 'golden time' he looks for. While Richard conceives of time as Machiavelli does, as the present affecting the immediate future, he is seen in the world of this play as an incarnation of chaos, destroying the rootedness of civilization in time. His own view of time is secular and pragmatic; that of his opponents mystical and prophetic. Margaret and Elizabeth continually remind us of this difference. In their speeches we see the old order of morality as it is affected by the new order of necessity.

It is Margaret who supplies a sense of the prophetic to the play. Richard's sense of time is historical and immediate. He does not feel the past pressing on him. All things are in flux, yielding to the will according to the power exerted upon them. He deals with time in an especially interesting way in his speeches; it is as if time were a commodity and he were a merchant who could exploit it any way he wished. The swirl of tenses in the following reveals that he moves from present to future in an inconceivably fluid way. For the while he is in fact the master of time:

> I am determined to prove a villain
> And hate the idle pleasures of these days.
> Plots have I laid, inductions dangerous,
> By drunken prophecies, libels and dreams,
> To set my brother Clarence and the king
> In deadly hate the one against the other:
> And if King Edward be as true and just
> As I am subtle, false and treacherous,
> This day should Clarence closely be mew'd up,
> About a prophecy, which says that G
> Of Edward's heir the murderer shall be.

Every variety of tense and mood is used; the effect is that of time itself absorbed into Richard's characteristic logic. Time for Richard would appear to be the mode of probability. He accepts the mysteries of prophecy only as some kind of vehicle for his purpose. For him there are no mysteries; prophecy is 'drunken' and part of irrational 'libels and dreams'. The contingencies of time fall into a scheme which stretches from past to future: he lives in the world of the conditional, in which things happen according to the direction imposed upon them. Time does not exist in this sense for the defeated. They think back on the 'pale ashes of the house of Lancaster' or toward the indefinite day of retribution. They invoke time as nemesis:

> If ever he have child, abortive be it,
> Prodigious, and untimely brought to light...

> If heaven have any grievous plague in store
> Exceeding those that I can wish upon thee,
> O, let them keep it till thy sins be ripe,
> And then hurl down their indignation.

> O, but remember this another day,
> When he shall split thy very heart with sorrow...

The defeated live in the midst of horror recollected and anticipated. The Queen can say simply, 'ay me, I see the downfall of our house', and, 'I see, as in a map, the end of all', and in these few words recognize a nightmare outside the moral order. She and Margaret live in a present overshadowed by past and future, immersed in tragic experience.

Margaret is especially a counterpart to the 'mounting spirit' of the protagonist. Whereas Richard looks forward only to 'the throne majestical' she is a kind of spokesman for the rottenness and not the ripeness of maturity:

> So, now prosperity begins to mellow
> And drop into the rotten mouth of death.
> Here in these confines slily have I lurk'd,
> To watch the waning of mine adversaries.
> A dire induction am I witness to,
> And will to France, hoping the consequence
> Will prove as bitter, black, and tragical.

Her function, consciously undertaken, is to provide in the court of time present a strong sense of the guilt of the past. She is the voice of an order of time which has its own laws of 'induction' and 'consequence'. The contrast to the rationale of Richard is complete.

There are dark intimations in the fourth act that the range of human experience is controlled by man's subservience to time. The two queens reveal that time is a wheel and fate its insentient expression:

> Thus hath the course of justice wheel'd about,
> And left thee but a very prey to time;
> Having no more but thought of what thou wert,
> To torture thee the more, being what thou art.

To exist is to be a 'very prey to time'. There is an illusory quality to all human expectation. Both actors and audience in the stage play of life are equally caught up by the great wheel:

> Thy Clarence he is dead that kill'd my Edward;
> And the beholders of this tragic play,
> The adulterate Hastings, Rivers, Vaughan, Grey,
> Untimely smother'd in their dusky graves.

Elizabeth is now a 'dream' and a 'breadth' of what she was. The mother of Richard herself sees that the hope of a birth was an illusion. Her interchange with her son is a bitter parody of that redemption which occurred outside of time:

> *Duch.*: Art thou so hasty? I have stay'd for thee,
> God knows, in anguish, pain and agony.
> *K. Rich.*: And came I not at last to comfort you?
> *Duch.*: No, by the holy rood, thou know'st it well,
> Thou camest on earth to make the earth my hell.

Yet, if his victims have been a prey to time, this will be the fate of Richard as well. For the future is now at hand. When Elizabeth asks Richard 'what canst thou swear by now?' he answers with characteristic logic, 'the time to come'. No response could be more accurate than the one she gives: 'that thou hast wronged in the time o'erpast'. The address of Richard to Elizabeth after this exchange is ironical in a sense he never intended:

> Plead what I will be, not what I have been;
> Not my deserts, but what I will deserve:
> Urge the necessity and state of times,
> And be not peevish-fond in great designs.

'The means will always be judged honourable', says *The Prince*, if the 'issue of the event' is successful. But if the apology of the Machiavellian hero looks to Fortune and futurity to set things right, it depends also on the unpredictable nature of both. 'Great designs' which are eminently rational have to reckon with a future that is ready to become the present. This Buckingham finds at his execution:

> This is the day that, in King Edward's time,
> I wish'd might fall on me, when I was found
> False to his children or his wife's allies;
> This is the day wherein I wish'd to fall
> By the false faith of him I trusted most;
> This, this All-Souls' day to my fearful soul
> Is the determined respite of my wrongs.

God gives now in earnest what was 'begg'd in jest'. The time to come will be a time of terrible expiation; as in *Doctor Faustus* there is a scene in which 'earth gapes, hell burns, fiends roar' for the soul whose bond of life has been cancelled.

If this is the understood fate of Richard, the time to come offers something else for the world he leaves. It holds the promise of a new creation:

> O, now, let Richmond and Elizabeth,
> The true succeeders of each royal house,
> By God's fair ordinance conjoin together!
> And let their heirs, God, if thy will be so,
> Enrich the time to come with smooth-faced peace.

Once again the natural order will assert its own laws, and time will become the agency of Providence. In *King John* Faulconbridge ends with devout submission to the 'lineal state' of the land. He and Salisbury assert the hierarchic nature of order with promises of 'faithful services', 'true subjection', and the 'love' which has been so conspicuously abused in the course of the play. The Bastard turns to the hope that history in England will once again manifest the divine will. Both plays end then with a kind of apotheosis in which history is visualized as the servant of law. They have confronted the egocentric, anarchic nature of the individual with the ideals of order. Yet their real issues have been neither the 'monstrosity' of Richard nor the ruthlessness of the Bastard, but the rationalism and materialism which are *representative* qualities of humanity.

NOTES

1. This and succeeding quotations are from the Hardin Craig edition (Chicago, 1951).

2. Lucretius, *The Nature of the Universe*, trans. R. E. Latham (1957), p. 125.

3. Niccolo Machiavelli, *The Prince*, trans. Luigi Ricci (New York, 1950), p. 63. From the famous 'In What Way Princes Must Keep Faith'.

4. *Ibid.* p. 24. (Italics mine.)

THE STAGING OF PARODY AND PARALLELS IN 'I HENRY IV'

JOHN SHAW

Considerable attention has been paid in recent years to the style of acting in Shakespeare's day. Though evidence is meagre and the problem a controversial one, we can nevertheless be rather certain about the matter in general. We are told that by the late 1590s acting was neither 'formal' nor 'natural', or, to put it the other way, that it was both 'formal' and 'natural'.[1] It was 'formal' in that stylized and conventional gestures would express specific emotions: '...an Elizabethan by means of gesture might validly communicate clearly and powerfully...what he was thinking, feeling, and willing to achieve when representing a character in an Elizabethan play'.[2] 'On cue, the actor could assemble detailed specific gestures into a visual emblem of an idea.'[3] We may find these gestures, derived from stage practices, in the handbooks on rhetoric. In regard to an awareness, too, of an overall thematic development, 'the literary product of the writer', Elizabethan acting was also 'formal', for imagery was projected by special emphasis.[4]

On the other hand, Shakespearian acting was also 'natural'. The actor played his role as if he were that character. He read his lines with the emotional and intellectual responses inherent in them. He expressed the feelings and desires of the character with utmost faithfulness. The same imagery that may have revealed the author's vision might also have expressed the character's ideas and emotions. In short, imagery was for the Elizabethan actor both poetic and dramatic;[5] and acting both 'formal' and 'natural'. In sum, Shakespeare's theatre 'possessed the capacity to accept mimetic action on two levels': the actor and character, the person representing (formal) and the person represented (natural).[6]

Moreover, in addition to accepting a view of acting which conveyed the author's vision, we now understand the Shakespearian stage to have been an 'emblematic' one in the tradition of the medieval cycles and moralities and later polemical interludes. In fact, 'the stagecraft of Shakespeare's theatre represented a climax to centuries of medieval experiments rather than a new beginning of Renaissance inspiration'.[7] Thus, scenes in Shakespearian drama were related to one another with didactic intent, much as the plays within the miracle cycles had been related to one another. And the liturgically minded playgoer of both eras would have had eyes to see and ears to hear these parallels, contrasts, and juxtapositions.[8]

Two questions can now be raised. First, to what extent might one speech or one scene in a Shakespeare play have been concretely related to another speech or scene by means of stage practices, voice, gesture, the use of properties and so on? and second, what effect might such overt connexions have had on the experience of the playgoer in the theatre? After all, does it not seem logical to expect deliberately contrived connexions on stage to spring naturally out of the action, when we grant Shakespearian stage conventions to be 'basically emblematic', the forms existing to express thematic meaning, and when we grant in the text the parallel construction of certain scenes? It would follow then that these connexions would participate in what

Professor Coghill calls the 'visual meaning' of the play, helping to create and modify the experience of the playgoer in the theatre.

Let us begin quite simply with a four line sequence. In *1 Henry IV* Prince Hal concludes scene three of the third act with the conventional couplet tag:

> The land is burning, Percy stands on high,
> And either we or they must lower lie. (*Exit*)[9]

Normally, according to Shakespearian dramaturgy, Falstaff would exit after Hal either without reply, or else with a routine rejoinder, such as 'We go, my lord'. For instance, in those scenes which do not conclude with words by the ranking character, we have such closing comments as, 'I will, my liege', or 'Pray God you do', or 'It must of force', or 'Good morrow, good my lord', each by the character of secondary importance. The true cadence to a scene is invariably spoken by the character of rank. But in this scene the case is different. Falstaff waits until Hal has gone and then adds his own scene-closer:

> Rare words! Brave world! Hostess, my breakfast, come!
> O, I could wish this tavern were my drum. (*Exit*)

Falstaff's words make no sense whatever, except in their comic relation to Hal's. That is, Falstaff's words are a parody of Hal's. Not that Hal's ideas are being ridiculed. It is the tone of the speech, Hal's heroic posture, that amuses Falstaff. After all, patriotism is all right (even for the heir of a usurper) and the rebellion must be defeated. But need we be quite so boyishly serious about it before breakfast?—and in the tavern!

About the projection of these two speeches from the stage, it would be foolish to argue that Falstaff's tone of voice could be much different from Hal's, both utterances being excited rhetorical ejaculations in form. The joke, of course, is that Falstaff's couplet has the rhetorical structure without the intrinsic emotional content, thus rendering the structure ridiculous. This is all quite obvious. But it must be laboured since our argument is based on the theory that gesture arises naturally out of rhetorical structure. If a set of gestures, a stylized stance, and a specific tone of voice accompanied the words of Hal, then the mimic Falstaff would certainly, with suitable exaggeration, have repeated these in his version of the heroic vaunt.

This scene, then, ends with a genuine flourish followed by a mock flourish, a decided departure from the usual scene ending, both in this play and in Shakespearian drama generally. What is the effect on the playgoer, seeing Falstaff burlesquing Hal's gestures while roaring his own nonsensical couplet? Suffice to say at this point that while we may laugh with Falstaff we do not therefore jeer at the Prince, or his words. His statement, 'The land is burning', stands. Rebellion is indeed afoot, political chaos has come, and the struggle is now to the death. Hal speaks with exhilaration, fully aware of his heavy responsibility and of the shortness of time. But the mimicry of Falstaff broadens the context within which we can experience these attitudes, a context which acknowledges the necessity for breakfast, among other values and choices. A wider view of 'nature' is afforded us in the mirror which Shakespeare holds up; nor is there much danger of shallow partisan propaganda when strenuous tones are matched by mocking ones in this manner. But more about the effects later.

Let us move to a more complicated problem before developing some of the evidence for the staging of scene connexions. In the same play let us examine the two interviews, the one between Falstaff and Hal, and the other between Hal and King Henry. Although there is scarcely need to review these two familiar passages in detail, several points about them need attention. For, though it is universally agreed that the two scenes are explicitly parallel,[10] the first a comic 'run-through' of the second, it is not generally recognized just how parallel they are. Let us pause here for a moment.

Needless to say, Shakespeare wrote the second, or serious, interview with the first, or comic, one very much alive in his mind. They are too alike to allow us to think otherwise. Each begins with the king, mock or real, seated in state on his throne. Each king first asks that the chamber be cleared as he turns from public to private matters. Falstaff says, 'Stand aside, nobility... For God's sake, lords, convey my tristful queen'. King Henry says, 'Lords, give us leave'. Each king speaks of his own sorrow over Hal's absence from the Court. Falstaff: 'for I must speak in passion...in tears...in woes also'. And King Henry:

> Not an eye
> But is aweary of thy common sight,
> Save mine, which hath desir'd to see thee more,
> Which now doth that I would not have it do,—
> Make blind itself with foolish tenderness.

Each king then addresses himself to the main point. Falstaff asks, 'Why, being son to me, art thou so pointed at?' King Henry charges Hal with being 'so common-hackneyed in the eyes of men, so stale and cheap to vulgar company'.

Actually, Hal's consorting with 'rude society' constitutes the chief substance of the two interviews. But it is interesting to note, also, that much emphasis is placed in both scenes on the father–son contrast. King Henry devotes a good deal of the interview to comparing his reputation to Hal's, and Falstaff facetiously dwells on the relationship between the king and his son:

That thou art my son, I have partly thy mother's word, partly my own opinion...if then thou be son to me...Shall the son of England prove a thief and take purses?

Finally, the two scenes conclude with similar assurances of reform on the part of Hal, the first spoken with gusto and good humour after Falstaff's 'Banish plump Jack, and banish all the world' ('I do, I will'), and the second expressed with the utmost sincerity of tones: 'I will redeem all this...' Then the two interviews are both cut off in precisely the same manner, by the intrusion of a hasty messenger:

(*Enter Bardolph, running*) O my lord, my lord, the sheriff with a most monstrous watch is at the door.
(*Enter Blunt*) *King:* How now, good Blunt? Thy looks are full of speed.
   Blunt: So hath the business that I come to speak of.

If these two scenes—both of an equal length, beginning and ending in the same manner, and concerned with identical details—were written, not as roughly similar episodes, but as precisely parallel scenes as a whole, can we assume any connexions were made between the two when produced on the stage? What evidence might there be to suggest that the physical staging of the two scenes, and the acting, emphasized and clarified their relationships? Certainly, in most contemporary productions, as was the case in those of the eighteenth and nineteenth centuries, the two scenes are treated as separate dramatic moments.[11] The great comedy of the Tavern these days is pointed toward the inevitable rejection of Falstaff, and the less dramatically engaging King Henry interview is run through quickly with many cuts. No attempt is made to bring out the parallels so skilfully incorporated into the pair of scenes by Shakespeare.[12]

Evidence to suggest that these two scenes were in Elizabethan days produced in such a manner as to clarify their relationship is scanty. One may argue, of course, that the very fact the scenes were written as identically parallel urges us to believe this aspect of their construction was not neglected in their original staging. But of more help is a glance at contemporary attitudes toward parody in general. First, we know a high value was placed on the talent for mimicry, or counterfeiting, by the 'quick comedians' during the latter half of the sixteenth century. Dick Tarlton, for example, was known for the 'power of his extempore wit', and in Chettle's portrayal of this famous comedian it seemed the obvious thing to have him improvise a brilliant parody of a Puritan condemning the stage: 'Fie vppon following plaies', Tarlton's mock denunciation begins.[13] Moreover in the sixteenth-century interludes we find occasionally that one actor definitely parodies another's movements. Thus, we have in *Jacob and Esau* two servants who elicit laughs by mimicking their master's voice and way of walking. We even have the following stage direction: 'Here he counterfeiteth [Esau] supping out of the pot.'[14] Again, in *Jack Juggler*, the clown Jack parodies the manners of the stupid servant Jenkins, especially his girlish way of walking.[15]

Altogether, we may say at least this much regarding the acting-out of the parallels of our two scenes, that to repeat actions or mimic voices on the stage would not have violated any convention of the Elizabethan stage; nor would it have been considered an innovation. On the contrary, staging the two scenes in order to bring out their parodic relationship might well have been expected.

Internal evidence can help here. Bertram Joseph's conclusions, as we have seen, relate acting techniques—the use of voice, gesture, movement—very closely to the emotional and intellectual potentials intrinsic to the lines. In the serious scene between Hal and the King, we see that King Henry has three points to make. He wishes to justify himself and his prudent actions; he wants to probe his son's true feelings, for he has heard vicious rumours; and he wants to shame Hal into rejecting his degenerate habits. At the same time, Hal's hope in this scene is to convince his father of his genuine loyalty. Both men speak sincerely and passionately, feeling deeply their alienation.

In the earlier comic scene the essential desires are roughly the same, though they are cloaked with complex, mocking ironies. Falstaff, like the King, wishes to justify himself. And he desires to probe Hal's true feelings, for he has an intuition about the future, and he hopes to win Hal's affection. At the same time, Hal desires to make it clear to Falstaff, as he indeed does, that the end of the fun is in sight. Banish Jack? 'I do, I will'. Though the words of this scene are facetious and the tone comic, yet the content of the scene might well call for a number of the same gestures and the same tone of voice, though here ridiculous, as the later scene. After all, Falstaff plays the King 'as like one of these harlotry players as ever' the hostess has seen. And upon his deposition Falstaff describes his own acting as done 'gravely...majestically, both in word and matter'. The point here is that these gestures would not be artificial or strained in either scene but arise quite naturally from the words.

Moreover, we have two 'thrones' and two 'sceptres', two 'crowns' and two interviews involving these properties. Surely, they could be handled on the stage in a like manner? I do not speak of exact copying between the two scenes of every action and manner, of course. But the general blocking, several of the gestures, and moments of the voicing (to which Elizabethans were sensitive, as Hamlet suggests in his advice to the players) would be enough to remind the audience of the comic preview during the serious scene. Let Falstaff's throne (the joint-stool) be placed in the central spot where King Henry's throne will later be; let Hal kneel in humble respect to his father, where he had knelt in mockery before Falstaff. Where Falstaff had gravely lowered his cushion upon his head, tapped his dagger on the table and turned to Hal to begin the scene, have King Henry now remove his crown in the same deliberate manner, place his sceptre on the same table, and turn to Hal to begin the scene. The fact that Falstaff might put on his 'crown' but Henry remove his (King Henry, who has been holding Court, is now the private man speaking to his son) is not important. Once a dramatist has established an expectation, the fulfilling of it or the failure to do so amount to the same thing: a subtle dramatic emphasis is generated in either case. Might we go so far as to have Falstaff arise from his 'throne' when he speaks of his tears and passion, and then King Henry arise from his throne when he speaks of his eye being blind 'with foolish tenderness'? The two scenes obviously contain the justification for similar stage movements latent within them, and, realizing that mimicry was one of an actor's most popular techniques, we cannot deny the strong possibility that the parallels were brought out in some such way.

In addition to speaking of Elizabethan attitudes toward stage parody, and of the inherent parallels between the two scenes under discussion implying similar stage treatment, we can support our theory with one or two other traces of evidence. Joseph Hall's satire on tragic actors, *Virgidemiarum*, I, 3, often regarded as a contemporary criticism of Marlowe's tragedies, or of the mixture of genres, actually offers some insight into the production of comic scenes like that of the Tavern as related to its later serious parallel:

> Now, least such frightfull showes of Fortunes fall,
> And bloody Tyrants rage, should chance appall
> The dead stroke audience, mids the silent rout
> Comes leaping in a selfe-misformed lout,
> And laughes, and grins, and frames his Mimik face,
> And justles straight into the Princes place.[16]

The framing of a 'Mimik face' and the phrase 'justles straight into the Princes place' suggest a parodying of gesture and blocking, if nothing else. One recalls (in *The Pilgrimage to Parnassus*) the clown drawn in with a rope, who, precisely because he cannot mimic facial expressions, is unable to play the king.[17] Also, returning to Joseph Hall, another reference occurs a few lines later in this same passage, to the relationship between clown and courtier:

> A goodly hoch-poch, when vile Russettings,
> Are match't with monarchs, & with mighty kings.

The usual sense in which we take this is that the lower class characters are *mixed* with upper class ones in an academically disreputable tragedy. But the term 'match't' also implies a controlled relationship of parody or burlesque, a faint suggestion of actual stage parallels of repeated action and gesture: 'vile Russettings are match't with monarchs'.

Turning now to the effects of the parallels made conspicuous by stage production, we may say again that the playgoer is made conscious of several aspects of a situation.[18] Dramatic scope is broadened, and value judgments, while more difficult, can be more accurately made, for the issues are seen within a wide context. The technique of multiple perspective on one situation renders experience more faithfully, nor would the ambiguities and ironies implicit in such treatment bother the audience. In the inclusive dramatic tradition of their day, Elizabethans were used to experiencing contradictory feelings simultaneously. For generations, after all, they had roared with laughter at Cain cheating in his tithing, while at the same moment they were aware of this action as prefiguring the killing of Christ.[19] As hard pressed yeomen they could sympathize with Cain, and as Christians they could at the same time be appalled by his wicked cheating. 'A popular audience...will attend to several diverse aspects of a situation, simultaneously yet without confusion.'[20]

The ironies inherent in the parallels between two scenes like the interviews in *Henry IV*, if forcefully emphasized by the staging, would have delighted the audience. A cushion for a crown! How fetching that implication for an audience of commoners, and, if vividly recalled by staging in the serious interview, how ironic in the light of Henry's solemn statements regarding responsibility. Similarly, how rich the irony of the dagger–sceptre equivalent, if carried through on the stage, for an audience schooled in the Wars of the Roses and the legalistic debate over Henry IV's claim in the Henry VI plays.

More important, however, the effect on the playgoer of the explicitly clear combination of scenes is to prepare him for the acceptance of Hal's resolve to reform. The dramatic impact of Hal's wonderful promise to redeem himself 'in the closing of some glorious day' is really quite stunning, if the playgoer has alive in his mind the earliest mock-innocent attitude of Hal when he pretends not to know whom Falstaff (playing the king) means by the 'virtuous man... noted in thy company'. Then it was play, but now it is in earnest. If one pauses for a moment to consider the King Henry interview without the Tavern scene preceding it, one realizes the dramatic difficulties of making Hal's statements to his father ring true. But hearing his jesting accents in the back of our minds as we listen to his resolute vows, we are readily convinced of his sincerity over the same matters in the latter case.

The use of comic preparation, of course, was traditional. In the Towneley *Secunda Pastorum* perhaps the best known example occurs, where the hilarious episode in Mak's cottage skilfully prepares us for the serious parallel of the Nativity. It is possible the identification was vividly carried through by use of the same crude cradle for the stolen lamb and for the Lamb of God.[21] Certainly, the rowdy, farcical domestic brawling (as the thunder roars) in the Towneley *Processus Noe Cum Filiis* serves as comic preparation for the serious and serene awe with which Noah and his wife, now in harmony, receive the miracle of their salvation. And in the *Woman Taken in Adultery* from the *Ludus Coventriae*, the long passage of noisy, obscene slapstick preceding the dramatically potent scene of Jesus quietly writing on the ground effectively highlights the serious conversation between Jesus and the Woman.[22] As A. P. Rossiter has pointed out, comic preparation not only gets an audience on the side of the dramatist: 'it makes an *audience of the people*'.[23] For laughter is public, disarming one's social and psychological defences, reducing one's restraints and aloofness. Shakespeare himself gives us one of the most effective moments of comic preparation of all in the wise fooling of the Clown who brings the asp to Cleopatra, immediately after which some of Shakespeare's most glorious poetry is spoken. The sincere basis of those lines beginning 'Give me my robe, put on my crown' must not be doubted by the audience, and the Clown's excellent comedy provides the right psychological preparation for the tragic speeches to come. And so it is in this light that we should see the entire Tavern parody in its 'matching' of the serious interview, not as a separate bit of comedy, nor as derisive criticism, but as comic preparation providing us with sharper awareness and a fresh alertness to the wider perspective and ironies with which we are to view the political and personal King–Prince relationship. Moreover, if the two scenes are staged so as to clarify the parallels, these effects are immediate; they become a part of the theatrical experience of the playgoer, adding depth of focus to his hearing and seeing of the events at the moment of perception. And dramatic meaning, of course, is enhanced in performance in a way the mere reading of the play could never accomplish.

Thus far we have dealt with two sets of parallel situations from *1 Henry IV* in an attempt to theorize about possible stage techniques in their original portrayals, and to assess some of their effects on the playgoer, if vividly connected. The question of whether these two pairs of parallel situations are indeed parallel has not been at issue; obviously they are. But would they have been *staged* as parallel? We have adduced a slight amount of evidence to support the assertion that they would have been. But the hypothesis that parallel situations were made clear by stage business may be most effectively developed if we consider two scenes whose parallels, if they are to be noticed at all, must be brought out by production. Such a situation we have in *1 Henry IV*, scenes iii and iv, 1–125, of Act II. The first of these is the Hotspur–Kate interview at Warkworth Castle (scene iii), and the second is the Francis–Hal foolery in the Tavern (scene iv, 1–125). Like the Falstaff parody of Hal's speech, with which this essay began, the entire Francis episode parodies the essential tone and atmosphere of the preceding Kate–Hotspur scene. But a reading of the two scenes does not at all make manifest their relationship, any more than a mere reading of Falstaff's parody, were it separated by fifty lines from Hal's speech, would make that relationship clear. In this case, we deal with two entire scenes; only a production emphasizing the relationship by business, blocking and voice can make the parody comprehensible. This is a bold interpretation and requires justification.

We must first be convinced the two scenes were written as complements for parody, that is, as two perspectives on a like situation. The two episodes are, in fact, constructed in precisely the same manner. Each has a brief passage of about thirty-five lines, mostly monologue, as a kind of introduction. Hotspur reads a letter, commenting here and there on the 'honourable action' his correspondent has decided to desert. In the comic parody Hal speaks to Poins, with easy contempt, about the 'honour' Poins has lost in not being with him 'in this action' of the drawers. Honour in the action of a rebellion, honour in the action with some drawers: these introductory passages first establish the parallel.

Then follows, in each case, about eighty-five lines of dialogue between Hotspur and Kate, first, and Hal and Francis, second, during which there is no real communication in either case. The basis for each of these interviews, the dramatic point of each, is the interaction of an earnest (Kate is and Hal pretends to be) questioner with a nervous, distracted listener. The

Hotspur–Kate scene is rather charming, though perhaps more romantic on the stage to us than it was to Elizabethans; the Francis–Hal scene seems absurd and pointless.

At the conclusion of the Francis–Hal scene, Hal makes an explicit comment about, almost an explicit comparison between, Francis and Hotspur:

That ever this fellow [Francis] should have fewer words than a parrot, and yet the son of a woman! His industry is up-stairs and down-stairs, his eloquence the parcel of a reckoning. I am not yet of Percy's mind, the Hotspur of the north, he that kills me some six or seven dozen of Scots at a breakfast, washes his hands, and says to his wife, 'Fie upon this quiet life, I want work'.

From Francis to Hotspur: so moves Hal's mind. He has associated 'my puny drawer' with Hotspur, as two men whose high-strung and agitated natures preclude their participation in a rich and full life. In Shakespeare's day this comparison between Hotspur and Francis would not strain the imagination. The potboy in the tavern, after all, draws drink, while the soldier was one who liked to draw his sword. Both, in their way, are drawers. We recall the association of the two in *Romeo and Juliet*:

Thou art like one of those fellows that when he enters the confines of a tavern claps me his sword upon the table and says, 'God send me no need of thee!' and by the operation of the second cup draws it on the drawer, when indeed there is no need.   (III, i, 5–10)

The Elizabethans would have seen the parallel, too, in the matter of both Hotspur's and Francis's eloquence being but 'the parcel of a reckoning'. For, as Madeleine Doran has pointed out, Hotspur, despite the poetic strength of his utterances, is not eloquent:

Hotspur despises poets and poetry from the bottom of his heart, yet who in the play speaks more wonderful poetry than he? It is a mistake, however, to smile indulgently at Hotspur and say that he is a poet whether he knows it or not. He is not, and Shakespeare does not mean him to be. As he is conceived, he could not sit down and speak sad epitaphs on the death of kings, as Richard, a true poet, does; imaginative as he is, he yet has no gift either of reflection or of controlled composition. The poetry he speaks is Shakespeare's poetry, a device for giving us all the color and vitality of Hotspur's bodily expressive temperament. It is an oblique device of style, completely unavailable when convention forces literal reproduction of the spoken word. Caliban, the brutish Caliban, incapable of being taught moral or spiritual beauty, is another example of the same thing...[24]

Detecting a comparison between Hotspur and Francis, then, would have been less difficult for Elizabethans than for us, placing a value as they did upon eloquence as the outward manifestation of a man's true essence.

After the bizarre procedure of shouting for Francis from the next room, Poins returns as mystified as today's audience. What has been the joke? 'But hark ye', Poins asks, 'what cunning match have you made with this jest of the drawer?' The word 'match' may very well refer to a game or wager, though it is not clear how this sense of the word could apply to what has happened with Francis. But we must recall Joseph Hall's use of the word in his phrase, 'vile Russettings...match'd with monarchs, & with mighty kings'. The 'cunning match' can, therefore, have been the comparison between Hotspur and Francis. For unbeknownst to him, Francis has in fact been counterfeiting Hotspur, like Jack Juggler mimicking Jenkins, and Hal, along with the audience if the production makes it clear, understands the 'match'.

The above analysis of the two scenes, despite their surprising congruence of form—same length, same shape of dialogue—must remain unconvincing. Only the staging of the parallels will reveal their relationship. Recalling that 'for the stage player the function of "external action" was to express naturally and completely what was felt truthfully by the speaker',[25] we can consider the two scenes on the stage. Unlike the two interviews between a king and a prince, in which a crown, a throne and a sceptre comprise properties useful for repeated action, these two scenes have little more than a table and chair on stage. But they both make use of one of the entrances on to the stage. This is the crucial point for the staging of the two scenes. After Kate's lovely, deeply troubled concern for Hotspur's 'heavy business', Hotspur must hurry to the door, for he shouts—and in reply to Kate!—to his servant:

> What ho!
>
> (*Enter a Servant*)
> Is Gilliams with the packet gone?
> *Serv.*: He is, my lord, an hour ago.
> *Hot.*: Hath Butler brought those horses from the sheriff?
> *Serv.*: One horse, my lord, he brought even now.
> *Hot.*: What horse? A roan, a crop-ear is it not?
> *Serv.*: It is, my lord.
> *Hot.*:   That roan shall be my throne.
> Well, I will back him straight: O Esperance!
> Bid Butler lead him forth into the park.
>
>   (*Exit Servant*)

Lady Percy's anxious question still hangs in the air. And so she asks again:

> But hear you, my lord.

A few lines later, and once again in response to the serious solicitations of his wife, Hotspur continues to call through the door:

> God's me! my horse!

Hotspur's rapid, nervous pacing from Lady Percy to the door and back would seem a likely bit of action arising naturally from the words and emotions of the scene. The same is true, of course, in the Francis scene:

> *Prince:* How old art thou, Francis?
> *Francis:* Let me see, about Michaelmas next I shall be—
> *Poins:* (*within*) Francis!
> *Francis:* —Anon, sir. Pray stay a little, my lord.
> *Prince:* Nay but hark you, Francis...

Using the same door Hotspur moved back and forth to, and the same general location for a table where Kate first and then later Hal are seated, the path of frantic pacing would be roughly the same in both scenes. It is possible, too, that a single gesture, clear and well-defined, would carry the identity of the two scenes home:

Hot.: That roan shall be my throne.
Well, I will back him straight: O Esperance!
(*Right arm out from chest to straight up in a rapid, triumphantly confident movement*)

Francis: O Lord, sir, I'll be sworn upon all the books in England, I could find in my heart...
(*Right arm out from chest slowly upward, and then falling limp with...*)...Anon, sir.

But the parody of Hotspur unconsciously hinted at by Francis need not be elaborate. With the stage uncluttered, the actors highly trained in rhetorical delivery, and the audience close at hand and responsive to meaning, a comic reminder of Hotspur could easily be projected. The main thing is that a pattern of serious question followed by comically irrelevant replies, with the 'parcel of reckoning' eloquence of both Hotspur and Francis made similar, be played with roughly the same blocking.

Regarding the staging of the Hotspur–Kate scene, one other point may be brought up. Kate's long opening speech is a curious one. Nearly thirty lines in length (and we have no reason to believe Kate is a garrulous woman), it is strangely out of place in this scene of rapid questions and rejoinders. It has reminded critics of Portia's twenty-line speech to Brutus, and the comparison is instructive.[26] For the rhetorical structure of the two speeches is significantly different. Portia's two long speeches to Brutus take the form of little narratives:

> And yesternight at supper
> You suddenly arose and walked about,
> Musing and sighing, with your arms across.
> And when I asked you what the matter was,
> You stared upon me with ungentle looks.
> I urged you further, then you scratched your head
> And too impatiently stamped with your foot.
> Yet I insisted, yet you answered not,
> But with an angry wafture of your hand
> Gave sign for me to leave you. So I did,
> Hoping it was but an effect of humour,
> Which sometime hath his hour with every man.

And Portia goes on to describe the symptoms of Brutus's 'sickness'. In Kate's somewhat longer speech, the material is developed not by narrative but by rhetorical amplification, first a series of questions and then an extended list of details:

> ...why are you...
> For what offence have I...
> what is't that takes...
> Why dost thou bend...
> Why hast thou lost...
> In thy faint slumbers I by thee have watch'd,
> And heard thee murmur tales of iron wars,

Speak terms of manage to thy bounding steed,
Cry 'Courage! To the field!' And thou hast talk'd
Of sallies, and retires, of trenches, tents,
Of palisadoes, frontiers, parapets,
Of basilisks, of cannon, culverin,
Of prisoners' ransom, and of soldiers slain,
And all the currents of a heady fight.

It is inconceivable that Hotspur would stand patiently still while poor Kate unravels the extra-ordinary list of items mentioned by him in his sleep. Besides of course helping to develop the strenuous mood of the romantic warrior and his preoccupation with the rebellion, and besides throwing light on the emotional relationship of Kate and Hotspur, the speech certainly illu-strates the limited eloquence of Hotspur—at least in his sleep! But, more important, does not this long speech, traditionally reduced by half in productions,[27] provide an opportunity for the display of Hotspur's excited anticipation of the rebellion? The speech is long simply so that Hotspur can ignore it! No other reason will suffice to account for the astonishing protraction of details. The speech, then, is a kind of stage direction for Hotspur: MOVE ABOUT. It is this 'industry...up-stairs and down-stairs' that Francis unknowingly mimicks in the next scene, reminding us and Hal of that 'paraquito' from the North.

While there is some evidence that Shakespeare did not view Hotspur as the completely attractive figure we so often find on our stage,[28] we must not assume Hotspur, because here 'counterfeited', to be the object of his ridicule. Though Hal may have laughed at him, we in the audience should be all the more aware of the threat he poses to the kingdom when we see his powerful striding in contrast to Francis's comic trotting. In this sense the parody helps build Hotspur into an antagonist of proportion. The Francis parody also establishes another perspective on the 'honourable action' for which Hotspur is willing to sacrifice 'this quiet life'.[29] It thus has its place in the kind of comprehensive pattern of incompatible attitudes found in so many of the plays of Shakespeare and his predecessors. But we need not labour this concept of multiple perspective and dramatic completeness. The important point is that the parody of Hotspur exists as part of the 'visual meaning' of the play, and that though Shakespeare wrote it into his text, its dynamic projection in the theatre is absolutely requisite to its recognition and consequent effect on the playgoer. It works without strain theatrically as a kind of 'double exposure', instantaneously modifying and ultimately enriching the playgoer's experience of the play.

If the above conclusions are acceptable, it would seem reasonable to argue, then, that some scenes in Shakespeare deemed to be parallel by literary critics might have been produced on the stage to emphasize their identical elements. Elizabethan acting theory, the Elizabethan emblem-atic stage, the experienced playgoer's expectations, and the very presence of these parallels in the text would all urge this hypothesis. Such might be the case, for instance, with the two challenge scenes in *Richard II* (I, i and IV, i), or with the two 'trial' scenes in *King Lear* (III, vi and vii).[30] Furthermore, it would seem valid to expect certain parallels which are not ordinarily thought of as resemblances to have been developed through stage practices. Perhaps a case in point would be Pistol's mock-vaunt to Nym in which he plays upon the word 'solus' (*Henry V*, II, i, 49 ff.). This speech cunningly matches Henry's brilliant vaunt to the French ambassadors which plays on the word 'mock', spoken some hundred lines earlier. Or in *Julius Caesar* the handshake of Brutus with each of the conspirators ('Give me your hands all over, one by one') might have been matched by blocking and gesture to the handshake of Antony with each conspirator ('Let each man render me his bloody hand').[31] Needless to say, not every affinity between two scenes would find its highlighting on the stage. Still, considering the tradition from which Shakespearian drama emerges, with its techniques of juxtaposing situations in order to bring out prefigurations and typological relationships,[32] and considering the 'native' tradition in miracle, morality and interlude of 'counterfeiting', it is not extreme to suggest that careful attention was paid to the blocking, the use of gestures and properties, and the use of voice in putting parallel scenes on to the stage, assuming as one always must with Shakespeare that no character violates his own dramatic integrity, and that no scene is distorted in the process. The resulting effects of such stagecraft on the playgoer would certainly have been to intensify expectations, rivet attention, and enrich the sense of ironies and ambiguities mirrored in the dramatic representation. And what for us, reading the play, must remain only an analytical and critical exercise would have been for the audience in Shakespeare's theatre a visually and intellectually stimulating, thoroughly dramatic experience.

NOTES

1. B. L. Joseph, *Elizabethan Acting* (2nd ed., Oxford, 1964), pp. 96 ff. Joseph opposes the use of the terms 'formal' and 'natural'. See also Alan Downer, 'Prolegomenon to a Study of Elizabethan Acting', *Maske und Kothurn*, x (1964), 626: 'We must avoid such familiar critical terms as formal, natural, for they mean nothing; or at least inevitably suggest the wrong things.'

2. Joseph, p. 47.

3. Downer, p. 634.

4. B. L. Joseph, *Acting Shakespeare* (1960), pp. 121 ff. and 160 ff.

5. *Elizbethan Acting*, pp. 3 ff. See also the recent discussion by William A. Armstrong, 'Actors and Theatres', *Shakespeare Survey 17* (1964), esp. pp. 191–8.

6. Glynne Wickham, *Early English Stages* (1963), II, viii.

7. *Ibid.* p. 3.

8. *Ibid.* p. 36. Professor Nevill Coghill's *Shakespeare's Professional Skills* (Cambridge, 1964) develops a number of interesting points founded on the basic assertion that in Shakespeare 'the scenes are designed, both internally and in relation to the play as a whole, with an intellectual power for which I can hardly find a parallel in other drama'.

9. We can assume that Hal leaves after his couplet, though the stage direction comes from Dyce, not Shakespeare.

10. Of special value to our discussion are the treatments by Brooks and Heilman, *Understanding Drama* (New York, 1946); Harold Jenkins, *The Structural Problem in Shakespeare's 'Henry the Fourth'* (1956), pp. 8–9 and 17; and A. R. Humphreys's Introduction to his New Arden *First Part of King Henry IV* (1960), esp. pp. xlv–lvii, where the riches of much scholarly and critical effort are brought together. Coghill, pp. 64–9, discusses the way in which many of the parallels in *Henry IV* work to generate meaning.

11. See C. B. Hogan, *Shakespeare in the Theatre* (Oxford, 1952 and 1957), I, 144 and II, 238, for lines cut during the eighteenth century in London productions. Generally, the mock interview was shortened by about fifty lines, while Henry's speeches to Hal were cut by about forty.

12. See, for instance, the review of *1 Henry IV* produced at Stratford, Connecticut, in *SQ*, XIII (Autumn, 1962), 537 ff. Also, note Arthur Colby Sprague's comments about this trend in *Shakespeare's Histories* (1964), pp. 63–4.

13. See M. C. Bradbrook's references to Tarlton, *The Rise of the Common Player* (1962), pp. 79 and 170–1; Henrie Chettle, *Kind-Hartes Dreame* (1592), ed. G. B. Harrison (1923), pp. 39 ff. For Shakespeare's attitude toward uncontrolled extemporaneous mimicry, see Armstrong, *op. cit.* pp. 194–5.

14. Robert Dodsley, *A Select Collection of Old English Plays*, ed. W. C. Hazlitt (1847–76), II, 215.

15. *Ibid.* pp. 114–15 and 117.

16. *Poems*, ed. A. Davenport (Liverpool, 1949), p. 15.

17. *The Three Parnassus Plays*, ed. J. B. Leishman (1949), pp. 129–30. This episode literally dramatizes Sidney's remarks about 'mingling Kings and Clownes', where clowns are 'thrust in...by head and shoulders, to play a part in maiesticall matters, with neither decencies nor discretion'. See *An Apology for Poetry*, in *Elizabethan Critical Essays*, ed. G. Smith (Oxford, 1904), I, esp. p. 199.

18. William Empson's discussion of 'double plotting' in *Some Versions of Pastoral* (1935), pp. 30 ff. and 103–9, has much to say about this sort of 'dramatic completeness'.

19. See G. R. Owst, *Literature and Pulpit in Medieval England* (Oxford, 1961), pp. 366 ff. In the York Cycle *Sacrificium Cayme and Abell* Cain actually strikes God's angel 'evyn on thy crowne', in a prefiguration of the Crucifixion.

20. S. L. Bethell, *Shakespeare and the Popular Dramatic Tradition* (1944), p. 28.

21. There seems to me to be doubt about the cradles since the Christ Child would appear to be on Mary's knee in the final scene of the *Secunda*:

Farewelle, lady, so fare to beholde,
With thy chylde on thi kne.

However, see J. Speirs, *Scrutiny*, XVIII (Autumn, 1951), 110; F. M. Salter, *Medieval Drama in Chester* (Toronto, 1955), p. 103; and A. P. Rossiter, *English Drama from Early Times to the Elizabethans* (1950), p. 72, in reference to the suggestion that the same cradle might have been used.

22. See Eleanor Prosser's discussion of the mixture of the comic and the serious in this play, *Drama and Religion in the English Mystery Plays* (Stanford, 1961), pp. 105 ff.

23. *Angel with Horns* (1961), p. 279. Rossiter's term designating the relationship between comic and serious elements in Shakespeare, 'interinanimation' (from John Donne's 'Extasie'), is a very useful one for emphasis of the stage depiction of these parallels.

24. *Endeavors of Art* (Madison, 1954), pp. 248–9. A. R. Humphreys, in his Arden edition of *1 Henry IV*, cites other examples of drawers being singled out for their 'meagre vocabulary'. See p. 61, note for l. 96.

25. Joseph, *Elizabethan Acting*, p. 8.

26. I believe Mrs Jameson was the first to make the comparison in *Characteristics of Women* (1832), quoted in the Variorum Edition of *1 Henry IV*, p. 475.

27. Hogan, I, 144; II, 238.

28. See Humphreys's discussion, Introduction, pp. xlvii–xlviii and lv–lvii.

29. Reviews of the Stratford-upon-Avon production of *1 Henry IV* in 1951 were unanimous in finding the most effective scene to be that of the Welsh music (III, i, 186 to end), and it was pointed out that this scene seemed a kind of still centre for the play, emphasizing a 'visual and temporal stillness' between the ceaseless hurry of preparations and the outbreak of fighting soon to follow. The Francis parody of Hotspur, had it been clarified in this production, might well have lent support to that interpretation. See J. R. Brown, 'Theatre Research', *SQ*, XIII (Autumn, 1962), 459–60.

30. In the Stratford, Connecticut, production of *King Lear* in 1963, Morris Carnovsky repeated a bold gesture of imperial authority, first struck on his entrance in Act I, upon which all the courtiers fell to their knees; and then struck, vaguely, at the query of Gloucester, 'Is't not the King?' (IV, vi, 108–9), whereupon the blind Gloucester and poor Edgar fell to their knees. The highly dramatic effects of this mimicked action were thought to be among the most effective of the entire production, according to Carnovsky himself. See review in *SQ*, XIV (Autumn, 1963), 438.

31. I am grateful to Miss Marion Jones of the University of Birmingham for calling this to my attention.

32. It is hardly necessary to point out that the miracle cycles and other liturgical plays, utilizing the technique of the prefiguration, so standard in medieval and Renaissance modes of thought, were still very vital in the early part of Shakespeare's lifetime.

SHAKESPEARE'S UNNECESSARY CHARACTERS

BY

ARTHUR COLBY SPRAGUE

'Shakespeare', Raleigh once wrote, 'sought first for a story.'[1] Most of the persons in his plays have things assigned them to do, things that belong to the plot. Others are commentators on what is done, or purveyors of information, the creatures and agents of a complex expository technique. No rigid classification is possible. What, for instance, are we to make of Benvolio in *Romeo and Juliet*? We remember Benvolio, a little vaguely, it may be, as the companion of Romeo and Mercutio, with one or both of whom he converses. He listens while Mercutio holds forth on dreams or characterizes Tybalt as a duellist, and through the kind of attention he gives can enhance the effectiveness of these speeches. He fights, seemingly with reluctance, in the turmoil at the beginning of the play, and going to Capulet's 'ancient feast', which he persuades Romeo to attend, presumably dances there. He tells of Romeo's solitariness and of Mercutio's death, and twice he explains to the Duke what we in the audience have seen happening. I have known an actor cast as Benvolio, through the impress of his own personality, make Mercutio's description of his quarrelsomeness take on new interest—as if Mercutio were not merely amusing himself by inventing a character for him. But why his mind was 'troubled', so that like Romeo he sought to escape company, walking very early by 'a grove of sycamore' to the west of the city, stirs little curiosity. What chiefly matters in the part is the variety of uses which it serves.

Some of the minor characters have, however, a quite limited and definable function. Balthazar in *Much Ado about Nothing* is introduced as the singer of a song, 'Sigh no more, ladies'. The words of the song, designed to weaken Benedick's resistance to the softer emotions, have dramatic significance. An assumed diffidence alone distinguishes the singer, and once his music is finished he disappears from the play. Amiens in *As You Like It* is a specialist of the same sort. The low comic characters in *Othello* (the easily forgotten Clown) and *Timon of Athens* (the regularly omitted Fool) are equally restricted in what they do.[2] So are certain of the numerous attendants and minor confidants who lend state to their superiors and supply them at moments with someone to talk to. Ursula in *Much Ado about Nothing* owes her being, we may suppose, to the desirability of enlarging the little group of women who discuss Benedick's hopeless infatuation, while Beatrice as they well know is listening (Ursula is, indeed, so strictly kept in her place that she is not even provided with a husband at the end of the comedy). In *The Tempest* the presence of Adrian and the almost mute Francisco reminds us that Alonso is a king, and without them the palace revolution attempted by Antonio might seem a little ridiculous.[3]

The lavishness with which small parts were added in *Macbeth* led, in course of time, to retrenchment. In a note on the messengers who tell Macbeth that he is Thane of Cawdor, Francis Gentleman wrote in 1773: 'The characters of *Rosse* and *Angus* have been judiciously blended at

Covent-Garden Theatre, into those of *Macduff* and *Lenox*, to make them more worthy the attention of good performers and the audience.'[4] The striking introduction of Macduff at this moment—Davenant's idea, originally, and long followed on the English stage—is not mentioned as such, though it may have commended itself to those who made the change. Rather, Gentleman is pointing out its practical advantages. As for Angus, his role is a curious one. He is present, though he does not speak, in two later scenes in the first act, then rejoins the cast only in Act v, when it is swollen with newcomers like Seyton, a second Doctor, the Siwards, Caithness and Menteith.

Macbeth, in other words, suggests an easy assurance on the playwright's part that the company for whom he wrote was able to cope with a great many minor roles, as many conceivably as he cared to insert. Nothing could have been easier, had he chosen, than to cut out a number of them, beginning perhaps with Angus and the nameless Lord with whom Lenox talks at the end of Act III. Far from being restricted in the size of his casts, Shakespeare wrote, on the one hand, *Twelfth Night* and *Othello*, which today any repertory company or little theatre of respectable strength can put on without strain, and, on the other hand, *Henry V* and *2 Henry IV*, which would be unthinkable for them to attempt without large reinforcements.[5]

That Shakespeare counted upon the frequent doubling of parts by his actors seems beyond question. Such doubling was facilitated, however, in many instances by the nature of the stories which he chose to dramatize. In *Henry V* the *dramatis personae* are exceptionally numerous. But in a tale of Agincourt the Bishops are needed, if they are needed at all, only at the beginning; the Ambassadors who insult the English King with the gift of tennis balls exist only for a particular occasion; and Cambridge, Scroop, and Grey depart from the play early and definitely. The availability of a valuable reserve of actors was thus established, almost we may assume without effort.

As for boy-actresses, it is commonly assumed that they were in short supply, as indeed they may have been. Shakespeare rarely used more than three or four. In his sources, however, whether chronicles, romances, or novellas, the women of any dramatic interest are few. Jane Shore might conceivably have appeared in *Richard III*, and does not. But her omission is exceptional, and Shakespeare not infrequently added women to those he found. Luciana in *The Comedy of Errors*, Audrey in *As You Like It*, and Mariana in *Measure for Measure* are among these; as are also, more impressively, Paulina in *The Winter's Tale* and the Countess of Rossillion in *All's Well that Ends Well*. For his immediate purposes he may not have felt greatly restricted even in this matter.

The freedom with which he introduced minor characters has not gone uncriticized. It was offensive to ideas of neatness and economy, whether those of neo-classicism or of the well-made play. Charles Gildon writes of *Richard II* in 1710 that 'the want of a regular Design brings in abundance of unnecessary Characters, of no manner of Use or Beauty, as the Groom in the fifth Act of this Play'.[6] Today his objection would not, I think, be widely shared. The arrested triumph of Ventidius in *Antony and Cleopatra* is more debatable. 'A brief scene, totally useless to the plot and purely satiric in its purpose', Bradley calls it; adding that at this point 'a painful sense of slowness oppresses us'.[7] To Granville-Barker, on the contrary, the episode was a 'notable and typical' instance of stagecraft, the full effect of which becomes perceptible only as we place ourselves in imagination before the unencumbered platform of the Globe.[8] There indeed, if no least pause intervened, the contrast with, and criticism of the revelling on Pompey's galley may have been explicit. In modern productions when the Parthian episode is kept it is with some risk of unintelligibility.[9]

Cinna the Poet, though he outlasted the Restoration era, had left the stage by 1770 when Francis Gentleman referred to his encounter with the mob as 'a most unessential scene, omitted in representation'.[10] The character could still be described as wanting in 1904, when a reason for his creation was discovered in the theatrical conditions of Shakespeare's time. The scene before needed the entire stage and that following was an interior for which the 'back-stage' must be re-set ('all interior scenes' were played there).[11] Eight years later Ben Greet in his acting edition of *Julius Caesar* ('The Ben Greet Shakespeare for Young Readers and Amateur Players') added a number of curious directions. To him the scene was quite simply an instance of comic relief, and in performance '*it must be made very funny*': through specified business and the make-up and behaviour of the protagonist. Horror is not so much as mentioned. To emphasize it deliberately, as we do today, would have been unthinkable.

A last flaring up of hostility came in 1919. William Archer in reviewing the productions of Bridges-Adams at Stratford-upon-Avon, that summer, found himself out of sympathy with the inclusion of 'a good deal of inert matter' in *The Winter's Tale* and with a performance of the entire text of *Julius Caesar*. The young director had even consented 'to mar the effect of the forum scene by retaining the irrelevant anecdote of the death of Cinna the poet'. If this sort of thing was to continue the actor would find himself playing to empty benches and 'be tutored in insincerity' by pretending to understand what he did not. Archer's criticism, which came out in *The Nation*, 9 August, was answered a week later by John Drinkwater, and Archer came back on the twenty-third. He had, he now protested, enjoyed hearing every word of *A Midsummer Night's Dream*, but not 'the retention of a good deal of grossness and puerility' in *Romeo and Juliet*. And he remained convinced that the Cinna episode 'let down' Shakespeare's effect.[12]

But if we dismiss almost casually the objections to this character, and to a scene which for us carries an almost oppressive weight of meaning, we may still remain puzzled by other characters for whose existence there seems no obvious reason. Some of the very inconspicuous persons in the plays are of this sort; some, that is, whose presence in the cast would be inconceivable had Shakespeare been forced to economize. Lovel in *Richard III* and Gloucester in *Henry V* are two such. Although each appears in several scenes, these two men have little to say (Lovel has a total of three lines; Gloucester, almost the same) and what they do say might have come equally well from someone else. Each served, even so, a commemorative purpose. Gloucester was that good Duke Humphrey, idealized in *2 Henry VI* as a loyal and disinterested public servant, whose assassination initiated a whole sequence of tragic happenings. Lovel would not have been so widely known. But Collingbourne's destructive couplet,

> The Cat, the Rat, and Louell our Dogge,
> Rule all England vnder an Hogge,

once heard is not easily forgotten.[13]

To Lovel and Gloucester I would join Cicero in *Julius Caesar*, though at first thought he may seem to be a character of far greater prominence. The terms in which he is mentioned are arresting. One listens, also, a little more closely—as an Elizabethan audience must have listened—

when Cicero is named. It is he who spoke Greek, ambiguously, when Caesar refused the crown; he who is not asked to take part in the conspiracy—

> For he will never follow anything
> That other men begin;

he whose death, as reported with that of many other Senators, wrings from Cassius the quietly poignant 'Cicero one?'. Yet he appears in only two scenes and speaks—less than ten lines in all—only with Casca in that of the prodigies. 'So important a man as Cicero', Thomas Davies wrote in 1783, 'should not have been introduced in a scene of so little significance... The players have very judiciously left it out in the representation.'[14] They continued to do so for many years.

There remain six characters to consider. Of these, four—the Third Murderer in *Macbeth*, the Second Poet in *Julius Caesar*, the Archbishop of York in *1 Henry IV* and Barnardine in *Measure for Measure*—are confined at least as speakers to a single scene each.[15] The other two appear much more frequently and one of them is almost but not quite a major figure.

The Third Murderer, unnamed like the First and Second, joins them as they are waiting to set upon Banquo. He is acquainted with the details of their plan; knows that their victim will approach the palace on foot; and recognizes him when he enters. He seems to question the wisdom of extinguishing the torch, an action which should have aided the assassins in their attack upon the formidable Banquo but which made possible the escape of his son. There is no reason to identify the Murderer with any other character in the play, though this has often been attempted.[16] He is certainly, as the following scene demonstrates, not Macbeth. He may be Seyton but is not so designated in speech heading or stage direction. His mission is an indication not only of Macbeth's suspicion of his own agents but also of his characteristic desire to 'make assurance double sure'.

The dramatic function of the Third Murderer can be inferred with some confidence. That of the Poet who interrupts Brutus and Cassius in *Julius Caesar* is less clear. In Plutarch his intrusion has no bearing on the course of the quarrel, which has paused, with both leaders in tears, before he enters, and is resumed, after fresh provocation, at a later time. In Shakespeare, harshness and violence have been succeeded by pathos. Then, as the Poet clumsily insists upon what is obvious, it is Cassius who is amused and tolerant, his friend who becomes impatient—

> What should the wars do with these jigging fools?

And just here, when we like Brutus least and feel that we know him best, he startles and awes us with the three words 'Portia is dead'. On the stage when the Poet is omitted, as he frequently is, the scene moves forward smoothly enough still, as we wait to see what will be made, if anything, of Brutus's hearing in turn what he has just told. The cut might, then, seem justified. It spoils, nonetheless, what appears to be a deliberately calculated effect.[17]

In *1 Henry IV* the Archbishop of York is several times mentioned before his single appearance, conferring anxiously with an unidentified Sir Michael, in Act IV, scene iv. This scene has rarely been performed except when, as at Stratford-on-Avon in 1951 and 1964, the play was given as one in a sequence of histories. A towering figure in Holinshed, the Archbishop is only a little less striking among Shakespeare's rebel lords in *Part Two*. His introduction here, before the decision reached at Shrewsbury, is a chief reason—one of the two best reasons—for thinking that the dramatist was already looking beyond the limits of a single play. It is only within these limits that the character may seem out of place, nor is he wholly without use even here. The battle lies ahead, its outcome already foreshadowed by the news that neither Northumberland nor Glendower will be with Hotspur when they are most needed. What the Archbishop says provides one more directive: repeating and clarifying what we have learned, confirming the impression of doom for those who oppose the King. That the Archbishop himself will not be with them is made clear, as well, and above all the imminence of battle:

> Tomorrow, good Sir Michael, is a day
> Wherein the fortune of ten thousand men
> Must bide the touch...[18]

To a Shakespearian scholar, mention of Barnardine carries with it memories of Hazlitt—Hazlitt at his characteristic best in writing of this defiant figure—of Raleigh, probably, as well ('He is a fine example of the aristocratic temper...He treats the executioner like his valet', etc.).[19] Even today Barnardine for a sensitive reader may become something like a personal symbol. Yet his inclusion in the play is commonly accepted as an artistic error on the dramatist's part, one corrected almost painfully. Even a respectful audience may show amusement at the Provost's convenient afterthought:

> There died this morning of a cruel fever
> One Ragozine, a most notorious pirate,
> A man of Claudio's years...[3]   (IV, iii, 75)

Shakespeare's original intention, it is supposed, was to have Angelo's cruel purpose satisfied by the sight of Barnardine's head, just as Shakespeare's original intention, as is equally possible, was to have Antigonus (in *The Winter's Tale*) perish in the storm which engulfs his ship, instead of being devoured by an unnecessary bear. The change of plan in the case of *Measure for Measure* came about through the character's somehow asserting himself and charming his author, as he fascinates us. But although this explanation may very well be a sound one it leaves out of account things that demand attention. For Barnardine's insensibility to the terrors of punishment in the life hereafter is not alone contrasted with Claudio's too vivid imagining of them. It is related to the larger theme of dying and death taken up by voice after voice in the central scenes of this sombre play. The Duke as Friar is heard first, speaking, it might be out of the fifteenth century, of the miseries of mortal existence. The simple preference of death to dishonour is expected of Claudio by Isabel, who would without pause give up her own life for his if this were of use. Claudio's outburst of terror follows. And it is Claudio who says, enviously, of the murderer Barnardine that he is:

> As fast lock'd up in sleep as guiltless labour
> When it lies starkly in the traveller's bones.   (IV, ii, 69)

Is it quite conceivable that the voice of this defiant man, once heard, was to be silenced by death; by death, what is more, at the hands of Abhorson and his cheerful new assistant? That the state of his spiritual health was desperate, that he was not, to borrow words from another play, 'fit and season'd for his passage', is recognized immediately by the Duke, who grants him at the last his measure of mercy.

Yesterday's critics of Shakespeare had not yet tired of examining for traces of individuality even the very least of his characters. Cumberland Clark tried hard to make something of Peto, only to be thwarted by want of material.[20] Some, too, of Peto's better moments, as those with Prince Hal at the close of the Tavern Scene in *1 Henry IV*, are likely to belong not to him but Poins.[21] What we are left with is an accepted if minor member of Falstaff's train. As such he reappears in the Tavern Scene in *Part Two* at a point where we are being reminded of the past: of Francis and his 'anon, anon, sir'; of Falstaff's inspired claim that at Gadshill he knew the Prince all along. Peto is associated with this last episode, as with the robbery itself. Poins, beforehand, names him with Falstaff, Bardolph, and Gadshill, as those from whom the booty was to be snatched by Hal and himself. They were two against four—four men who might have been too hard for them but fled wildly, possessed with fear. Three, for dramatic purposes, would not have been enough. Peto, I suggest, came into being to complete their strength: 'Then did we two set on you four and, with a word, outfac'd you of your prize, and have it...'

Herbert Farjeon in a moment of fine candour asks who and what Fabian is, and why he was introduced into *Twelfth Night:* 'Here is a Shakespearean mystery that has been left unexplored. Is there any character with so many words to say who remains so completely characterless?' And he adds, without too great risk of contradiction: 'Nearly all the lines that Fabian speaks could be spoken equally well by some other character on the stage.'[22] As a consequence of this uncertainty Fabian has become what might be called a 'director's character': one, that is, upon whom a variety of shapes can be imposed at will. I have seen him as a cook, a coachman, a dignified old family retainer, and a rival jester threatening to displace Feste. And I have seen his entire part in the Letter Scene appropriated by Maria.

Recognition of what Fabian's position in a noble household would have been throws light on some of the dubious things about him. As 'a gentleman in the service of Olivia' he might have discussed with propriety the inditing of a challenge and other preliminaries to a duel.[23] There is a dash of chivalry in the account he gives of the conspiracy against Malvolio, an account which spares the lady in the case by placing responsibility on himself and Sir Toby. His respectful bearing towards both knights, his complaint that Malvolio had brought him 'out o' favour with my lady', and Olivia's impatient 'sirrah' as she asks him to read the Steward's letter are all in keeping. His age is indeterminate. Granville-Barker, who notices that he is 'the cautious one', would have him 'not a young man',[24] though Sir Toby at one point calls him 'lad' (III, ii, 58).

The indefiniteness of the role all but ceases when we reach the theatre and Fabian is embodied by a particular actor. In the theatre, his enjoyment of the comic proceedings not only accompanies but intensifies our own. An old friend, Mr Allan Wilkie, who played the part under Ben Greet, writes me of the assistance Fabian can be to the other characters—'though always overshadowed by them. The one opportunity he gets of an individual nature—and that a very small one—is when he comes forward and apologetically explains the situation to Lady Olivia'. It is Fabian, too, with his quiet 'more matter for a May morning', who leads us forward from the pleasure of Malvolio's discomfiture to the headier joys of the duel. There his presence, like that of Peto during the robbery, is imperative. For while Toby on one side of the stage is holding Sir Andrew, someone—who can scarcely be Feste—must be holding Viola. Neither must escape.

SHAKESPEARE'S UNNECESSARY CHARACTERS

Not many years ago when the traditions of precise craftsmanship carried forward from Pinero and the 1890s were still recognized, an essay on Shakespeare's unnecessary characters might have been, not sharply critical, for Shakespeare was an exception to all rules, but a little condescending. In a play, we were convinced, not only should every stroke tell: a skilled dramatist must accomplish more than one thing at a time. Somerset Maugham's fine comedy *The Circle* would have been finer still without that unnecessary Mrs Shenstone near the beginning. From this point of view Shakespeare's prodigality in the introduction of minor characters could only seem primitive. Yet these parts served, as we have seen, a variety of purposes; now technical, as with Peto; now, as with Cinna the Poet, closely related to the gravest concerns of the play. Sometimes, once more, the purposes are easy to detect. But sometimes we can only guess at them—and with no great confidence that we have guessed right.

NOTES

1. *Shakespeare*, 'English Men of Letters' (New York and London, 1907), p. 133.

2. The last-named I have still to see after five productions of *Timon*. His sallies fill a time interval in II, ii, much as do those of the Clown in *Othello*, III, iv.

3. Francisco's part is actually shorter than that of the notoriously taciturn James Gurney in *King John*.

4. Bell's Edition, I, 6.

5. In his learned and engaging lectures, *Shakespeare and his Theatre*, Professor G. E. Bentley offers a different opinion. 'The cast of any play of Shakespeare's', he writes, 'is determined in the first instance not by the fertility of the imagination of the playwright, but by the available personnel of the company' with which he was associated. He had in each case to provide roles for all, or most of them. 'He could never create any role for which there was not already a suitable actor' (Lincoln, Nebraska, 1964, p. 39). But is there any reason to suppose that Shakespeare would have preferred smaller casts than those he used (even such a neat, unprofessional tragedy as Daniel's *Cleopatra* has ten characters besides its chorus), or that some of his actors might not have been glad of an occasional rest between plays?

6. 'Remarks on the Plays of Shakespear', in Rowe's edition, VII (1710), p. 343.

7. *Oxford Lectures on Poetry* (1920), p. 291.

8. *Prefaces to Shakespeare*, ed. M. St Clare Byrne (1963), II, 9, 10.

9. This was true, I should say, even of Mr Frank Hauser's production at the Oxford Playhouse in October 1965, when the pains taken to secure the right effect included stylization.

10. *The Dramatic Censor*, II, 12; see also Gentleman's note in Bell's edition of *Julius Caesar*, p. 53.

11. *Julius Caesar*, ed. Charlotte Porter and Helen A. Clarke (New York, 1904), pp. 149–50.

12. The controversy to which both Shaw and Granville-Barker were to contribute lasted on through September. I first learned of it through a reference by Dr John Ripley in his Shakespeare Institute dissertation (1963) on the stage history of *Julius Caesar*.

The restoration of Fortinbras by Forbes-Robertson, after a long absence from the boards, was not received with cordiality by some critics; but neither Richard Dickins (*Forty Years of Shakespeare on the English Stage*, 1907, p. 86) nor William Winter (*Shakespeare on the Stage*, p. 393) goes as far as to call the character unnecessary.

13. Holinshed gives it, and Fabyan; and Lovel is a character in *The True Tragedy of Richard III*.

14. *Dramatic Miscellanies* (1783), II, 213. Some of the noble names of minor characters were assigned them, I cannot help believing, almost at random—as Essex in *King John*, I, i, 43–44–46 (but cf. notes in the Variorum and New Shakespeare editions).

15. Helenus and Deiphobus in *Troilus and Cressida* might also be mentioned; and, not to go further, the two Friars in *Measure for Measure*, if they are really two.

16. One of the latest treatments of this unprofitable subject was by C. B. Purdom, 'Who Was the Third Murderer in "Macbeth"?', *The Shakespeare Stage*, no. 6–7 (September–December, 1954). For summaries of early attempts, see the Furness Variorum Edition (the matter was argued through many issues of *Notes and Queries* in 1869) and Kenneth Muir's note in the New Arden *Macbeth*, p. 90.

17. George Skillan has an excellent note on the passage in French's Acting Edition (1937), p. 77. Gentleman could make nothing of it: unless its purpose was 'that of turning a noble reflection into ill-timed unprofitable laughter'.

18. The scene is ably defended by H. Edward Cain in *Shakespeare Quarterly*, III (1952), 31, 32.

19. *Op. cit.* p. 149.

20. *Falstaff and his Friends* (Shrewsbury, 1935), p. 52.

21. See especially the Variorum Edition, pp. 172, 241. That Falstaff at IV, i, 10, refers to Peto as his lieutenant is rather confusing than otherwise.

22. *The Shakespearean Scene, Dramatic Criticisms* (1949), p. 76.

23. Cf. John W. Draper, *The Twelfth Night of Shakespeare's Audience* (Stanford, California, 1950), pp. 160–4. I do not accept Professor Draper's contention that Sir Toby's 'thou' and 'thee' to Fabian, in their first scene together, implies no difference in rank. This is to ignore Fabian's consistent 'you' to the two knights and his 'thou' to Feste at v, 1, 1.

24. *Twelfth Night*, Acting Edition (1912), p. viii. It is a temptation to consider still further characters. The Lord who succeeds Osric as the King's emissary just before the fencing in *Hamlet* is one. He appears, interestingly, in the Second Quarto but not in the Folio.

WALTER WHITER'S NOTES ON SHAKESPEARE

BY

MARY BELL

The 1794 edition of Walter Whiter's *Specimen of a Commentary on Shakspeare* is notable for its anticipation of much that is regarded as modern in the criticism of Shakespeare's language and imagery. Because of his interest in Locke's theory of the association of ideas, Whiter is able to discover the underlying chain of thought in many of Shakespeare's characteristic expressions; and because of his etymological interests, he is often able to throw light on the problem of the individual word in Shakespeare's text. A collection of notebooks and loose papers (Cambridge University Library, Catalogue Number Oo, vi, 103–106)[1] contains further comments on textual and interpretative problems in at least twenty-four of Shakespeare's plays, excluding some of the histories and all of the Roman tragedies.[2] These notes follow the general pattern of the *Notes on 'As You Like It'* in the first section of the *Specimen*. Some are mere jottings and quotations; others are presented as complete essays on a variety of topics. What follows is a selection of some of this additional material not used in the *Specimen*.

In the unpublished notes, as in the *Specimen*, there is much to demonstrate Whiter's allegiance to Malone. Thus he is at all times concerned rather to restore the readings of the Folio ('the old Copy') than to condone the emendations of the 'ingenious commentators'; and, wherever possible, he seeks to justify these restorations by analogy with the phraseology of Shakespeare's contemporaries or by allusion to 'customs long since disused and forgotten'.[3] One instance which illustrates this habit of using contemporary sources to support his reading or to suggest the interpretation of an obscure phrase or image is found in Notebook 2, in which he relates Mercutio's jest, 'for the bawdy hand of the dial is now upon the prick of noon' (*Romeo and Juliet*, II, iv, 118), to Prince Hal's reply to Falstaff in *1 Henry IV*, I, ii, 7–13:

What a devil hast thou to do with the time of the day? Unless hours were cups of sack and minutes capons and clocks the tongues of bawds and dials the signs of leaping houses and the blessed sun himself a fair hot wench in flame-coloured taffeta, I see no reason why thou shouldst be so superfluous to demand the time of the day.

Whiter's comment observes:

The imagery is remote: yet the following passages will lead us into the same train of ideas.

(Oo, vi, 104: Notebook 2)

Although such supporting quotations are not always drawn from other plays of Shakespeare, a similar note on *The Two Gentlemen of Verona* (Oo, vi, 104: Notebook 1) traces a connexion between the shepherd/sheep imagery of Proteus' exchanges with Speed in I, i, 73–106—

Indeed a sheep doth very often stray,
An if the shepherd be a while away—

83

and Edgar's mad song in *King Lear*, III, vi, 42–5.[4] More usual, however, are the following examples taken from *The Merry Wives of Windsor* in which other dramatists are quoted:

'Else you had look'd through the grate, like a *geminy of baboons*' [II, ii, 8]. There is something meant here which the Commentators are not aware of: tho' I do not understand precisely what it is. When *Subtle & Face* in The Alchemist have made up their quarrel *Dol* says: 'Why, so, my good *Baboons*!' (Act I. S.i. page 212. Ed. 1692).

'I will stare him out of his wits; I will awe him with my *cudgel*: it shall hang like a meteor o'er the cuckold's horns' [II, ii, 292].

'*Meriel*. Yes; and then Springlove, to make him madder, told him that he would be his proxy, and marry her for him, and lie with her the first night, with a naked *cudgel* betwixt them.'

(The Merry Beggars. Old Plays 10. p. 409)
(Oo, vi, 104: Notebook 1)

Sometimes the authority cited is more learned, and the following note on *1 Henry IV*, I, iii, 106 (opening with a misquotation)[5] collects a number of allusions:

'the crisp head of the Severn'

See The Underwoods 550. See Shak. 8. 98 & The Tempest pag. 78.

'The rivers run as smoothed by his hand:
Only their *heads* are *crisped* by his stroke.'

(Jonson's Vision of Delight. 601)

See Old Plays 2. 281. See Hurd on Imitation p. 184. Jonson p. 374. Warton 70 n. & 98–100.

'crack'd crowns,
And pass them CURRENT too.'

(A.2. S.3. p. 163)
(Oo, vi, 104: Notebook 2)

Such a note takes a deal of deciphering, and I have not been able to trace the Warton references. The Shakespeare references, however, relate to *Timon of Athens*, IV, iii, 183 ('below crisp heaven'—with a note giving 'curled, bent, hollow') and *The Tempest*, IV, i, 130 ('Leave your crisp channels'); 'The Underwoods' to Jonson's *Celebration of Charis in ten Lyrick Peeces*, poem IX, *Her man described by her owne Dictamen* ('with crisped hair Cast in a thousand snares'); and the 'Old Plays' to Kyd's *Cornelia* (Act IV: 'Turn not thy crispy tides like silver curl'). The Jonson reference towards the end of the note relates to *The Irish Masque at Court*, and the final quotation is taken from *1 Henry IV*, II, iii, 97 (Malone, vol. v).

Another indication of Malone's influence on Whiter lies in the many passages in which he attempts to relate his criticism to his knowledge of the Elizabethan theatre. In a notebook comment on the 'noddy' passage in *Two Gentlemen of Verona*, I, i, 119 ff. he is clearly examining his material with an eye to the business of staging. The force of the argument depends on the physical symbol of assent by nodding, which renders unnecessary the explanatory clause 'Did she nod?' added by Theobald; and Whiter's note continues:

This addition has destroyed the little conceit, which was intended. To the question of Protheus [*sic*] of what said she; Speed replies by a nod, with a sound which generally accompanies the action like *Aye* or *I*. Protheus then cries out *Nod, I* repeating the same sound which Speed had made use of, as much as to say what do you mean by such an action & such a sound: Speed again nods repeating the accustomed sound, meaning to assert by way of answer to Protheus that his Mistress nodded. Protheus then says '*Why that's Noddy*'. In the first Folio there is no Stage direction, & Nod, I? is written *Nod-I*. The next speech of Speed explains the process of the transaction & shews my explication to be right. '*You mistook, sir; I say, she did nod, and you ask me if she did nod; and I say, I.*'

(Oo, vi, 104: Notebook 1)

Other passages in the notebooks indicate that Whiter, unlike Johnson, does not feel obliged to censure Shakespeare for using language and imagery drawn from his own profession:[6] and in Notebook 5*b* he uses the 'acting' passage in *Winter's Tale*, v, ii, 86—

The dignity of this act was worth the audience of kings and princes; for by such was it acted—

as an introduction to a series of examples of Shakespeare's distinctive habit of personification: 'Death' in the song in *Twelfth Night*, ii, iv (with Johnson's note: 'Though *death* is a *part* in which every one acts his share, yet of all these actors no one is so true as I'); 'engrossing Death' in *2 Henry IV*, iv, v, 80;[7] the 'cloak of Night' in *Richard II*, iii, ii, 45; and the pun on squires and knights in *1 Henry IV*, i, ii, 28:

let not us that are squires of the night's body be called thieves of the day's beauty.

In Notebook 5 he adds similar personifications of 'Night stealing away' from *Cymbeline*, iii, v, 69 and *All's Well*, iii, ii, 131; and refers also to Milton's *Comus*, l. 285[8] in which the word 'fore-stall' is used as in *Cymbeline*. Elsewhere in his loose papers, Whiter has lengthy discussions of other theatrical topics, as Pageants and 'the Imagery of the rising Sun and the Morning connected with the Pageant'.

A similar visual and theatrical interest underlies the many passages in which Whiter refers to the tapestry hangings in the Elizabethan great halls (and in the Elizabethan theatre)[9] and to the paintings and statuary with which Shakespeare must have been familiar.[10] Many examples are given in the *Specimen*, and a jumbled note in the 'Little Book' collects a number of other allusions,[11] prefaced by direct references to the 'Cain-colour'd beard' in *Merry Wives* (i, iv, 23), 'Imogen's Chamber' in *Cymbeline* (ii, ii), the 'Room in the Taming of S.' and 'The Portraits in Hamlet' (iii, iv). On the next page Whiter adds the following brief note:

Patience on a Monument smiling at grief. This might be perhaps taken from an ancient monument... See Henley's note that our Poet sometimes takes his images from the prints of books.　　(4. 122)[12]

Despite his observation of Shakespeare's personifications and his undoubted interest in things theatrical, neither in the notes nor in the *Specimen* does Whiter reveal any great interest in Shakespeare's methods of characterization. Only twice in the notebooks does he make any comment on Shakespeare's skill in this matter. The first refers to Shylock and observes:

It is remarkable that Shakspeare in drawing the character of the Jew has made him explain the metaphorical expressions he had made use of. So, 'But stop my house's ears, I mean, my casements'. (Is there anything characteristic in this?)

(Oo, vi, 104: Notebook 1)

Whiter then goes on to quote the similar construction of Shylock's remark in i, iii, 25—'water thieves and land thieves; I mean pirates'. The second note refers to Shallow (*2 Henry IV*) and is equally perceptive:

Those who are not accustomed to *jesting humour* or *metaphors* explain them.

(Oo, vi, 105: 'Little Book', p. 52ᵛ)

Although an interest in characterization is one of the main preoccupations of his 'romantic' contemporaries, Whiter remains outside this new movement of the late eighteenth and early nineteenth centuries.

In his attitude to the pun, too, Whiter is closer to the age of Johnson than to the age of Coleridge. Although he does not go out of his way to discuss this particular figure of speech, the play on words comprises one of the four categories of association described in the *Specimen* (p. 70):

Certain terms containing an equivocal meaning, or sounds suggesting such a meaning, will often serve to introduce other words and expressions of a similar nature;

and his illustrations of such associations are clearly examples of unconscious puns. (In the *Specimen* Whiter quotes several passages in which the word 'weed' is taken in its double significance of 'plant' or 'dress' and leads on to a string of related terms.) Among his loose papers, on a sheet headed *Sp. of a Com. on Sh.*, he has added another example:

Our Poet has again quibbled on this word—In All's Well etc. we have 'Virginity, like an old Courtier, wears her cap out of fashion: richly suited but unsuitable' p. 361 [i.e. Malone, vol. III: *All's Well*, I, i, 169]. In Comedy of Errors we have

> Adr.: What is he arrested. Tell me at whose suit.
> Dro. S.: I know not at whose sUIT he is arrested, well;
> But he's in a suit...   [IV, ii, 44–5] (Oo, vi, 106: Folder 6)

While these conscious and unconscious puns are interesting as a reflexion of the associative processes of the author, Whiter cannot wholly approve them, and there is a grudging note in his comment on Petruchio's threat to Grumio in *Taming of the Shrew*, I, ii, 16:

> Faith, sirrah, an you'll not knock, I'll *wring* it.
> (He wrings Grunnio [*sic*] by the ears)

The pun in this passage has not been observed by our Commentators: Poor as it is, we ought not to conceal it.

(Oo, vi, 104: Notebook 4)

By way of illustration, Whiter goes on to quote other instances of the use of the word 'ring' to imply 'what we should now call the Knocker', including a passage from Jonson's *Silent Woman* (II, i: 'You have taken the ring off the street door') and a refrain from one of Percy's *Old Ballads* (Vol. III, 2nd ed.: 'She knocked at the ring'). The note continues:

(Shakspeare's quibble we see, such as it is, is compleat. The *ringing* of the ear is alluded to by Shakespeare.)

Why Mr Malone should read 'I'll *wring* it' (with a w) I cannot see: the Editor of 1785 reads *ring*. So, does Mr Capell & even in the marginal direction he has 'rings him by the ears'.—See page 339. vol. 10.

> *Knock* is a phrase belonging to a peal of bells.

(Beaumont & Fletch. vol. 8. p. 152)

> 'She will not stick to *ring* my ear'

(Shakesp. 10. 339. See page 337)

See Toup's Emendations on Suidas vol. 1. p. 178.

> *Nym:* Pray thee, corporal, stay; the knocks are too hot...
> *Pist.:* ...*Knocks* go and come; God's *vassals* drop and die;
>
> And sword and *shield*,
> In bloody field,
> Both win immortal fame.

[Henry V, III, ii, 8]
(See Shak. vol. 8. 336)
(See Beaumont & F. Love's Pilgrimage. A. 2. S. 1.)

Observe humour is connected with *knocking*—with *liegers* in Cymbeline 8.336—with *Rebus* in Jonson's New Inn. 'I will maintain the *rebus* 'gainst all *Humours*' (p. 724) There is certainly some connection between *Heraldry* (*Rebus—shield—vasselage—knock.*)

(It is curious to trace the intermediate idea by which words have been originally connected with each other in the formation of phrases; & to mark the accident by which they afterwards convey a similar idea, tho' with a metaphor entirely different to that, by which they were associated in their original formation. The phrase *ringing at a* door in an ancient writer, by the accident of a *bell* being employed for that purpose would be now perfectly understood in its true meaning, tho the allusions connected with the original metaphor would have no affinity to those which related to the present.)

This entire note is interesting as an illustration of Whiter's usual method of quoting from contemporary sources and offering direct criticism of the readings of other editions.

The development of Whiter's theories leads him also to the realization of what has come to be known as 'iterative imagery'. The third of his categories of association in the *Specimen*[13] anticipates both Professor Spurgeon's apparent 'discovery' of Shakespeare's peculiar connexion of 'heels', 'spaniel', 'fawn', 'candy' and 'melt'[14] and the 'image clusters' exposed by E. A. Armstrong in his study of *Shakespeare's Imagination* (1946). In the *Specimen* Whiter comments on every use of the word 'candy' in the Shakespeare canon; and in Notebook 5*b* he adds a further reference to the passage in *Much Ado*, IV, i, 321—

But manhood is *melted into courtesies*, valour into compliment, and men are only turn'd into *tongues* and trim ones too!—

under the significant heading of 'Candy'—here represented by the more elaborate term 'Count Comfect'. Although Whiter does not go on, like Professor Spurgeon, to relate these 'iterative' images to the theme or atmosphere of the play (or plays) in which they occur, this idea is at least implicit in his comment on *Romeo and Juliet*, III, iii, 132:[15]

The idea of gun-powder has seized on the poet in this play. (Oo, vi, 104: Notebook 2)

Later critics have commented on the relevance to the tragi-romantic theme of the play of such images of sudden flashes of light against a dark background of night; but the suggestion is already there in Whiter's unpublished notes.[16]

For the rest, Whiter is concerned to analyse the mental processes of the creative writer in the light of Locke's theory; and in his notes and loose papers he explores other groups of associated ideas which seem to him to mark an unconscious train of thought belonging distinctively to Shakespeare.[17] One of the most interesting of these essays is concerned with the theme of Love and Death: and he quotes a variety of passages in which Death is presented in the form of a lover, embracing his chosen prey and thereby inflicting the 'stroke of death'. Many instances of this can be found in *Antony and Cleopatra*. Thus Antony boasts:

> The next time I do fight
> I'll make *death love me*;   (III, xiii, 192–3)

and again: I will be
> A *bridegroom* in my death, and run into't
> As to a lover's bed.   (IV, xiv, 99–101)

Cleopatra uses the same language in her reflexion on Antony's death:

> If thou and nature can so gently part,
> The *stroke* of death is as a lover's pinch,
> Which hurts, and is desired.   (V, ii, 297–9)

Whiter's commentary continues:

But what will the reader say, when he reads the following passage in the same play spoken of the same person? who is herself the speaker in the present.

  'Cleopatra' (says Enobarbus) ['] catching but the least noise of this, dies instantly; I have seen her die twenty times upon far poorer moment: I do think, there is *mettle in death, which commits some loving act upon her*, she hath such a celerity in dying['];   (I, ii, 144–9)

and, as he points out, the image is carried right to the end of the play in Charmian's final tribute to her mistress:
> Now boast thee, death! in thy possession lies
> A lass unparallel'd.   (V, ii, 318–19)

Similar quotations are produced from *Romeo and Juliet*. Romeo tells the Friar:

> Do thou but close our hands with holy words,
> Then love-devouring death do what he dare;   (II, vi, 6–7)

and Juliet uses the same image when she hears of Tybalt's death:

> I'll to my wedding bed,
> And *Death*, not Romeo, *take my maidenhead*.   (III, ii, 136–7)

Old Capulet tells Paris that: the night before thy wedding day
> Hath Death lain with thy wife...
> Death is my son-in-law, Death is my heir;   (IV, v, 35–40)

Juliet longs for the arrival of 'loving, black-brow'd night' (III, ii, 20); and in the last scene of all Romeo declares:
> Death, that hath suck'd the honey of thy breath,
> Hath had no power yet upon thy beauty:...
>   ...Shall I believe
> That unsubstantial death is amorous;
> And that the lean abhorred monster keeps
> Thee here in dark to be his paramour?   (V, iii, 92–3, 102–5)

Whiter finds other examples of this particular chain of ideas in *Henry V*, II, i, 65 ('and doting death is near'), *King John*, III, iv, 25–36 ('O amiable lovely death... I will kiss thy detestable bones...and I will think thou smil'st,/And buss thee as thy wife!') and *Measure for Measure*, III, i, 83–5,

> If I must die,
> I will encounter darkness as a bride,
> And hug it in my arms.

A similar idea is repeated in Whiter's last published book, *A Dissertation on the Disorder of Death* (1819), in which he collects a number of references to what he describes as 'the lovely appearance of beautiful females after death' and the 'lightening before Death' referred to in *Romeo and Juliet*, v, iii, 85–90:

> For here lies Juliet, and her beauty makes
> This vault a feasting presence full of light...
> How oft when men are at the point of death
> Have they been merry! which their keepers call
> A lightning before death.[18]

To illustrate his notion of the 'Sleep of Death and the Death of Sleep' (*Dissertation on Death*, pp. 102–3) Whiter draws on *Lucrece*, 400–6,[19] and *Macbeth*, II, ii, 7–8.[20]

Among his loose papers, still on the same general theme of death, Whiter has an essay on 'the colours of Death and the Cheeks', which leads him to a discussion of 'Masks, Patches, Colours, Flags and Ensigns'. Here he is playing on the double significance of 'colours', both as cheeks or complexion and as flag or ensign: and he illustrates these associations from the last scene of *Romeo and Juliet* and from Daniel's *Complaint of Rosamond* (1594):

> And nought-respecting *death* (the last of paines)
> Plac'd his *pale colours* (th'*ensign* of his might)
> Upon his new-got spoil...
> Decayed roses of discolour'd cheeks
> Do yet retain some notes of former grace,
> *And ugly death sits faire within her face.*

In a later note he connects a pale face with the 'lenten colours' of *Twelfth Night*, I, v, 5–13;[21] and he goes on to relate this idea to the theme of war, as in *Merry Wives*, III, iv, 82–6:

> I must advance the colours of my love

or, in a different sense, in *Julius Caesar*, I, ii, 22:

> His *coward* lips did from their *colour* fly.[22]

Another long note quotes from *Spectator* Essay No. 81 (2 June 1711) which describes the facial patches worn by women during their visits to the theatre, and which refers also to the 'Colours or Flags...displayed at the top of the [Elizabethan] Theatre' during the performance of a play. Whiter's note continues:

The *Black Patches* or *Masks* seem to have been cut into the forms of the *Sun-Moon & Stars*, & hence the *Brows* of Females are consider'd as the *Heaven* or *Sky*. The *Brows* thus converted into the *Heaven* or *Sky*, are then supposed to be darken'd & disturbed by *Clouds & Storms*. Sometimes figures of *Flags* or *Colours*, as they are called, appear to have been represented on the *Brows & Cheeks*, & hence we shall find, strange as the union may seem, that the Brows of Females have been associated with the *Theatre*.

It is a short step from this to the assumption that

when Juliet talks in a strange-wild speech, of cutting Romeo into little *Stars* in order to make 'the face of heaven' fine, & the *Night* lovely, the mind of the Poet is impressed with the exhibition of *Stars* on the masque'd or Black *Brow* of a Female.

To support this claim Whiter refers to 'black-brow'd night' (*Romeo and Juliet*, III, ii, 20–5), the 'beetle-brows' of Mercutio's mask (I, iv, 29–32) and the mention of black masks in *Romeo and Juliet*, I, i, 236–7, *Measure for Measure*, II, iv, 78–81, and *Love's Labour's Lost*, II, i, 124–5; IV, iii, 253–61; V, ii, 295–7. Further illustrations are cited from Dodsley's *Old Plays*—*The Hog Hath Lost his Pearl*, *The Roaring Girl* and *A Mad World my Masters*.

Another interesting collection of passages (Oo, vi, 104: Notebook 4) relates to 'Title and Intitled—terms belonging to Lovers',[23] and, still on the theme of Love, in his loose papers (Oo, vi, 106: Folder 5) Whiter has brought together a series of references in which Love is 'associated with a *Mansion, House, Building* etc. & with the *Ruin-Destruction* etc. of *Buildings* etc.'. The opening quotation is taken from *Romeo and Juliet*:

> O, I have bought the *mansion* of a *love*
> But not possess'd it;   (III, ii, 26–7)

and the remaining passages[24] collect a number of associations already noted by Malone, Steevens and other of Shakespeare's earlier editors. Still others of Whiter's loose papers deal with such topics as 'The term *Flecked* connected with the Morning and with a Drunkard', 'Ideas relating to Love and a Female connected with Ships and Sailing' and a full-length essay 'On the customs —habits etc. attached to Servants in the days of Shakespeare'.

Elsewhere in his unpublished papers Whiter's interest in language and etymology leads him into a detailed discussion of certain individual words. In Notebook 2 he comments at length on the word 'brach' in Thersites' scornful retort 'I will hold my peace when Achilles' brach bids me' (*Troilus and Cressida*, II, i, 125–6):

'The folio and quarto read' (says Dr Johnson) 'Achilles' *brooch*. *Brooch* is an appendant ornament. The meaning may be, equivalent to one of Achilles' *hangers-on*.' Dr Johnson is certainly right.—Brock is explained by Mr Steevens in the 12th. Night [*sic*] *Badger*. That surely cannot be the meaning. Mr Malone sometimes thinks that *brock* may possibly be the word in Troilus & Cressida; & that Achilles' *brock* means that overweaning conceited coxcomb, who attends upon Achilles. I am convinced that *brock* is but another mode of spelling *brooch*; and that as it signifies in one sense a *fashionable* or perhaps in our Poet's time a *fantastick* appendage to the dress, so in the other it might mean a *coxcomical hanger on* or even a finical attendant upon a person. Mr Malone quotes a passage from the Jests of George Peele.

'This self-conceited *brock* had George invited'—

The reader will pardon me for venturing upon a laughable conjecture. Whence is derived the expression of *badgering* for *troubling* or disturbing? *Brock* we know is the name likewise for a badger; & as *Brock* (derived from Brooch) might easily signify a *troublesome* or *impertinent attendant*, & as it likewise might be consider'd as synonimous with badger, when brock became obsolete *badger* would then be used in the same sense.—Our language abounds with quaint apellations [*sic*] of men from animals—*Bear —Dog—Cock—Boar—Buck*—perhaps *Blood* (vol. 2. 366: [i.e. *L.L.L.*, IV, ii, 4])—*Brach—Tyke—Trundle-tail, Rake, Puppy, Bitch*—(not to mention the abstract *Brute-beast*)—*whelp—Beagle—Rascal—Cur*—

Hound—cat—colt—Bull—Mongrel—cat. (Old Plays, v. 2. 44: [i.e. *Gammer Gurton's Needle*, III, iii]). *Badger* may be derived however from the *baiting him.* Cock & pie is an instance which confirms the first sense. Rake (vol. 7. 146: [i.e. *Coriolanus*, I, i, 24]). *Rascal* (vol. 7. 152: [i.e. *Coriolanus*, I, i, 163]).

It is interesting that, although modern dictionaries make no connexion between 'brock' and 'brooch', the first recorded use of 'badger' as a verb is given as 1794, the exact year of Whiter's original *Specimen*. One other note which shows a similar linguistic interest relates the description of Hotspur (*1 Henry IV*, III, ii, 139) as a 'CHILD of *honour* and *renown*' to 'This CHILD of *fancy* that Armado hight' in *Love's Labour's Lost*, I, i, 171 and to the enigmatic line, 'Child Rowland to the dark tower came' in *Lear*, III, iv, 177 (Oo, vi, 104: Notebook 2). As Whiter points out, both the former passages and a later description of Armado (*L.L.L.*, I, i, 179)[25] contain the word 'Knight'.[26]

This interest in language overflows at times into an interest in proverbial phrases: and one such instance occurs in Notebook 5*b*, with a cross reference to '*Specimen* 109':

The Fish lives in the Sea

Is there any phrase in the language about the fishes of the eyes. 'One of the prettiest touches of all, & that which angled for mine *eyes* (caught the water, though not the fish) was' etc.

(Winter's Tale, v, ii, 90)

If there is such a passage it will account for the imagery & will be no more extraordinary that [*sic*] the virgins of the eyes in Longinus—or the *babies* in the eyes in Shakespeare.

A later reference in Whiter's 'Little Book' (Oo, vi, 105) suggests that he is here thinking of the passage in *Timon of Athens*, I, ii, 115–16:

> Joy had the like conception in our eyes
> And at that instant like a babe sprung up;

and he goes on to refer to *Merchant of Venice*, III, ii, 46–7:

> my eye shall be the stream
> And watery death-bed for him

and *Romeo and Juliet*, III, v, 133–4:

> For still thy eyes, which I may call the sea,
> Do ebb and flow with tears,

as well as quoting from two plays by Beaumont and Fletcher (*The Woman's Prize*: 'To look gay babies in the eyes' and *The Woman Hater*: 'Mine eyes look'd babies in...') and from 'Sir John Harrington's Ms. Poems in his Ariosto in the Public Library': 'To his wife of love without lust' ('And lookst chast babies in my wanton eyes'). Brewer's Dictionary cites a similar phrase from Heywood's *Love's Mistress* ('Toyed with his locks, looked babies in his eyes') and suggests that 'Love is the little babe Cupid, and hence the conceit, originating from the miniature image of oneself in the pupil of another's eyes'.

Whiter has other notes relating to the eyes: and in the same notebook (5*b*) he relates *Much Ado*, IV, i, 123–5 (story—printed—eyes) to *Pericles*, I, i, 15 ('Her face the book of praises') and Malone's note on *Macbeth*, I, v, 39–48: 'The raven himself is hoarse...' etc. (Malone IV, p. 295). The passage from *Pericles* is specifically assigned to the *Specimen*, p. 116, and the whole note is included in the comment, 'This ought not to have been omitted in the Specimen.' A few pages earlier in *Macbeth* occurs the phrase:

> There is no art
> To find the mind's construction in the face,　　　　　　　(I, iv, 11–12)

which Whiter does not appear to have noticed: nor does he comment on the sustained 'book' imagery in *Romeo and Juliet*, I, iii, 81–92, although in his 'Little Book' he transcribes a couplet from this speech:

> The fish lives in the sea; and 'tis much pride
> For fair without the fair within to hide.

One other reference to the eye occurs in Notebook 2 and relates to the same kind of imagery in *Lucrece*, 133–6:

> And Tarquin's *eye* may read the *mot* afar.

Whiter's note, however, strikes off on another line—

Modern Editors read *mote*. Mr Malone restor'd *mot* the *motto* or word. This is undoubtedly right; & the general allusion is from heraldry. The *eye* however reading the mot was suggested by the *mote* in the *eye* as it is found in Scripture—

and is followed by the usual train of associated quotations—*Love's Labour's Lost*, IV, iii, 155 ('Your eyes do make no coaches'), *Hamlet*, I, i, 112 ('A mote it is to trouble the mind's eye') and Jonson's *Masque: Part of the King's Entertainment in passing to his Coronation*.

Whiter's habit of making notes on Shakespeare appears to have persisted all through his life, extending to the *Dissertation on Death* and even to the unpublished volumes of his *Etymologicon Universale*. In his notes for a proposed volume to be called *Nova Tentamina Mythologica*, but which he did not live to complete, Whiter has two further references to Shakespeare which are worthy of preservation. In the course of a discussion of the relation, since ancient times, between schools and gardens, places of learning and places of worship (in which he refers to the 'Mystic Gardens' of mythology, the 'groves' of the classical Academies and the cloisters of old Cambridge), Whiter observes that

the ancient custom of Philosophers frequenting the Temples for the purpose of Education is retained among us by the practise, which formerly prevailed of having Schools in Churches. Shakspeare, as we remember, alludes to this practise when he talks of *A Pedant, that keeps a School in a Church*.

　　　　　　　　　　　　　　　　　　　　　(12th, Night A. 3. 2) (Oo, vii, 44: Folder 16)

Again, under the heading of *Epiphanies of the Gods*, he draws an interesting parallel between Macbeth's haunting vision of 'Pity, like a naked new-born babe, Striding the Blast' (I, vi, 21–2) and the revelations of the mystics, as described by Orpheus:

Sometimes to see fiery appearance extending with skipping motions over the (swelling) concave of the heavens—sometimes we have fiery meteors without shape in flashes darting across the sky—Sometimes you have a full rich blaze of light rolling or rattling on—sometimes you see a horse, all glittering with fire, or a Boy of fire riding on the swift back of a horse—now cloathed with gold, and again all naked and sometimes standing on his back and darting with his bow.　　　(Oo, vii, 44: Folder 9)

It has been possible to give here no more than an indication of Whiter's methods and discoveries: but even a brief glance through his unpublished notes supports the opinion of many twentieth-century critics that the author of the *Specimen* was a man of wide learning and considerable perception. Even where he is wrong, his ideas are provocative and stimulating, and Whiter deserves more credit than he is usually allowed for having laid the foundations of many so-called 'modern' trends of thought on Shakespeare.

NOTES

1. Oo, vi, 103: an interleaved copy of the *Specimen*, containing notes and additions for a proposed second edition—this has recently been edited by Alan Over and Mary Bell (1967). Oo, vi, 104: five notebooks containing notes on Shakespeare and Rowley, much scored through but containing the first draft of much of the material used in the *Specimen*. Notebook 5 has two insertions, 5*a* and 5*b*. Oo, vi, 105: a thick octavo volume composed of several copy books bound together and referred to as the 'Little Book'. Oo, vi, 106: a bundle of loose papers containing the rough draft of several brief essays on Shakespearian topics.

2. Whiter has left no comments on *Henry V, Henry VI* or *Henry VIII*; but it is at least possible that these notes may have been recorded in a separate notebook which has not been preserved. Inscriptions on the flyleaf of the interleaved *Specimen* refer to a *Journal* and a *Commonplace Book*; and in Notebook 3 Whiter speaks of 'my folio book'. None of these has been identified.

3. See Malone, *Preface to Shakespeare* (1790).

4. Sleepest or wakest thou, jolly shepherd?
   Thy sheep be in the corn;
   And for one blast of thy minikin mouth,
   Thy sheep shall take no harm.

5. The passage should read:
   Three times they breathed and three times did
      they drink,
   Upon agreement, of swift Severn's flood;
   Who then, affrighted with their bloody looks,
   Ran fearfully among the trembling reeds,
   And hid his crisp head in the hollow bank
   Bloodstained with these valiant combatants.

6. See, for example, Johnson's notes on *Midsummer Night's Dream* (Raleigh, pp. 67–70), or his comment on *Henry V*, III, vi, 133–4—'Now we speak upon our cue' (Raleigh, p. 130). Line references in this article are to the 'Globe' edition.

7. This quotation is used by Whiter to support the belief, voiced in his 'Little Book', that 'Shakespeare had some employment in the *law* when he was in the country'.

8. 'May/This night forestall him of the coming day' (*Cymbeline*); 'Come, night; end, day!/ For with the dark, poor thief, I'll steal away' (*All's Well*); 'Perhaps fore-stalling Night prevented them' (*Comus*). Whiter adds the query: 'Something is surely meant here. Is *fore*STALL to steal before hand?'

9. See *Specimen*, pp. 153 ff.

10. It is interesting to compare Whiter's concern with the influence of tapestry paintings on Shakespeare with John Hookham Frere's description of Whiter's own home: see the poem, 'Journey to Hardingham' (*Complete Works of John Hookham Frere*, I, pp. 278–80, ed. 1872):
    Alighting now, we pass the hall
    And view the parlour snug and small;
    The fire of logs, the tapestry wall.

11. These references include Falstaff's description of his conscripts in *1 Henry IV* (IV, ii, 27–9) as 'slaves as ragged as Lazarus in the painted cloth, where the glutton's dogs licked his sores'; his later argument with Mistress Quickly in *2 Henry IV* (II, i, 152–9)—

    Hostess: I must be fain to pawn both my plate and the tapestry of my dining chambers.

    Falstaff: Glasses, glasses is the only drinking: and for thy walls, a pretty slight drollery, or the story of the Prodigal, of the German hunting in water work, is worth a thousand of these bed-hangings and these fly-bitten tapestries—

    and Costard's objection to Sir Nathaniel during the Pageant of the Nine Worthies: 'O, sir, you have overthrown Alisander the conqueror. You will be scraped out of the painted cloth for this' (*L.L.L.* v, ii, 576–8). Whiter also includes the less obvious examples of Paulina's description of Leontes' baby daughter (*Winter's Tale*, II, iii, 97–9) and Lady Macbeth's assurance to her husband:
    the sleeping and the dead
    Are but as pictures: 'tis the eye of childhood
    That fears a painted devil.   (*Macbeth*, II, ii, 54–6)

12. See *Specimen*, pp. 34 ff.

13. 'The resemblance of a familiar phraseology, of a known metaphor, or of a circumstance not apparent in the text, will often lead the writer into language or imagery derived from these sources; though the application may be sometimes totally different from the meaning & spirit of the original' (*Specimen*, p. 70).

14. *Shakespeare's Imagery and What It Tells Us* (Cambridge, 1965), pp. 194–9.

15. 'Thy wit, ...Like powder in a skilless soldier's flask,/Is set a-fire by thine own ignorance.'

16. See also *Specimen*, p. 124: 'There is scarcely a play of our Author, where we do not find some favourite vein of metaphor or allusion by which it is distinguished.'

17. Whiter, like Coleridge and the romantic critics in general, recognizes in Shakespeare the greatest example of the creative writer (see *Specimen*, p. 64) and hence the fittest object for his study. Apart from this, however, he shows little or no awareness of the imaginative beauty of Shakespeare's poetry.

18. Other quotations are taken from *Cymbeline*, IV, ii, 206–18 ff. (description of Fidele, supposed dead, of which Whiter remarks: 'We have here a case of suspended animation, where appearances of Life in its most lovely though placid form are described'); *Pericles*, III, ii, 87–9

> Death may usurp on nature many hours,
> And yet the fire of life kindle again
> The o'erpressed spirits;

and *Romeo and Juliet*, IV, i, 93–106 (the Friar's description to Juliet of the effects of the potion).

19. Showing life's triumph in the map of death,
> And death's dim look in life's mortality:
> Each in her sleep themselves so beautify,
> As if between them twain there were no strife,
> But that life lived in death, and death in life.

20.   I have drugg'd their possets,
> That death and nature do contend about them,
> Whether they live or die.

21. Whiter goes on to describe the 'lean' times of Lent by a quotation from *Hamlet*, II, ii, 27–9 ('what lenten entertainment the players shall receive from you').

22. A note in the 'Little Book' collects together a number of passages in which the colours of the cheeks themselves appear to make war with each other, as in *Coriolanus*, II, i, 232–4, *Taming of the Shrew*, IV, v, 30, *Lucrece*, 71–2, and *Venus and Adonis*, 345–6. In some of

these instances, Whiter observes, 'The war of *Red* and *White* in the cheeks alludes to the *wars* of the Houses of York and Lancaster.'

23. The passages cited include *Love's Labour's Lost*, V, ii, 821–2:

> If this thou do deny, let our hands part,
> Neither INTITLED in the other's heart;

Taming of the Shrew, III, ii, 124–5:

> When I should bid good-morrow to my bride
> And seal the TITLE with a lovely kiss?

Richard III, IV, iv, 340–50:

> *Q. Eliz.*: Under what TITLE shall I woo for thee...?
> ...To wail the TITLE as her mother doth.
> *K. Rich.*: Say I will love her everlastingly.
> *Q. Eliz.*: But how long shall that TITLE, 'ever' last?

Cymbeline, I, v, 95–7 ('You may wear her in TITLE yours...'); *All's Well*, II, iii, 124, 137–8 (''Tis only TITLE thou disdain'st in her...' 'The property by what it is should go,/Not by the TITLE') and *Lucrece*, 890–3:

> Thy secret pleasure turns to open shame,
> Thy private feasting to a publick fast;
> Thy smoothing TITLES to a ragged name;
> Thy sugar'd tongue to bitter wormwood taste.

24. Taken from *Troilus and Cressida*, IV, ii, 109–11:

> the strong base and building of my love;

Merry Wives, II, ii, 223–6:

Like a fair house, built on another man's ground; so that I have lost my edifice by mistaking the place where I erected it;

Comedy of Errors, III, ii, 1–4:

> Shall love, in building, grow so ruinous?

Two Gentlemen of Verona, V, iv, 7–12:

> Leave not the mansion so long tenantless,
> Lest, growing ruinous, the building fall;

and Sonnet X:

> For thou art so possess'd with murderous *hate*
> That 'gainst thyself thou stick'st not to conspire,
> Seeking that beauteous *roof* to *ruinate*
> Which to *repair* should be thy chief desire.
> O, change thy thought, that I may change
>   my mind!
> Shall hate be fairer *lodg'd* than gentle *love*?

25. 'A man of fire-new words, fashion's own knight.'

26. Whiter concludes with the unexpected remark that '*Fancy's child* is adopted in another sense by Milton in characterizing our great Poet. He was not aware of the force of the expression'. (See also *Specimen*, p. 175 n.)

SHAKESPEARE'S 'ROMEO AND JULIET': ITS SPANISH SOURCE

BY

OSCAR M. VILLAREJO

Mr Paul Morgan has shown in a recent essay that two of William Shakespeare's intimate friends —Leonard Digges and James Mabbe—were residing in Spain between 1611 and 1614 and had occasion in the year 1613 to comment upon the wide popularity of Shakespeare and Lope de Vega in their respective countries as renowned poets of the age. Interesting in this respect is the fact that Digges and Mabbe were so well acquainted with Spanish that in 1622 both published English translations of two notable Spanish picaresque romances.[1] Another of Shakespeare's friends, who was also his collaborator—namely, John Fletcher—is known to have employed two plays by Lope de Vega for the composition of *The Loyal Subject* (1618) and *The Prophetess* (1622).[2] Moreover, Fletcher's associate, Francis Beaumont, is believed by many critics to have made use of the first Spanish edition of *Don Quixote* (1605) for the composition of *The Knight of the Burning Pestle*.[3]

As for the distinct influence of the literature of Castile in the writings of Shakespeare himself, it is well known that the main plot of *The Two Gentlemen of Verona* is based, directly or indirectly, on the episode of Felix and Felismena in the Spanish pastoral romance, *La Diana* (Valencia, 1559?) of Jorge de Montemayor. It follows that if Shakespeare had acquired a knowledge of Jorge de Montemayor in the middle of the 1590s, he could scarcely have failed to learn about another Spanish author whose fame had eclipsed even that of Montemayor. The majority of critics who are familiar with the achievements of the *Fénix de los ingenios* in drama are inclined to agree that by the turn of the century (1600) the name of Lope as an author of plays—unlike Shakespeare's—had become proverbial not only in his native country but also in Italy, France, Portugal, the Netherlands, and the distant lands of the Spanish Indies.[4]

Less well known to the critics in regard to the influence of Spanish literature upon the works of Shakespeare is the example of Lope de Vega's play *Castelvines y Monteses*. In 1874 the German literary historian Julius Leopold Klein set forth in one of the volumes of his comprehensive history of the drama of Europe a series of striking parallels extracted from Lope's *Castelvines y Monteses* and Shakespeare's *Romeo and Juliet*. In the course of declaring that the parallels in question proved to his satisfaction Shakespeare's intimate knowledge of Lope's *comedia* prior to the period in which the English tragedy was composed, Klein stated with some asperity in the face of the hostile critics who could not agree to his novel theory that *Castelvines y Monteses* was certainly written by the year 1603 and, in his opinion, much earlier.[5] Klein's assertion that Lope's play must be dated for an unknown period antedating 1603 is only slightly inaccurate. In a study of Lope's theatre which was published in 1965 for the *Revista de Filología Española*, the author of the present essay showed that Lope's famous list of the titles of 448 of his plays had appeared in manuscript form before 29 July 1604.[6] Since *Castelvines y Monteses* is the 395th title in Lope's list of plays of 1604, one can presume that Shakespeare's *Romeo and Juliet* (*c.* 1595)—a play which treats of exactly the same subject matter—could have followed and not preceded *Castelvines y Monteses* in the history of the European theatres.

Among the parallels cited by Klein is the one involving the moonlight scene in the garden, an episode found in Lope's *Castelvines y Monteses* (I, x, xi) as well as in Shakespeare's *Romeo and Juliet* (II, ii).[7] As will be shown later, this particular garden scene does not appear in any of the known sources which might have been available either to Lope or to Shakespeare (viz. Brooke, Painter, Boaistuau, Bandello, Luigi Groto, etc.). Such being the case, the following verbal similarities emerge from an examination of the Spanish and English texts at comparable points of the garden scene presented by both dramatists:

Julia: Que el nombre en ajena boca	
Alegra, enternece y mueve.	(Lope: I, ix)
Jul.: O, be some other name!	
What's in a name? that which we call a rose	
By any other name would smell as sweet.	(Shakespeare: II, ii, 42–4)
Roselo: Querida enemiga mía,	
Luz del alma que aborreces.	(Lope: I, ix)
Rom.: My name, dear saint, is hateful to myself,	
Because it is an enemy to thee.	(Shakespeare: II, ii, 55–6)
Julia: No jures; que los que juran	
Mucho del crédito pierden.	(Lope: I, ix)
Jul.: Do not swear at all;	
Or, if thou wilt, swear by thy gracious self...	(Shakespeare: II, ii, 112–13)

Neither the parallels nor the other points in the analysis set forth by Klein could persuade the English scholars of his day to accept the thesis that Shakespeare had been indebted to a contemporary Spanish dramatist for the composition of *Romeo and Juliet*. Albert R. Frey went to considerable lengths in his forty-one-page essay entitled 'William Shakespeare and Alleged Spanish Prototypes', *Publications of the New York Shakespeare Society*, paper no. 3 (New York, 1886) in an endeavour to show that the parallels cited by Klein represented only an accidental conjunction of writings by two different authors who had no knowledge of each other while using the same or similar sources. Among other arguments presented by Frey in support of his thesis was that 'the Spanish drama, and that portion of it written by Lope in particular, was defective' (p. 39); hence, Shakespeare would not 'find it necessary to copy from such unfaithful forms' (p. 41). Later, H. H. Furness published his heavily annotated text of *Romeo and Juliet* for his Variorum edition of Shakespeare's plays (Philadelphia, 1899), being careful to include in that volume (pp. 470–80) a summary of Lope's *Castelvines y Monteses*, together with selected passages of that work translated into English. Furness makes no mention of Klein's parallels in the Variorum edition. Instead, he takes note (p. 470) in his summary of Lope's play of 'the different treatment that the same story received in the hands of Shakespeare's greatest dramatic contemporary out of England'. Furness also remarks on the same page that he had extracted his summary from a complete English translation of Lope's *comedia* entitled *Castelvines y Monteses. Tragi-comedia. By Frey Lope Félix de Vega Carpio. Translated by F. W. Cosens...* (1869). Presumably, the translation was made from the only known Spanish work of the seventeenth century containing this play in its contents. The title page of the volume is cited below.[8] *Castelvines y Monteses* is the seventh of the twelve plays printed in this *Parte XXV* (Zaragoza, 1647) of Lope de Vega's *comedias*.

From its structure, *Romeo and Juliet* appears to have originated from a continental type of play which has little in common with ordinary English plays of the same period. We refer to the predominant characteristics of the Spanish *comedia de capa y espada*, of which Lope's *Castelvines y Monteses* is very typical. To those who are familiar with the Spanish drama of the Golden Age, *Romeo and Juliet* recalls immediately by virtue of its sword play—between Sampson and Abram (I, i); between Tybalt and Benvolio (I, i); between Tybalt and Mercutio (III, i); between Romeo and Tybalt (III, i); and, finally, between County Paris and Romeo (V, iii)—that particular trait of Spanish plays of 'cloak and sword' which requires the deadly thrust and counter-thrust of swords by hot-blooded young gallants at critical points of the action.

Another trait of the Spanish *comedia de capa y espada* is the frequent presentation of a duenna who carries messages between lovers in an atmosphere heavily charged with intrigue. In this respect, Shakespeare's Nurse presents a more than superficial psychological resemblance to Celestina, the satanic old woman with the insinuating tongue whose influence pervades every scene of the *Tragicomedia de Calisto y Melibea* (Burgos, 1499); and, indeed—as the German critic Gervinus says—'much of *Romeo and Juliet* is found in this work'.[9] An English translation of this same *Tragicomedia* was published at London in 1631 by Shakespeare's friend, the hispanist James Mabbe.

Many critics have pointed out that numerous Spanish plays of the Golden Age (e.g. Lope's *Fuenteovejuna*, *Peribáñez*, etc.) conclude with the entrance of a higher authority (usually the King) to resolve with finality the issues in dispute portrayed in the preceding scenes of the action. In Lope's *Castelvines y Monteses*, this function is performed by 'El Señor de Verona' (III, x), and Shakespeare seems to follow the Spanish example: for his 'Prince of Verona' appears at the conclusion of *Romeo and Juliet* (V, iii) in order to compose the remaining differences between the Montagues and the Capulets. Still another trait of the Spanish *comedia* is the portrayal of a Don Juan type of lover (e.g. Lope's Roselo in *Castelvines y Monteses*) who is accustomed to visit his lady's bedroom at night by climbing a wall or vaulting over a balcony in the manner that Romeo does in Shakespeare's play. Lastly, it is of importance to note that the element of *pundonor* (a point of honour) which is found in numerous Spanish *comedias* of 'cloak and sword' is reproduced with fidelity in Romeo's speech after the death of Mercutio (III, i, 114–20), particularly in the words: 'my reputation stain'd with Tibalts slaunder...'[10] It might be remarked, in connexion with the lines spoken by Romeo cited above, that his words seem to show that he understands the concept of honour (reputation rather than virtue) which is found in many Spanish plays of the Golden Age.

The complex topic of Shakespeare's available sources for the composition of *Romeo and Juliet* is the subject which next claims our attention. There can be no doubt, as many scholars assert, that Shakespeare had at hand Arthur Brooke's long narrative poem called *The Tragical History of Romeus and Juliet* (1562) when he composed his text for *An Excellent conceited Tragedie of Romeo and Juliet...London. Printed by John Danter. 1597*.[11] However, J. J. Munro, in his exhaustive study of 1908 concerning the sources of *Romeo and Juliet*, has this to say in respect of the relationship of Brooke's poem to Shakespeare's play:

Here, then, we are led to believe again that there was a source from which Shakespeare drew, other than Brooke; and we have to remember that this was precisely the conclusion we arrived at, from a consideration of Luigi Groto, Boaistuau, and the Italian novels...[12]

Munro advances compelling reasons for his belief that there was a second source for Shakespeare's *Romeo and Juliet*. He also thinks that this second source was a play rather than a novel. Munro's patient and unsuccessful efforts in his essay, therefore, to identify the second source of Shakespeare's play are necessarily related to the identity of Lope's immediate source for the composition of *Castelvines y Monteses*. Munro is apparently in error when he says that *Castelvines y Monteses* originated exclusively from Bandello's *Novelle* (Lucca: Busdrago, 1554).[13] In 1918 Wolfgang von Wurzbach, in the introduction of his German translation of Lope's *Castelvines y Monteses*, made a minute analysis of the source of the Spanish play and concluded, after examining the relevant texts, that an intermediary text between Bandello (II, 9) and Lope must have been the source of *Castelvines y Monteses*.[14] He denies that this source could have been, for example, either Masuccio or Luigi da Porto. Instead, he cites the following Spanish translation of the *Tragical Tales* of Bandello via Boaistuau and Belleforest as the most probable source of Lope's play: *Historias Tragicas exemplares, sacadas de las obras del Bandello Verones. Nueuamẽte traduzidas de las que en lengua Francesa adornaron Pierres Boaistuau, y Francisco de Belleforest...En Salamanca...En casa de Pedro Lasso. 1589.*[15] Arthur Brooke, it will be recalled, employed the original French version of Boaistuau and Belleforest's translation of Bandello's *Tragical Tales* for the composition of his *Tragical History of Romeus and Juliet* (1562), a source which Shakespeare undoubtedly used in composing *Romeo and Juliet*. Thus, Lope could very well have employed as early as 1589 a version of the old Italian tale of Romeo and Julietta which approximated very closely in its form to the materials which Shakespeare had at his disposal when he made extensive use of Brooke's poem for the composition of *Romeo and Juliet*.

As Wurzbach has shown in his analysis of the text of *Castelvines y Monteses*, Lope's play could have been written as early as 1589. One of the indications found in the Spanish play which inclines us to believe that such is the date of Lope's original is the following: appearing in the cast of *Castelvines y Monteses* in its present text—altered to an unknown degree from its original version[16]—are two characters named Belardo and Dorotea. As many Spanish scholars have pointed out (viz. H. A. Rennert, J. Blecua, J. de Entrambasaguas, etc.), the pseudonym 'Dorotea' is the one which Lope employed during the period 1583–8 in order to designate the Spanish actress Elena Osorio. The final rupture of relations between Lope and the actress took place in February 1588. The amatory dialogues relating to Belardo (the pseudonym of Lope himself in many of his plays) and Dorotea (the pseudonym of Elena Osorio) which appear in certain scenes of *Castelvines y Monteses* could easily mean, therefore, that the original version of Lope's *comedia* was written in the period 1588–9. One might add to the previous remarks that Émile Gigas refers to a Spanish translation of Bandello's *Tragical Tales* via Boaistuau and Belleforest which was published at Salamanca in 1584, but Gigas says: 'Je ne l'ai pas vue.'[17] If such a volume were ever found, it might sustain the theory that Lope could have written his play even before 1589.

Turning now to Munro's essay concerning the unknown second source of Shakespeare's *Romeo and Juliet*, we note that the chief focus of attention in his essay is upon the Dutch play of *Romeo en Juliette*, written in Alexandrine couplets by Jacob Struijs in 1630, but not published until 1634. Munro makes much of the fact that the play by Struijs agrees exclusively with Shakespeare (i.e. with none of the usual suggested sources for the tale of Romeo and Julietta, such as Brooke, Painter, Boaistuau, Bandello, Luigi Groto, and the like) on at least seven different counts, all of them important. Munro also advances excellent arguments to show that Struijs could not have copied any part of Shakespeare's play.

It is unfortunate that Munro did not make an analysis of either of the two Spanish plays set forth in his chart (pp. xlvii–xlix) in an endeavour to find the unknown source of the Dutch play by Struijs. Apparently, Munro did not study their texts nor did he ascertain their approximate dates. If he had done so, he would have found that, except for one instance, each of the seven parallels which he isolated from the text of Struijs and designated by means of the letters *a*, *b*, *c*, *d*, *e*, *f*, and *g*[18] finds its equivalent in the play by Lope de Vega, *Castelvines y Monteses*, as well as in Shakespeare's *Romeo and Juliet*.

As one would expect, an examination of the respective texts of Lope's *comedia*, and the play by Struijs of 1634, reveals that the latter is only another Dutch adaptation of the exceedingly popular plays of Lope de Vega in the Netherlands at this time. *Romeo en Juliette* by Struijs, therefore, should be properly listed with the thirty-odd plays of the Low Lands of the seventeenth century which, according to Jonas van Praag, are translations of or adaptations from the *comedias* of Lope de Vega, Luis Vélez de Guevara, and of other Spanish dramatists of the Golden Age.[19] In other words, the Dutch play by Struijs reminds us of the manner in which Johannes Serwouters wrote an adaptation of Lope de Vega's *La nueva ira de Dios y Gran Tamorlán de Persia* (1583–6) at an unknown date in the seventeenth century entitled *Den grooten Tamerlan, met de doot van Bayaset de I. Turks Keyser. Door J. Serwouters...1719*.[20] In this instance, as an examination of the relevant texts will show, the Dutch play originated from Lope and not from Christopher Marlowe's famous drama on the same subject matter. Thus, the exhaustive inquiry made by Munro in search of his second source for *Romeo and Juliet* ends, finally, with *Castelvines y Monteses*, a tragi-comedy written by Lope de Vega with a disappointingly incongruous ending. Since the play was published in an unauthorized edition of the *comedias* twelve years after the dramatist's death, one has additional reason to suspect that Jornada III and other portions of the play disclose a badly corrupted text and not Lope's original as he wrote it.

In regard to the seven parallels which Munro has established between *Romeo en Juliette* by Struijs and Shakespeare's *Romeo and Juliet*—parallels which cannot be connected in any way with the conventional suggested sources which Munro has examined minutely, such as Brooke, Painter, Boaistuau, Bandello, Luigi Groto, and the rest—the following notations are cited here to show why *Castelvines y Monteses* must be linked to Shakespeare's play:

(a) *Romeo's description of Juliet at the feast*
1. (Struijs: I, i). See Fuller, *Modern Philology*, IV (July 1906), 26–7.
2. (Lope de Vega: I, ii, iii, iv). See *Biblioteca de autores españoles* (Rivadeneyra, LII), 2–4.
3. (Shakespeare) I, iv, v.

(b) *The moonlight scene in the garden*
1. (Struijs: I, ii). See Fuller, p. 27.
2. (Lope de Vega: I, x, xi). See *BAE* (Rivadeneyra, LII), 6–7.
3. (Shakespeare) II, ii.

(c) *The conference with Friar Laurence*
    1. (Struijs: III, iii). See Fuller, pp. 29–30.
    2. (Lope de Vega: III, viii), pp. 17–18.
    3. (Shakespeare) III, iii.

(d) *Tybalt's desire to attack Romeo at the feast*
    1. (Struijs: I, iv). See Fuller, p. 28.
    2. (Lope de Vega: I, iv), p. 2.
    3. (Shakespeare) I, v.

(e) *The death of Tybalt* (called *Thibout* in Struijs and *Octavio* in Lope)
    1. (Struijs: III, ii). See Fuller, p. 29.
    2. (Lope de Vega: II, ix), p. 10.
    3. (Shakespeare) III, i.

(g) *The parting of the lovers*
    1. (Struijs: IV, i). See Fuller, p. 30.
    2. (Lope de Vega: II, xvii, xviii, xix, xx), pp. 12–13.
    3. (Shakespeare) III, v.

In Parallel (a) cited above, Lope's Roselo falls instantly in love when he confronts Julia at the feast in exactly the same manner and in exactly the same physical setting as Romeo is presented with in the play by Struijs and in Shakespeare's *Romeo and Juliet*. In other words, the darkness, the torches, the masquers, and the unreal, surcharged atmosphere found in Lope's presentation of the feast at Verona are reproduced unmistakably in the corresponding scenes written by Shakespeare and Struijs. As noted previously, no scene depicting Capulet's feast is found in Brooke, Painter, Boaistuau, Bandello, etc. Similarly, one finds in the other parallels a consistent portrayal of episodes, settings, and characters which makes it clear, as Munro says, that Shakespeare's second source was probably a play rather than a novel—that is to say, Lope's *Castelvines y Monteses* of date 1589. One might note, for example, in Parallel (c) that the conference with Friar Laurence is found in the identical portion of the text (III, iii) of the respective plays by Struijs and Shakespeare. It is also clear that, in Parallel (d), Thibout's attempted attack on Romeo occurs in I, iv, of the Dutch play and in exactly the same act and scene (I, iv) of Lope's *comedia*. In Shakespeare's play, Tybalt's attempted attack upon Romeo takes place only one scene later (I, v). Evidence such as this must mean that Munro was correct in saying that Shakespeare's second source was probably a play rather than a novel.[21]

It may be mentioned that a number of astrological allusions, treated in the Spaniard's typical manner, are found in Lope's *Castelvines y Monteses* as well as in Shakespeare's *Romeo and Juliet*. In spite of the fact that *Castelvines y Monteses* apparently suffered extensive changes before it was finally printed in its edition of Zaragoza, 1647, one finds the following astrological allusion in Jornada II (p. 311 *b*) which is still intact:

> *Ros.:* Que calle, pues tu no ves
> que en la creciente, y mudança
> de la luna hablan los locos?

In another astrological reference found in Jornada I (p. 295 *a*), Roselo speaks in terms of a hidden but benign celestial power which gives approval to the mutual love exchanged between himself and Julia:

> *Ros.:* ...mira que por dicha el cielo,
> nos proboca ocultamente
> a este amor honesto, y santo,
> con que todos en paz queden.

These verses remind us of the fact that in Lope's autobiographical novel *La Dorotea* (composed 1585–8), Fernando (Lope de Vega) speaks about Dorotea (the actress Elena Osorio) in the following terms: 'I do not know what star propitious to lovers was then in the ascendant, but we no sooner saw each other than we fell in love.'[22] Since astrological references of this type are notably absent in Brooke, Painter, Boaistuau, Bandello, and other suggested sources of *Romeo and Juliet*, one is led to inquire in what source, other than Lope, Shakespeare could have found the inspiration for his famous line 'star-crossed lovers'. Lope's interest in astrology was exceedingly marked in the early years of his career. The poet's strong interest in astrology is seen very clearly in Book v of *La Arcadia* (Madrid, 1598), in which horoscopes and signs of the zodiac predominate in large portions of the text.[23] Furthermore, J. de Entrambasaguas cites one of Lope's early sonnets (which is studded with astrological references) as a proof that the sonnet was written while the poet was studying mathematics and astrology under Juan Bautista Labaña and Ambrosio Onderiz at the Academy of Mathematics at Madrid between 1583 and 1586.[24]

The reader might ask, too, why it is that Shakespeare employs the phrases 'King of cats' and 'rat-catcher' in order to characterize Tybalt. Neither one of these phrases nor anything resembling them is found in the conventional sources cited by the critics for Shakespeare's tragedy. Students of Lope de Vega, however, detect at once in the phrases one of the hallmarks of Lope's youthful writings. It is not surprising, therefore, to find the following provocative lines in the text of *Castelvines y Monteses* (Jornada 1; p. 280a):

> *Mar.:* Pues los gatos tan ayrados
> andan en sus vandos juntos,
> que hazen compaña por puntos
> las cozinas, y texados.
> Si mahullan es por fin
> de declarar su interes,
> porque unos dizen Montes,
> y otros dizen Castelvin.[25]

Since nothing has ever been said hitherto by the critics regarding the possible source, or sources, of the phrases 'King of cats' or 'rat-catcher' as applied to Shakespeare's Tybalt, the question arises as to whether Shakespeare could have seen these particular lines by Lope. As is shown by the verses just cited, Marín remarks drily to his master, Roselo, that the roving bands of cats skulking in the kitchens and woodsheds of Verona had also become fierce partisans in the ancient feud between the two noble families of the town, for one band called themselves the Monteses and the other the Castelvines. It is therefore appropriate—all things considered—for Shakespeare to have referred to Tybalt as the King of one of the two roving partisan bands who were disturbing the tranquillity of Verona. The evidence in favour of such a point of view is not weakened, either, when one reads the following lines in the letter which Lope addresses to his son in the earliest known edition (Madrid, 1634) of *La Gatomaquia* ('The War of the Cats'):

> Y escucha mi famosa *Gatomachia*:
> Así desde las Indias a Valaquia
> Corra tu nombre y fama...[26]

A previous edition of Lope's mock heroic poem, *La Gatomaquia*, might have been printed prior to 1634; for otherwise Lope would not have been referring in these stanzas to a work whose renown had extended in its time from the Indies to Wallachia (Romania). The probability is that numerous editions of Lope's burlesque epic have been lost and that one or more of them had reached England as early as the nineties of the sixteenth century.[27] It is known, at least, that F. Sales states in the introduction of his *Selección de obras maestras dramáticas de Lope de Vega y Calderón de la Barca...* (Boston, 1844; Library of Congress: PQ6439.E7), pp. ix–x, that during Lope's service as a soldier aboard one of the galleons of the *Gran Armada* in its attack upon England (1588), the Spanish poet had occasion to compose 'el más celebrado de los poemas jocosos que posée nuestra lengua, la famosa *Gatomaquia*...' Such an early text of Lope's burlesque poem about the 'War of the Cats' could very well have been published shortly after 1588, inasmuch as in Ignacio de Luzán's *La poética* (Madrid, 1789), I, 308, one finds the following lines quoted by the author from *La Gatomaquia*:

> Hechó Marramaquiez de furia lleno
> Una mano al papel, otra al relleno.

The lines in question represent a variant from the equivalent ones found in Silva II of *La Gatomaquia* (Madrid, 1634)—that is to say, in the only surviving text of Lope's burlesque poem known to us. The lines from Silva II in this latter text read thus:

> Tan gran traición, colérico arremete,
> Y echa veloz, de ardiente furia lleno,
> Una mano al papel y otra al relleno.

Taking into consideration the fact that such a textual variant is known to exist in Lope's poem, one might infer from this variant that, prior to 1789, Luzán might have consulted an extremely early edition of *La Gatomaquia* (1589?) which is now lost, for the unorthodox verses from Lope that he quotes in *La poética*.

The argument of this essay depends on an early date for *Castelvines y Monteses* and there is some testimony to show that the play was written in 1588–9. Internal evidence within the play appears to reveal its date as 1588–9. The Spanish play closely parallels in its plot the events of Lope's own life; for, according to the biographical account given by the poet himself in *La Dorotea* (originally composed 1585–8),[28] he, like his hero Roselo and like Shakespeare's Romeo, fought a duel, received a grievous sentence of banishment from the kingdom in which he was born, and abducted his young bride in the face of opposition from both families. Lope's biographer Montalván mentions the incident of Lope's duel with an unknown *hidalgo* in his account (Madrid, 1635) of the career of Lope de Vega.[29] If Lope and Montalván are accurate in their facts, the duel in which our poet participated took place between 1585 and the beginning of 1588, at which time *La Dorotea* was completed in its original form.

'ROMEO AND JULIET': ITS SPANISH SOURCE

The horoscope prognosticated by Caesar (Luis Rosicler) in *La Dorotea* is related very clearly to the plot of *Castelvines y Monteses*; for the astrologer Caesar predicts in the horoscope that Lope will soon be persecuted and banished from the kingdom but that he will find happiness in his marriage to a high-born lady of the court, although with the strong disapproval of Lope's family and of hers.[30] Since Lope received a ten-year sentence of banishment from Castile by the court of Madrid on 7 February 1588[31] and since he unlawfully abducted and married by proxy (10 May 1588) Doña Isabel de Alderete, the daughter of Don Diego de Urbina, a king-at-arms in the court of Philip II,[32] one can understand why the plot of *Castelvines y Monteses* stresses in particular the formidable family barriers preventing the marriage of Romeo and Julietta in the old Italian tale. Accordingly, one might infer from Lope's personal situation in the year 1588 that he had a strong incentive to write such a play as *Castelvines y Monteses* towards the end of 1588 (after Lope's return as a soldier from the Armada expedition in December)[33] or early in 1589, when the poet was residing at Valencia as a highly successful author of plays. In the last analysis, the date of the play seems to be 1589; inasmuch as Lope appears to have made use of a Spanish translation of the *Tragical Tales* of Bandello via Boaistuau and Belleforest of date 1589 for the composition of his drama. If these last statements are in accordance with the facts, large portions of the surviving text of Lope's *Castelvines y Monteses* were written at Valencia several years before the date of composition of Shakespeare's *The Tragedy of Romeo and Juliet* (*c*. 1595).

According to the evidence presented in this essay, and especially in relation to the analysis made by Munro in 1908 concerning the sources of Shakespeare's *Romeo and Juliet*, the German literary historian Julius Leopold Klein was probably correct when he stated in 1874 that Shakespeare must have had an intimate knowledge of Lope's *Castelvines y Monteses* when he composed his tragedy of *Romeo and Juliet*.[34]

NOTES

1. Paul Morgan, *Shakespeare Survey 16* (1963), 118–20.

2. Fletcher's *The Loyal Subject* (1618) is an adaptation of Lope's *El gran duque de Moscovia* (1617), while Fletcher's *The Prophetess* (1622) and Massinger's *The Roman Actor* (1626) are both derived from Lope's *Lo fingido verdadero* (1621). See O. M. Villarejo, *Lope de Vega and Three Jacobean Plays* (Master's thesis: George Washington University, 1949), Library of Congress: PR655.V5, as well as the doctoral dissertation of the same author entitled *Lope de Vega and the Elizabethan and Jacobean Drama* (Columbia University, 1953).

3. For a typical comment upon this subject, see F. W. Moorman (ed.), *The Knight of the Burning Pestle* (1942), p. vii.

4. Cervantes states in 1605 (*Don Quixote*, pt. 1, ch. xlviii) that Lope 'has filled the world with his fame' (*tiene lleno el mundo de su fama*) through the unprece-

dented number, quality, and variety of his *comedias*. Lope likewise states in the prologue of *El peregrino en su patria* (Seville: Clemente Hidalgo, 1604) that his plays are well known in Portugal, Italy, France, and the Indies.

5. Julius Leopold Klein, *Geschichte des Dramas* (Leipzig, 1874), x, 347–8.

6. O. M. Villarejo, 'Revisión de las Listas de *El Peregrino*, de Lope de Vega', *Revista de Filología Española* (Madrid, 1965), XLVI, 343–99. See also by the same author, 'Lista II de *El Peregrino*: La lista maestra del año 1604 de los 448 títulos de las comedias de Lope de Vega', *Segismundo* (Madrid, 1966), III, 57–89.

7. Klein, *op. cit.* x, 347.

8. *Parte veintecinco, perfeta y verdadera de las comedias del Fénix de Espana, Frey Lope Félix de Vega Carpio... Çaragoça, Viuda de Pedro Verges*, 1647. Copy in the University of Pennsylvania: 868.C pt. 25.

9. Julio Cejador y Frauca (ed.), *Fernando de Rojas: La Celestina* (Madrid: *Clásicos castellanos*, XX), I, xxxiii.

10. For an excellent definition of the Spanish concept of honour during the Golden Age, see Edward M. Wilson, 'Othello, a Tragedy of Honour', *The Listener* (5 June 1952), XLVII, no. 1214, 926–7.

11. See Geoffrey Bullough, *Narrative and Dramatic Sources of Shakespeare*, I (1957), 274, or Kenneth Muir, *Shakespeare's Sources* (1957), p. 23.

12. J. J. Munro, *Brooke's 'Romeus and Iuliet' Being the Original of Shakespeare's 'Romeo and Juliet'* (New York, 1908), pp. xlvi–xlvii.

13. *Ibid.* p. xlvii.

14. Wolfgang von Wurzbach, *Ausgewählte Komödien von Lope de Vega* (Strasbourg, 1918).

15. Eugène Kohler, 'Lope et Bandello', *Hommage à Ernest Martinenche* (Paris, 1939), pp. 117, 135. For a photographic facsimile of the title page of the Spanish translation (Salamanca, 1589) of the *Tales* of Bandello mentioned by Kohler, see the *Catálogo de la Biblioteca de Salvá* (Valencia: Ferrer de Orga, 1872), II, 115.

16. M. Ménendez y Pelayo notes numerous missing lines in the Zaragoza, 1647, text of *Castelvines y Monteses*. See the Spanish Academy edition of Lope's plays, XV (1913), 316a, 326b, 339a, and 354b.

17. See Kohler, *op. cit.* p. 135, n. 16.

18. Munro, *op. cit.* p. xliii.

19. Jonas A. van Praag, *La comedia espagnole aux Pays-Bas au XVII et au XVIII siècle* (Amsterdam, 1922), pp. 43, 81.

20. Lope's *La nueva ira de Dios y Gran Tamorlán de Persia* is found in *Parte 33 de varios autores* (Valencia: Claudio Macé, 1642), of which a copy is owned by the British Museum. The Dutch play by J. Serwouters is listed in the Library of Congress (Washington, D.C.) under the class mark: PT 5497.T6 (vol. 12, no. 7).

21. Brooke tells us that he had seen a dramatic version of the story of Romeo and Juliet before 1562, but this could not have been Lope de Vega's play since he was born in that year.

22. Hugo A. Rennert and Américo Castro, *La vida de Lope de Vega* (Madrid, 1919), p. 9. For the English translation of these lines, see Hugo A. Rennert, *The Life of Lope de Vega* (Glasgow, 1904), p. 8.

23. *Biblioteca de autores españoles* (Rivadeneyra, XXXVIII), 435 ff.

24. Joaquín de Entrambasaguas, *Vivir y crear de Lope de Vega* (Madrid, 1946), I, 59–61.

25. It is interesting to note that Lope's very early play *La nueva ira de Dios y Gran Tamorlán de Persia* not only contains numerous astrological references but also the following lines describing 'el gato Tamorlán' in fol. 103ᵛ of the Valencia, 1642, text found in the British Museum:

> Ozm.: ...somos ratones los dos
> que procuramos yo y vos,
> su vida y su buen suceso.
> Llega *el gato Tamorlán*,
> Y sin hazer mas procesos
> muele nuestra carne y huesos,
> con los moços de vn batan.

The previous lines find an interesting parallel with the following verses alluding to Lope's banishment (*destierro*) of 1588, as quoted by Francisco Rodríguez Marín (pp. 62, 198) in his 1935 edition of Lope's *La Gatomaquia* (Madrid, 1634):

> Pues de sus manos se escaparon pocos,
> Llamándolos traidores Mauregatos;
> Que, levantando una cuchar de hierro,
> A eterno condenándolos *destierro*,
> Fue *Tamorlán de gatos*.

The source of Lope's play *El Gran Tamorlán de Persia* is the well-known narrative about Tamerlane the Great and Bajazeth, the emperor of the Turks, by Pero Mexía which was published at Seville in 1582. References to Tamerlane and Bajazeth are found in Act V, Sc. iii of Lope's *La Dorotea* (1585–8), as well as in Book III of Lope's *La Arcadia* (Madrid, 1598). Accordingly, the fact seems to be well established that Lope's interest in cats for literary themes could very well antedate the year 1589.

26. F. Rodríguez Marín, *op. cit.* p. 4. But see his note (pp. 101–2) in reference to the phrase 'y escucha mi famosa *Gatomachia*'.

27. Doña Teresa Verecundia addresses Lope as the famous poet 'el licenciado Tomé de Burguillos' in a laudatory sonnet prefixed to the text of *La Gatomaquia* (Madrid, 1634), but Lope refers to himself as the poet 'el maestro Burguillos' in IV, iii, of *La Dorotea* (composed 1585–8); and in this latter work he alludes to the subject matter of cats by such expressions as 'y de los gatos se saca algalia' and 'por lo que tiene de gato, y al fin lo vendrá a ser de tus doblones' (see José M. Blecua, ed. *La Dorotea*, Madrid, 1955, pp. 346–7). The reference to Lope's banishment (*destierro*) mentioned in our note 25 above, as well as the astrological allusions relating to Garfiñanto (see Marín, pp. 24, 128) in *La Gatomaquia*, represent verses which Lope could have composed before 1589. As might be expected, owing to the early date of *La Dorotea*, astrological references abound in that work. Aside from all this, Marín takes note of missing lines (pp. 9, 112) in the 1634 text of *La Gato-*

maquia. One can presume, therefore, that this is not the original edition but a reissue in print of an old but famous poetical work of Lope's.

28. Blecua, *op. cit.* pp. 407, 498. See also Rennert, *Life of Lope de Vega*, p. 18.

29. Juan Pérez de Montalván, 'Fama póstuma...del Doctor Frey Lope Félix de Vega Carpio', *Biblioteca de autores españoles* (Rivadeneyra, XXIV), x. See also 'Lord Holland's Account of Lope de Vega', *The Edinburgh Review...for Oct. 1806...Jan. 1807*, as reprinted in New York City by Eastburn, Kirk, & Co., IX (1816), 225.

30. Blecua, *op. cit.* pp. 575–6.

31. Rennert, *op. cit.* p. 36.

32. *Ibid.* pp. 55–9.

33. *Ibid.* p. 64.

34. This article was in the press before the appearance of T. J. B. Spencer's ed. of *Romeo and Juliet* (New Penguin Shakespeare, 1967). For 'King of cats' (cf. p. 101 above), see Spencer's note on II, iv, 19 (p. 214).

THE GRIEVES SHAKESPEARIAN
SCENE DESIGNS

BY

SYBIL ROSENFELD

During the quatercentenary celebrations at Stratford an exhibition was mounted at Hall's Croft by Mr John Carroll of designs by the Grieves purporting to be for performances of Shakespeare's plays. This exhibition first drew public attention to a collection of over six hundred Grieve stage designs in the University of London Library, from which a large proportion of the exhibits were drawn. A closer examination of this collection, however, reveals that only eight are actually assigned to Shakespeare plays in contemporary hands, though some others may well have been for performances for which the Grieves painted scenery. Unfortunately there is no evidence to substantiate these. Two hands are involved in the captions, excluding modern additions: one is small and generally in ink on the mounts; the other is large and either in ink or pencil, generally on the drawings themselves but occasionally also on the mounts. Even with the eight captioned designs a caveat must be entered: these are sketches and may have been considerably modified on the stage. *All's Well*, however, is cut out as a model and 'Shylock's House' is squared for enlargement.

This article is confined to the work of the Grieve family up to the death of J. H. Grieve in 1845. The later work of his son Thomas for Charles Kean at the Princess's in the 'fifties is well known and amply documented. According to Edward Fitzball[1] the family of J. H. Grieve and his two sons, Thomas and William, was remarkably united and the sons always looked up with deference to their father's talents. The three, working as a team, made Covent Garden famous for its scenic effects.

J. H. Grieve was first employed at Covent Garden in the winter of 1806 and his earliest known Shakespeare design is for *The Tempest*, brought out on 8 December that year (Plate III). This monochrome sketch in the Victoria and Albert Museum is inscribed, according to the catalogue,[2] 'First Sketch of Prospero's Cave. Painted C.G. for Jnº Kemb.' The playbill advertises Phillips, Whitmore, Hollogan and assistants as the painters so that Grieve must have been given this assignment as an assistant.[3] If the design is for John Philip Kemble it could only have been for this production and it therefore has claims to be the earliest extant one we have for a Shakespearian performance, antedating Capon's *Richard III*[4] by five years. The next *Tempest* at Covent Garden was for Macready in 1821 when Grieve also designed a Prospero's Cave along with ten other scenes; his partner Charles Pugh supplying the other four.[5]

In 1821, J. H. Grieve, who had been joined by his two sons, had three Shakespeare productions to his credit, the two others being *2 Henry IV* and *The Two Gentlemen of Verona*. This latter was in a musical version by Reynolds and Bishop who had already collaborated with Grieve in their *Comedy of Errors* in 1819. Scenically it was distinguished by a set of four new scenes of carnival in the square of Milan. The pretext for this is in the Duke's words:

> Come let us go: we will include all jars
> With trumpets, mirth, and rare solemnity,

duly adapted to 'Now, on to Milan; where will end all jars'. The four scenes were: (1) the four seasons and four elements in procession with Cleopatra's barge sailing down the Cydnus; (2) palace of the hours, morning, noon, evening and night by Wright; (3) an artificial mountain in the gardens of the Duke of Milan which exploded and discovered (4) the Temple of Apollo. This pageantry lasted half an hour, though subsequently curtailed, and necessarily involved much cutting of the text. Opinions on the scenery differed. The *Theatrical Observer*[6] considered it 'exceedingly splendid and beautiful' but the critic in *Drama*[7] was carping: he surmised that the scenery had been painted for some Venetian play and merely used for *The Two Gentlemen*. He found alarming errors at a time when topical accuracy was the vogue: 'There is a view of St Mark's palace, which is admirable in every respect but the church, which is a very indifferent representation' since its west front had been carelessly supplied with seven doors instead of the actual five. The error, he continues, could have been avoided if the scene painter had viewed Barker's panorama in the Strand.[8] Worse was to follow: 'The scene announced in the bills as the *grand square of Milan*' was guilty of including what was obviously the Venetian Doge's Palace with an opening leading to St Mark's. As for Cleopatra's galley, it 'filled the whole frame of the stage' and the writer concluded in a vein of admiration: 'this play has borne the arts of stage machinery and scenic decoration to the highest pitch'. The *Morning Post*,[9] after defending the musical version on the ground that it restored an unattractive play to popularity, added that the production was 'distinguished by one of the most gorgeous pageants that can be conceived...a representation of the Carnival with all its gaieties and amusements'. The audience is said to have risen to the spectacle and shaken the house with applause. Indeed it was so popular that it was later detached from the play and presented with the coronation spectacle from *The Exile*.

Very different was the Grieves' scenery for *1 Henry IV* which opened on 3 May 1824. This was the second of Charles Kemble's archaeological Shakespearian productions with costumes by Planché. The preceding *King John* of 1823 does not appear to have been accorded any new scenery, only new dresses. But for *Henry IV* the reconstruction was more thorough and the scenery was 'mostly new'. Six new scenes are listed on the playbill.[10] Of these we have the design for the third which is inscribed in the small hand on the mount: 'Hotspur's Camp—near Shrewsbury. C.G.' (Plate IV A). The tents are gaily painted in blue, crimson and yellow. This encampment scene together with the night scene of the inn yard and castle at Rochester were selected for special praise both by the *Examiner*[11] and the *Times*.[12] The second design is inscribed in the large hand 'Henry 4th. C.G.T. 1st Part. May 1824' and is of the King's canopied throne for the new scene in the King's tent (Plate IV B). It is painted in crimson and gold with green lined draperies, a blue band on top and yellow poles.

Archaeological exactitude was more suitable for the historical plays than for the legendary *Cymbeline*, produced on 5 May 1827, with Charles Kemble as Posthumus. The brilliantly coloured drawing for this is inscribed in the small hand on the mount 'Cymbeline. C.G. 1827' (Plate V A). It shows an iron-age Britain with a cromlech covered with a red and yellow drapery and surrounded by a stone circle; a hut, red shields and a harp. Of the many authorities quoted, Samuel Meyrick and Charles Hamilton Smith's *The Costume of the Original Inhabitants of the British Isles* (1815) has coloured plates illustrating stones similarly draped and the same type of hut.[13] Doubtless the Grieves made use of these engravings. But, as a critic pointed out, antiquarianism was not a satisfactory solution for the mixed atmosphere of the play:

We do know that there is at least a general correctness in most particulars in which mere antiquarian lore is concerned, with not unfrequently a very absurd departure from poetical sense and the intention of the bard. *Cymbeline* is a play of no time, only of place, so far as it is necessary to give to general humanities 'a local habitation and a name'. It blends in character the ancient Briton, and the modern Italian—the villain of the 16th century with the contemporaries of Augustus Caesar...We expect next to see legitimate authority produced for the dressing of Puck and authenticated wings allotted to Mustardseed.[14]

It is a well-deserved rebuke and leads one to wonder in what fashion the Italian scenes were set.

A design inscribed in the small hand on the mount 'Shylock's House' has nothing Venetian about it (Plate VB). It is squared for enlargement and may have been used for Charles Kemble's production in 1830 for which new scenery by the Grieves was advertised. One has only to compare it with the magnificent design for Charles Kean's production in 1858 to realize how much further William Telbin had gone in elaboration, splendour and topographical atmosphere. For Kean's production there is also a rather faint preliminary sketch for the last act inscribed 'Merchant of Venice. P.T. 1857' in pencil in the large hand on the mount (Plate Vc). If this is compared with Thomas Grieve's final version in the Victoria and Albert Museum, it will be seen that, whilst the elements of mansion, flight of steps, bridge and water are there in both, very considerable alterations were made in the arrangement of them on the stage.

For Charles Kemble's presentation of *Henry VIII* in 1831 the three Grieves were assisted by Finley, Thorne and Augustus Pugin who was a scene painter in his youth. The four new scenes were: the Palace at Westminster with a view of the Thames and Lambeth Palace; St Paul's and London Bridge as in 1533; the west front of the Abbey as it was left unfinished by Abbot Islip, and the interior of the choir of the Abbey looking up the nave. According to the catalogue of the Victoria and Albert Museum, their models for *Henry VIII* are for this production. However, they do not represent any of these scenes and are connected rather with Charles Kean's spectacular presentation at the Princess's in 1855 which introduced the panorama of London ending at Greenwich Palace. Among the models is a replica of this in eight parts.

After this antiquarian effort the managers returned to a fantastic, operatic hotch-potch for *All's Well* in 1832.[15] In Act I a masque was introduced called 'Oberon and Robin' which included, in addition to the name roles, the quartet of lovers from *A Midsummer Night's Dream*. The design for this masque is inscribed in the large hand on the mount: 'All [sic] Well That Ends Well. Masque of Robin Goodfellow' (Plate VIA). It is cut out in two parts, the proscenium arch and the moonlit backcloth with a temple, lake and trees thus representing a theatre in which the singing and dancing took place. The arch and columns are brown, the drapes red, and the background blue and green. The mixture was not much approved. The *Times*[16] pointed out that the operatic members of the cast were unfit to speak Shakespeare's verse and condemned the masque as having 'as little meaning as usual with such affairs'. The writer admitted that there was some good scenery 'and the dresses are splendid, tasteful and appropriate'. The *Morning Post*[17] agreed that the singers were inadequate and revealed that the play, which the critic considered 'the least worthy of Shakespeare's productions', was reduced by more than half and was obscured by the attempt to veil the 'indecency' of the plot. The masque 'though by no means what it might or should have been, was the most pleasing part of the performance'.

Speaking of the revival of *Hamlet* at Drury Lane in 1838, the *Times*[18] remarked how shameful it was that 'while thousands are thrown away on the ornaments and decorations of a paltry

French melodrama, the works of Shakespeare have hardly ever been honoured with a new dress or a new scene' and went on to commend the liberal outlay for this production. This may have been true of Drury Lane but it was not true of Covent Garden where the Grieves had hitherto worked. They moved to Drury Lane in October 1835 and *Hamlet* was the first play of Shakespeare's that they mounted there. The new scenes consisted of: a platform of the castle; another part of the platform; theatre in the court; Queen's closet; churchyard; state apartment. Of these the opening scene, the Queen's chamber and the churchyard were picked out for commendation. A monochrome design inscribed 'Hamlet's Castle' in the small hand on the mount (Plate VIB) may have been for this production as no new scenery is recorded for those of 1843 at Covent Garden or 1844 at Drury Lane. It is a curious design with a platform but no battlements and most un-Danish mountains in the distance. Two other designs[19] are inscribed in pencil at the back 'Hamlet TRDL'. The actual inscriptions on the mounts have been cropped and all that remains legible is 'TRDL' on one. These beautiful designs do not seem suitable for *Hamlet* as they are of a Russian-looking castle in the snow by starlight and a romanesque court-yard also in the snow.

The Grieves also painted for Charles Kean at Drury Lane *Richard III* and *Othello* in 1838. The new scenes for the former are listed by Odell.[20] It is most probable that two designs are for this production though there are no inscriptions. One shows the White Tower and gardens (no. 495) which would illustrate Act I, scene i, of the Cibber version, 'A View of the Keep and Gardens of the White Tower'. The other, of a large draped tent on the right, shows a recumbent figure and some blue apparitions in the opening of the tent at the back (no. 497). This would illustrate v, v, 'Richard's Tent', in the Cibber version where the ghosts appeared only to Richard. We know that when Edmund Kean played the role, the back of the tent opened and discovered the ghosts[21] and this piece of staging was probably retained by his son. It is possible that some models in the Victoria and Albert Museum (E. 2129-60-1927) may be connected with this production. If so, the scene of the White Tower is considerably modified. The funeral procession may be that for Henry VI and a vaulted chamber that in the White Tower. There are camp and tent scenes, especially two of an encampment beside a mill before and after a battle which may represent Bosworth Field. Some cut out figures of dead and wounded soldiers which belong to these scenes are marked on the back 'Richard III'. These models are a puzzle and are possibly replicas used by a juvenile theatre publisher as they are crudely drawn and dead looking, quite unlike the delicate, lively work of the Grieve sketches.

In the autumn of 1839 the Grieves returned to Covent Garden under the management of Mme Vestris and executed entirely new scenery for *Love's Labour's Lost* which she presented on 30 September. The following year they painted some new scenes for *Romeo and Juliet*. Though we can assign no actual designs to this production, we have five sketches of them made in the theatre by George Scharf.[22] They are of a Verona street for I, i; the ballroom; the balcony by moonlight; Juliet's chamber and the tomb for the last scene. The *Morning Post*[23] appreciated the expenditure of pains and labour on the dresses, appointments and scenery and considered the play 'beautifully illustrated and costumed'. The *Times*[24] went further: 'The dresses were very beautiful and the scenery, though not exclusively new, skilfully and artistically arranged so as to break through the more conventional manner in which this play is invariably produced.' The more's the pity that Jane Mordaunt was a complete failure as Juliet and Anderson made but a ranting Romeo.

On 30 April 1840, Mme Vestris and Mrs Nisbett appeared as the wives in *The Merry Wives of Windsor* with new scenery by the Grieves. For this we have a green-blue monochrome design inscribed in the large hand 'Herne's Oak' with an added annotation in pencil 'Moon 14 ft fr. Gdn &c. centre' (Plate VIc). Windsor Castle on its hill and the Thames can be discerned in the middle distance. Mme Vestris is said to have displayed her usual taste and judgment in the *mise en scène*:[25] 'The costumes and scenery were exceedingly beautiful and appropriate. A scene laid in Windsor Forest with the Castle in the distance, was a superb specimen of the art of scene-painting' and the scene of Ford's house was 'also beautifully painted'.

Later in the year the Grieves designed *A Midsummer Night's Dream* for Vestris. They remained under her management until Wallack took over Covent Garden in 1843, when they returned to Drury Lane. William Grieve died in 1844 and his father in 1845, leaving Thomas who later led the team of scene painters for Charles Kean's celebrated productions at the Princess's.

It must be borne in mind that many Shakespearian representations used what Planché condemned as 'make-shift' scenery whilst others were a mixture of stock with new scenes. On a few occasions completely new scenery and costumes were provided during the regime of the Grieves.

Shakespeare productions are always a guide to the taste of the times. The Grieves were called upon to satisfy the urge to instruct by means of antiquarian and topographical exactitude and the desire to illustrate the plays with spectacular scenes, some of which had little or nothing to do with the text. They were not always successful on the first count, as has been seen, but on the second they enraptured their contemporaries. Something of their brilliant effects comes through in the sketches for *Cymbeline* and *Henry IV* and of the soft beauty for which they were renowned in those for *The Merry Wives* and *All's Well*. Without doubt, they did a great deal to raise the standard of scenic embellishment of the plays in the first half of the nineteenth century.

© SYBIL ROSENFELD 1967

NOTES

1. *Thirty-five Years of a Dramatic Author's Life* (1859), II, 124.

2. Presumably on the back and no longer visible owing to mounting.

3. Only two payments are recorded to him in the Covent Garden Account Books (Egerton 2305) for 1806–7, the first being on 20 Dec. for £5. 19s. 0d. for 7 days' work and the second on 3 Jan. 1807, for 11 days, £9. 7s. 0d. (i.e. 17s. a day). He must at the beginning have been only an occasional painter.

4. In Leicester Public Library, reproduced in *Theatre Notebook*, x, opp. p. 118.

5. For list see G. C. D. Odell, *Shakespeare from Betterton to Irving* (1920), II, 160.

6. 30 Nov. 1821.

7. II, 45.

8. See H. A. Barker and T. Burford, *Description of the View of Venice, with a Representation of the Carnival, now Exhibiting in their Panorama* (1820).

9. 30 Nov. 1831.

10. Odell, *op. cit.* II, 174.

11. 10 May 1824.

12. 4 May 1824.

13. Pls. XI, XIII.

14. Unidentified cutting, Enthoven Collection, Victoria and Albert Museum.

15. For songs see Odell, *op. cit.* II, 145.

16. 12 Oct. 1832.

17. 13 Oct. 1832.
18. 9 Jan. 1838.
19. Nos. 493, 494.
20. *Op. cit.* II, 216.
21. *King Richard III with the descriptive notes recording Edmund Kean's Performance made by James H. Hackett,* ed. Alan Downer, Society for Theatre Research (1959), p. 90.
22. Enthoven Collection, reproduced in *Theatre Notebook,* XI (October 1956), pl. 2.
23. 17 March 1840.
24. 17 March 1840.
25. *Morning Post,* 1 May 1840.

SHAKESPEARE ON THE MODERN STAGE: PAST SIGNIFICANCE AND PRESENT MEANING

BY

ROBERT WEIMANN

I

The criticism of Shakespeare's plays on the modern stage is practised from so many (and some-times quite conflicting) angles and is so often overloaded by descriptive detail that, to begin with, it may seem worth while to ask some more general questions of method. During the last four decades literary criticism has so strenuously pleaded for standards of evaluation that the discussion of criteria by which to judge past plays on the contemporary stage may seem a trifle anachronistic. Theatre criticism, however, is not normally burdened by considerations of value or method; it is written so spontaneously, or with a view to reporting information, that it may appear almost ungrateful to look for more than a fair record of spontaneous impressions received on the evening of the performance. But if the performed play is by Shakespeare (or Racine, or Calderón) this, perhaps, is not enough. Of course it is difficult to generalize about the criticism of Shakespeare productions, since the professional theatre critic's approach is sometimes quite different from that of the Shakespearian scholar. The former, for instance, is perhaps more apt to be impressed by the originality or the unique style of a production. In things theatrical there is plenty of room for *tempérament*, but the originality of either director or critic can be an unreliable basis on which to assess his performance. It is true, no one wants to see the mediocre reproduction of once-famous formulas, and theatre (or criticism) without discovery is unthinkable. The nature and the object of such discovery are, however, a legitimate and, it may be claimed, urgent matter of debate.

On the other hand there is the theatre criticism of the Shakespearian scholar, and the first thing that should be said of this is that it absorbs a tiny fraction of his energies, which are usually quite swallowed up by his textual and historical research or his approach to Shakespeare's plays as dramatic *poems*. Although there are brilliant exceptions and although *Shakespeare Survey* as well as *Shakespeare Quarterly* have, with some success, attempted to cover both theatrical and academic aspects, the gap that still remains is surprisingly wide. If an outstanding scholar does write about the contemporary staging of Shakespeare's plays, his point of view is likely to be worlds apart from that of the professional critic or, for that matter, of the producer. Instinctively (and it is difficult not to sympathize with him) he feels called upon to defend the Shakespearian text against alterations in the script, transposition of scenes and over-elaborate theatrical effects. Against the producer's argument that Shakespeare has to be 'vitalized' (Tyrone Guthrie) and that modern audiences 'have to be persuaded that Shakespeare is anything but a dead classic without modern urgency or personal appeal' (Margaret Webster) his reply is that of a sceptic historian: 'There is no use in pretending that the Renaissance play is not a

113

Renaissance play. It may be true that there is no audience for the Renaissance play, but it is difficult to see how this may be determined unless it is occasionally performed.'[1] From this, quite a different frame of reference emerges: Shakespeare's plays are considered 'persuasive and vital in their own right, as well as self-interpretive' (Alfred Harbage). The standards of evaluation are definitely not the director's originality or vitality, but rather the Shakespearian text as it stands, 'Shakespeare's work as it is' (Kenneth Muir). The objective text is stressed as against its subjective reading, the historical play as against its modern interpretation, and its past significance as against its present adaptation.

This alternative is of course too neat a simplification, but perhaps it will serve to suggest that in Shakespearian theatre criticism and production there are today at least two extreme points of reference: the historical (and scholarly) and the contemporary (or experimental). While the latter is concerned with the *interpretation* of Shakespeare, the former feels concern over the interpretation of *Shakespeare*. Each represents a different system of values. The concept of authenticity, for instance, can be given two entirely different directions. The scholars, although they do not wish to see archaeological productions, would presumably consider them authentic in so far as they achieve the tone and tenor of Shakespeare's theatre: Hamlet will be a historical figure, the play's message an Elizabethan one in the sense that its past significance has priority to its present meaning. The 'interpretive' producer (who may occasionally be, like Mr G. Wilson Knight, a literary critic) has a different concept of authenticity which is primarily related not to the Elizabethan theatre, but to the modern sensibility that the play is meant to evoke. From this angle, a production would be 'authentic' as long as it achieves the tone and tenor of our own age: Hamlet will be a modern symbol and the play's message a contemporary one in the sense that its present meaning has priority over its past significance. Hence results 'a vital recreation' which entitles the producer to 'a development in a new medium of some central idea of wholeness in the original...Such understanding gives him full powers to cut, adapt, even, on rare occasions, transpose, according to circumstances; he has to consider his stage, his company, his audience'.[2]

Actually, the two points of reference may not be so diametrically opposed, but the contradiction involved is an objective one. No matter what the approach is, there remains the almost four-hundred-year-old script in the hands of modern actors; on the one hand the author's Elizabethan text and meaning, on the other the producer's modern understanding and interpretation. The resulting contradiction has to be resolved, and the way this is done determines the nature of the production in one of its most important aspects.[3] There is no getting away from this inevitable tension between the Elizabethan and the modern points of view, and no one-sided solution is feasible. The most learned and historically-minded producer cannot physically re-create the Globe; he would still have to do with the conditions of the modern theatre, its twentieth-century audience and actors and their social relationships that are quite different from those which, in Shakespeare's public theatre, then constituted part of the play's meaning.

As we can neither produce nor experience the plays quite as Burbage's company and its audiences did, it may—especially to theatre people—appear tempting to dispense with the historical perspective altogether. Why not consider Shakespeare as our contemporary? Why not so treat the plays that their various settings and figures appear as images of our own world, our friends and enemies? No doubt it gives a pleasant thrill of recognition to observe teddy boys among the Montagues, or to see a Roman mob as proletarian revolutionaries. Theatre folk are practically minded people: if Hamlet can be viewed as an angry young man, Brutus as an existentialist, Macbeth as a fascist, and Lear's realm as a kingdom of absurdity, then, surely, Shakespeare has come to life again, and the gap between the Elizabethan theatre and the modern world has at last been closed.

This kind of argument is extremely persuasive, especially when an outstanding artist lends his hand to give it a living reality. In the last resort, however, this solution poses more problems than it answers. No matter how consistent or sensitive the modernized version will be, there still remains the Shakespearian text whose verbal and poetic structures are conditioned by a different system of reference. Now it is not a question of mere academic pedantry, and it is not to claim any superiority in learning, when one wishes to see this historical order of things respected; for the historical element of the play is nothing external, but has gone into the very essence of its composition and meaning. It informs the parts and the whole, with all that their relationship stands for. The play's maximum effectiveness today depends on an awareness of its past genetics; its supreme integration as a work of art can never be achieved *against* the 'form and pressure' of the age which gave it birth and shape.

Since it is just as impossible to perform Shakespeare without an interpretation as it is to have an interpretation without Shakespeare, we cannot have either a genuine Elizabethan production (and this already contained an interpretation of the text) or one which makes us believe that *Hamlet* is a modern play. Today *any* Shakespeare staging has to come to terms with the tension between Renaissance values and modern evaluations. But this contradiction is not necessarily frustrating, and it may well be said that it constitutes an important element in the resulting production. Viewed from the angle of the drama as a work of art, this contradiction involves an inevitable friction of the various functions of the drama—the friction, that is, between the expressive and the affective aspects, between the significance of what Shakespeare *expressed* in plot and character, and the changing impact of this on the *affect* of the contemporary spectator. (The expression and representation of honour, chastity, and degree, for instance, may affect a modern audience in a different way from an Elizabethan one.) Yet these two aspects have to be re-integrated if the rift between the drama's past genesis and its present reception is to be overcome. From an abstract point of view this, then, is an essential task of theatrical interpretation: the expressed content has to find its affective equivalent, and this involves, on a different level, a corresponding correlation between the mimesis and the moral qualities of the play. To re-create the *mimetic* and the *expressive* dimensions is impossible without reference to Shakespeare's world and his intentions; to re-assess their *affective* and *moral* effects is impossible without reference to our audience and *Wirklichkeit*. Thus, in the contemporary Shakespearian theatre, both the modern and the Elizabethan world interact; a modern perspective confronts a Renaissance vision, and to ignore the friction of these two different view-points is not helpful. On the contrary, the tension between the Elizabethan vision and our perspective must be understood in order to be turned into a source of strength.

For the director (and for the critic who evaluates his work) the question, then, is not *whether or not* to accept both worlds as points of reference, but rather *how* to relate them so as to obtain the maximum effect. To put it like this may appear provocatively superficial, but to resolve the contradiction one cannot minimize the conflicting elements when each is—in its different world— so inevitable and necessary. The 'maximum effect', then, can mean no more and no less than this: to have the play as 'Elizabethan' as possible and, at the same time, as modern as is feasible; to have as much of the historical and as much of the contemporary merged into a new unity.

If this is to mean more than merely to have it both ways, the relationship between the Elizabethan vision and its modern perspective will have to be indicated with greater precision. For reasons that are, or will become, obvious, Shakespeare's text and not the 'modern sensibility' will have to be the initial point of reference.[4] To have the moral before the mimesis recalls the methods of propaganda, not art; and only when we understand the dramatist's intention and expression can we achieve the drama's maximum effect. But merely to contrast the various functions in this way makes things far too abstract and cannot adequately define the quality of the relationship between Elizabethan values and their modern interpretations. In order to grasp its dialectic, it is as well to remember that it is not entirely a case of opposites. On the contrary, it would be a grave mistake to overlook those many points of contact and identity, where Shakespeare's Renaissance and popular values can today be considered valid. This area of identity may of course differ radically between a Marxist production and one directed from the premises of Jacques Maritain's neo-scholasticism. But if the Renaissance heritage is not repudiated, there is bound to be a wide range of common territory, in which Shakespeare's views are as valid as on the first night in the Globe. Nor is this common territory, which of course is also one of humanity and derives from man's anthropological status, confined to the Renaissance tradition. We are all, Shakespeare, his producers and his critics, characters in history; our own points of reference are, like Shakespeare's, products of history. In this, our present values emerge from the same historical process which is both reflected in, and accelerated by, Shakespeare's contribution. This is even more obvious in the history of literature, which can only be written in reference to a scheme of values that (among other things) has to be abstracted from its great objects, including Shakespeare's dramas. Their greatness has been confirmed by the very contribution they have made to furnishing us with criteria by which to judge, and to judge not only modern plays but also the history of the drama as a whole.

As this area of identity may be accepted as given, the relationship between Shakespeare's vision and its modern perspectives cannot simply be described as one of conflict or opposition. The difference between his world and ours is obvious enough, but it does not exclude some kind of concurrence. As Dr Kettle has remarked, 'the best way to emphasize the value of Shakespeare in *our* changing world is to see him in *his*, recognizing that the two worlds, though very different, are at the same time a unity'.[5] This unity is at the basis of all our veneration for Shakespeare; without it, the impact of his work would not be possible. At the same time, this unity does not preclude a contradiction which is at the basis of all our conflicting interpretations. In very much over-simplified terms: the unity creates the need of our interpretations of *Shakespeare*; the contradiction accounts for the need of our *interpretations* of Shakespeare. But actually each is contained in the other, and the production as a whole can only succeed when these two aspects are inextricably welded into one. (In itself the production can of course, according to its point of view, either enhance or reduce the sphere of unity or the area of contradiction, but it can never entirely annihilate either.)

Once this relationship (although here still oversimplified) is understood more deeply, the theatre criticism of Shakespeare's plays has gained at least two negative standards of evaluation:

the modernized Shakespeare is no more acceptable than the museum version. This may not be saying anything new, but perhaps it helps to recover certain assumptions which might prove acceptable and practicable to both the Shakespeare director and the Shakespeare scholar. If the rift between them could thus be narrowed, the audience might be saved both embarrassment and boredom. Richard III, then, need not become Goebbels in order to convince, nor would it be necessary, as Martin Walser thinks it is, to produce the play 'in order to show us what things were like formerly' (*um uns zu sagen, wie es früher war*).[6] If the past can be conceived, neither in its identity with, nor in its isolation from, the present, a meaningful relationship could evolve which might also be *theatrically* effective. This needs neither textual alterations nor scenic transpositions but involves interpretation in the sense of selection and emphasis. No topical effects are wanted, but a sense of history which can discover permanence in change but also change in seeming permanence; the past in the present but also the present in the past. Hence the 'timeless' would result through a sense of time and history. It is in this sense that Shakespeare is 'for all time' precisely because, as Jonson also said, he was the 'soule of the Age'. In this view, Shakespeare's Elizabethan vision can be made to yield a contemporary meaning. Its past significance was achieved because, at the time, it was contemporary and *then* incorporated the experience of the present. The meaning of Shakespeare today can only be discovered through this past present, or that part of it which—although past—is still present and meaningful in a contemporary frame of reference. Thus, past significance and present meaning engage in a relationship which, in its interdependence, may illuminate either—the past as against the present and the present against the background of the past.

II

These points of method and evaluation open up a host of practical questions which do not very well bear a generalized treatment. Instead, two examples may perhaps serve which, despite their obvious limitations, can illustrate some of the more immediate problems of producing Shakespeare's meaning from a specifically modern perspective. The illustration is taken from the GDR, the play is *Hamlet*, the theatres being Deutsches Theater, Berlin (formerly Max Reinhardt's) and Städtische Theater, Karl-Marx-Stadt. (See Plates VII–VIII.) Their productions of *Hamlet* were first presented in 1964 and were still running in 1966. Nor were they the only productions of *Hamlet* in this country. Statistics for the 1964–5 theatrical season revealed that Shakespeare was played more often than any single German or any contemporary author: sixteen plays were shown in 45 productions, totalling more than 790 performances, including Brecht's adaptation of *Coriolanus*. (See Plates IX–X.) Among the tragedies, *Romeo and Juliet* saw 6 productions with 90 performances, the only one seriously to rival *Hamlet* which remained (as could be predicted) the most intensively discussed single play: three of its six different productions were partially televised, with interspersed commentaries by their respective directors. Besides Schlegel's classical text, two modern translations were used (by Rudolf Schaller at Karl-Marx-Stadt and, at Greifswald, by Hamburger and Dresen) and both proved remarkable for their stage-effectiveness.

Against this background the Berlin production (directed by Wolfgang Heinz) has to be seen. Even before its flexibly managed stage was revealed in black, with a huge tapestry in the rear displaying a Boschian vision of a world 'out of joint', a reading of the play's story was printed out like a subtitle on an over-sized playbill attached to the front curtain. There it was announced as 'a tragedy which shows how Hamlet, called upon to avenge the murder of his father, comes to learn that he lives in a murderous world; how he begins to understand that this world has to be changed, and how and why he is defeated'. Although this synopsis seemed reminiscent of some of Brecht's epic devices, the general style of the production was more conservative, yet straightforward and lucid. As the first scene unrolled, it became clear that the 'state' was shown 'to be disjoint and out of frame' (I, ii, 20) with 'some strange eruption' (I, i, 69) imminent. Against this Hamlet (Horst Drinda) entered as the representative of a new era, and his task was not conceived to be premature. Nor was his frame of mind that of a coward or a weakling. On the contrary, his capacity for action and self-defence was stressed; this was especially so in the 'To be or not to be' speech which was delivered with sword in hand by a man determined to meet the danger of a possible ambush. Nor did the physical preparedness exclude the inward concentration and self-searching; these were brought out by the other great monologues, and also in his encounter with the ghost: the ghost, in shining black armour, stood right behind Hamlet who, in a trance of intuition and surprise, himself spoke the words that are assigned to the spirit. But as the Prince was so noble in mind and full of fortitude, why then did he delay the 'eruption' that was so ripe? The answer, as the production suggested it, was not quite convincing: Hamlet's problem turned out to be that of how to use the force which had been known to him only by its abuse. He shrinks away from it, searches for a bloodless solution and thereby misses his opportunity. Feudal Fortinbras, the unprincipled warrior who has no such scruples, can take over.

Although this concept was brought across with an admirable intelligence which allowed for both precision and pathos, the production got itself entangled into several contradictions. The Danish court, Horatio and the soldiers were all conceived in close reference to the Renaissance text. So was Hamlet, except for the interpretation of his central dilemma. To discuss the strategic use of force may yield excellent lessons, but here it amounted to a modern perspective which did not square with the Renaissance vision. It was, partly, a case of moral versus mimesis, and the modern interpretation could not find room enough in the structure of the play itself. Consequently, two passages from *Measure for Measure* had to be grafted upon Schlegel's text, and the play had to come to an end despite, rather than through, Fortinbras's arrival. (If you assume that Shakespeare's age is one in which 'the ruling feudal class' is ripe to be overthrown, a triumphant feudal usurper must indeed be embarrassing.) But as the *historical* assumption was questionable in the first place, its *dramatic* correlative could not be discovered in terms of Shakespearian mimesis and expression. Consequently, in this aspect a modern perspective (and the contemporary 'affect') had to be produced against, rather than from, the Renaissance intention and expression.

Apart from that, the Berlin production contained many admirable things: the fine ensemble acting and a swift sense of movement produced beautiful results in such moments as the play within the play, which—like most of the larger court scenes—were satisfying in many respects. In this, the larger stage of the Deutsches Theater had a natural advantage over the much smaller one in Karl-Marx-Stadt. There the director (Hans Dieter Mäde) had to break up the proscenium line in order to provide for an additional entrance area; but in spite of the utmost economy the lively movement of the players' full orchestra had to be toned down almost to the requirements of a chamber recital. In the midst of this, sudden flashes of strength had a powerful, but sometimes inordinate effect. This was all the more so since Hamlet (Jürgen Hentsch) was most consistently seen as the Renaissance prince and Wittenberg humanist. This indeed was the courtier, the soldier, the scholar; not an existentialist or a frustrated revolutionary, but one whose historical stature allowed subdued contemporary pathos. The breadth of the generalization was such that Hamlet emerged as a Renaissance representative of values which—although utopian at the time—have remained relevant to this day.

These values were defined entirely in terms of Hamlet's dramatic speech and action. In this, the various relationships were extremely well differentiated: his attitude towards Horatio, the soldiers, the gravedigger and Fortinbras's captain had none of the flippancy, arrogance and cynicism that he displayed at court. This differentiation was based on a careful reading of the text, and its use as a means of defining the character's personality yielded a result both immediate and convincing. Nothing was vague; for at Court Hamlet challenged forces of adversity that were shown (and that he knew) to be dangerous and frightfully real: Polonius was less of a fool (though not nearly so brilliantly acted as in Berlin); Osric more vicious than ridiculous and, above all, Rosencrantz and Guildenstern had nothing clownish about them: two clever students going in for a courtly kind of careerism (hence resulted superb drama in the recorders-scene!).

Thus, Hamlet's tragedy developed not from any modernized dilemma, but from a contradiction, built up from the text itself, between his advanced view of man (as defined in monologues and relationships) and the over-mighty courtly powers that thwarted his plans and ideas about the world and how 'to set it right' (I, v, 190). To bring out this meaning, not a single line had to be altered, and no scene was transposed or forced into some topical context. In that sense, it remained a Renaissance play whose modern perspective was achieved not by ignoring or distorting but by probing its historical content more deeply. This implied an approach to history as a living continuum; in this view, the Renaissance world could be brought into a meaningful relationship with the present, and Elizabethan pathos had not to be disowned as modern bathos. Hamlet was no 'immature' neurotic attempting 'to escape from the complexities of adult living', but was shown as a hero, and the reserve and the consistency with which this was done were admirable. The surprising thing was that, from a purely theatrical point of view, it was all so rewarding. The director's hand was omnipresent, yet unobtrusive; his concept simple, but not superficial. The absence of anything sensational or merely pretentious was an engaging feature in an ensemble of actors whose strength was a perfect *unisono* rather than the *solo* virtuosity of any one star.

Despite the considerable difference in approach and the various degrees of success, the Berlin and the Karl-Marx-Stadt productions both drew from similar areas of strength, but they also shared a common bias. As indicated, the *strength* stemmed from a willingness to take Hamlet's humanist background seriously and to explore the position and the dilemma of the hero in terms of his contrasting social relationships. The resulting figure was neither an 'ambassador of death' (as G. Wilson Knight sees him) nor the 'fundamentally immature' adolescent (that L. C. Knights has observed).[7] On the other hand, and this was the *bias*, the role did not reveal the presumable bases in the text from which these symbolical and psychological verdicts are so questionably generalized. These premises are, one would suggest, neither symbolical nor consistently psychological, but may partly be found in the tradition of 'mad' release and reckless licence which—as the Prince's reference to himself as 'John-a-dreams', etc., underlines—was a popular and quite anachronistic element. As such, it goes hand in hand with his incessant word-play, his richly proverbial speech, and his antic version of 'impertinency' (*King Lear*, IV, vi, 175) which both reflect and provoke a certain loss of illusion, a heightened awareness of the audience, and that 'exaggerated play-acting', which Mr Knights interprets psychologically and as a 'quality of moral relaxation'. All these elements, which find a surprising echo in later Vice-figures such as Haphazard,[8] form an important aspect of the hero's dramaturgy, and in both performances this aspect was quite ignored. Although at Karl-Marx-Stadt the proscenium line was broken up and although this did establish an easier contact with the audience, the main actor had none of that theatrical awareness or that clownish licence which are part of Hamlet's 'antic disposition'. In Berlin, Hamlet's rashness was perhaps more forcibly represented and occasionally he did seem to address the audience, but his theatrical sense of 'relaxation' and 'play-acting' did not come across. To be sure, it took a Shakespeare to merge the humanist and the popular dramatic traditions, and the modern theatre may (like so much modern criticism) shy away from the sheer magnitude of the problem that this incommensurable synthesis poses. Still, it is an outcome of the Elizabethan 'gallimaufry' (Lyly), and to take its past significance seriously may be one way of discovering the present range and meaning of Shakespeare's universality.

© ROBERT WEIMANN 1967

NOTES

1. Alfred Harbage, 'The Role of the Shakespearean Producer', *Shakespeare Jahrbuch*, XCI (1955), 171; see also Kenneth Muir, 'Some Shakespearean Productions in England 1960–61', *Shakespearovski Sbornik* (Moscow, 1961), pp. 349–56.

2. G. Wilson Knight, *Principles of Shakespearian Production* (Penguin ed. 1949), pp. 35 ff.

3. To be sure, it would be an over-simplification to see the problem merely in terms of past significance and present values. There always was, and will be, the problem of how to translate a verbal imagination into visual reality. To proceed from letter to sound, from word to gesture, from text to performance must involve interpretation—in the Elizabethan playhouse just as on the modern stage. In this sense, the Elizabethan production must have been an interpretation. Accordingly the modern producer of a Shakespeare play has to face a similar problem, only *his* interpretation has to come to terms with the *additional* tension between the Elizabethan and the modern points of view.

4. Here one need scarcely plead for an infinite respect—based on knowledge—for the world's greatest dramatist; Shakespeare cannot be improved. And even though Brecht's dictum may be true ('wir können den Shakespeare ändern, wenn wir ihn ändern können'), any attempt to change the script is to create something different in the sense that *The Three-Penny Opera* is different from *The Beggar's Opera*. The resulting play is no longer Gay's or Shakespeare's, and hence cannot illuminate the relationship between a historical dramatic vision and its modern perspective in production.

5. *Shakespeare in a Changing World*, ed. Arnold Kettle (1964), p. 10.

6. Martin Walser, 'Für einen neuen Realismus', *Theater heute*, Januar 1965; this gifted modern dramatist suggests, 'Shakespeares Stücke nur als Vergangenheit zu spielen'!

7. G. Wilson Knight, *The Wheel of Fire* (1959 repr.), p. 58; L. C. Knights, *Explorations* (Penguin ed. 1964), p. 81.

8. *Apius and Virginia*, in *A Select Collection of Old English Plays*, Hazlitt–Dodsley, IV (1874), 118. The echo, which I have not seen mentioned, is worth noting: The antic, quibbling, proverb-mongering 'mad' (p. 148) Haphazard refers to himself as 'a scholar', 'a student, or else a country clown', or 'a fishmonger', and 'a dreamer, a drumble' (p. 118). Prince Hamlet, also a scholar, calls himself 'a rogue and peasant slave' (II, ii, 543) and his phrase 'John-a-dreams' recalls (as J. Dover Wilson's note suggests) 'John a Droynes, a country bumpkin'.

SHAKESPEARE IN BRAZIL

BY

BARBARA HELIODORA C. DE M. F. DE ALMEIDA

The short and sad story of Shakespeare in Brazil is, by and large, the story of a few translations that often are either un-Shakespearian or not stageworthy (or both, which is worse). The burden of the rhymed alexandrine weighs heavily on Brazil's literary and dramatic past (which is only natural, since all its literary vogues come from Portugal, which had them from France). The problem still exists, and we shall see that in the Brazilian theatre Shakespeare has been more a patron saint than a fellow-worker.

The first professional performances of Shakespeare in the country date from about 1835, in the form of Portuguese translations and adaptations of French adaptations. The records do not speak of *Romeo and Juliet* but of ' *The Tombs at Verona* or *Juliet and Romeo* ', and of ' *The Terrible Effects of Hatred and Vengeance* or *Juliet and Romeo* ', as well as of ' *Coriolanus in Rome* ' and, somewhat later, of ' *Ducis's Othello* '.

The first actor to be identified with Shakespearian roles—and the only one, in fact, for over a century—was João Caetano dos Santos, the most famous name of the Brazilian theatrical past. Surprisingly (or, to be more precise, regrettably) enough, although in 1835 João Caetano is said to have been acting in a direct translation from the English original of *Hamlet*, by 1840 he was using Ducis's adaptation, which the public found much more enjoyable than the sombre tones of Shakespeare's tragedy. In short, it will hardly be news to anyone that Ducis was historically justified.

Even then, however, there were exceptions to the rule, people who knew their Shakespeare and who could tell that Ducis was not up to the Master. Among them was Luis Carlos Martins Penna, the major Brazilian playwright of the nineteenth century, who among his many delightful comedies has one called *The Jealousies of a Footsoldier* (*Os Ciumes de um Pedestre*) in which the excesses of the Ducis *Othello* are ridiculed by further underlining of morbid, ridiculous jealousy. In the same one-act play Martins Penna gives evidence of his knowledge of Shakespeare by solving a rather intricate plot by means of the arrival of 'three argosies richly laden'.

But for a century after João Caetano's unsure attempts the rest is indeed silence as far as Brazilian productions are concerned. It was the visitors who came to Rio and São Paulo from Europe that kept the Shakespearian fires burning, always with a French or Italian accent, since it was not until 1962 that for the first time Brazil was (somewhat dubiously) honoured with the visit of English professional actors.

Most of the big names, thanks to the reversal of seasons, came to South America for their summer vacations throughout the second half of the nineteenth century and the regularity of these visits lasted until the years between the two world wars. The fact that they gave performances did not alter the essential spirit of these pleasure cruises. So Brazil saw most of the big French and Italian names in Shakespeare even if perhaps not always in top form: Salvini, Rossi, Zacconi, Bernhard doing *Hamlet*, Novelli. Alexander Moissi also came, as well as Jean-Louis Barrault, the Stabile di Genoa and the Piccolo Teatro di Milan in more recent years. And the big names of the Portuguese theatre at the end of the last century and the beginning of the present one also contributed their quota of Shakespeare on the Brazilian stage. It must be noticed also that quite often the performing visitors were surprised by the extremely demanding standards of both the public and the critics.

The long Shakespearian silence on the stage does not mean, however, that he was unknown or forgotten. Practically all major Brazilian writers read, quote or echo him, and surely he is nowhere as consistently and enchantingly present as in the works of Machado de Assis, the exquisite novelist now being discovered, through translations, by the English-speaking world.

Shakespeare has also been present as the patron saint of practically every significant stage of development of the Brazilian theatre. It was in the 'thirties that the profound changes began which would eventually reshape the Brazilian theatre so thoroughly that it is unlikely that one could so easily identify, anywhere else, two 'generations' of actors, authors, directors and set-designers. So clear-cut is this division, in fact, that it creates overwhelming problems when casting parts for characters who are 45 years old, or more.

One of the basic features of this renewal was a movement of amateur theatre, and in 1938 the 'Teatro do Estudante do Brasil', led by Paschoal Carlos Magno, a Brazilian diplomat deeply impressed by the English theatre, presented, as its first production, *Romeo and Juliet*. It was an epoch-making event, even though not a great reading of the text. The Onestaldo de Pennafort translation, though occasionally over-sentimental, worked better than most on stage, and has been done more often by amateurs than any other play in the canon.

Still the professional theatre did not dare to do Shakespeare and in 1948 it was again the students who shook the Brazilian theatre with an extraordinarily successful and romantic *Hamlet*. The translation by Tristão da Cunha has a few felicitous passages, but the actor is often defeated by this twentieth-century translator's misplaced scholarship which attempts to render Shakespeare into seventeenth-century Portuguese. Nonetheless, the sheer impact of the talent of Sergio Cardoso, who played the title-role, was enough to make up for a pseudo-archaic translation, assorted periods in costume, an appallingly romantic line of direction given by the German Hoffmann Harnisch, and the obvious lack of technique on the part of all the actors. This amateur *Hamlet* crowded an 800-seat theatre for fifty performances, becoming, overnight, the major cultural event of Rio. Both production and actors were over-praised, but the importance of the performance is undeniable; the general picture was no doubt hectic, but the results were extremely healthy. It was from then on that Shakespeare began to gather strength to set himself up in business in the Brazilian theatre. In 1949, with a much smaller measure of success (having no further major talents to reveal), the Teatro do Estudante staged *Macbeth*, *A Midsummer Night's Dream* and a new version of *Romeo and Juliet*. Many actors from the *Hamlet* cast abandoned their proposed careers as doctors, lawyers or dentists to turn professional, opened their activities with a slightly altered production of the same play, and still met with considerable success.

The professional stage, meanwhile, had taken giant steps with the creation, in São Paulo, of a stable, privately-owned group named Teatro Brasileiro de Comédia. Franco Zampari, a wealthy man of industry, decided to finance a high-quality permanent repertory theatre, and to this day the splendour of the early years of the 'TBC', as it was always called, is mentioned with awe. The 'TBC', for the first time, permitted professionals to mature while acting together, and naturally enough they thought of doing Shakespeare. The problem of translation came up, and a new *Macbeth* was commissioned from Manuel Bandeira, a major name in modern Brazilian poetry. The result is not as fully satisfactory as one might expect, but it is still many cuts above what had gone before. Unfortunately, even though it was commissioned a good ten years ago, the translation has yet to be tested on stage: by the time it was ready the 'TBC' people were discovering, much to everybody's amazement, that, if one spends a great deal of money over a long period of time, eventually one may run out of it. And soon after, the group began to break up: too many (for Brazil) 'big' names had been brought together. At least two new companies, formed by actors leaving the TBC, started their activities with Shakespeare: Sergio Cardoso again played *Hamlet* professionally, using a new translation by Pericles Eugenio da Silva Ramos, which is uncannily faithful to the original in everything except poetic and dramatic quality: using unrhymed alexandrines Mr Ramos falls prey to his considerable erudition, and the result is a scholarly work that actors cannot speak and audiences often cannot understand at one hearing. Its success was very limited.

The other set of TBC alumni that went in search of Shakespeare was composed of Adolfo Celi, director, Tonia Carrero, actress, and Paulo Autran, actor. They commissioned a new translation of *Othello* from Onestaldo de Pennafort; he worked under pressure and the result is adequate but not brilliant. The production was exceptionally well received and ran for over 130 consecutive performances in Rio alone, finding a similar welcome when the new company presented it in São Paulo.

This was 1956, and—whether it was the poor quality of the translations, the inadequacy of training, or the severe economic limitations of the Brazilian theatre—it was not until the year of the Quatercentenary that any professional group attempted Shakespeare again. The state-owned theatre company of the southern state of Paraná was the only professional group to stage Shakespeare in 1964, and it was a good thing to see the Millor Fernandes translation of *The Taming of the Shrew*, ready since 1961, finally get its chance to be tested on stage. The result was highly satisfactory for both the actors and the public; since the translator was not tampering with a major poetical text, whatever liberties he took with *The Shrew* seemed fully justified, and for once the public became aware of the fact that one may laugh while seeing Shakespeare. After a tremendous success in Paraná, the production was in Rio for just a few days, and was very well received. Other than that it was the amateurs who honoured Shakespeare: *A Midsummer Night's Dream* received two fairly good productions (again a new translation, by Maria da Sauda de Cortesão, which sometimes fails to work because it betrays the translator's Portuguese-from-Portugal diction); *Macbeth* was attempted in Pernambuco and Goiás; various other people presented scenes from the play, and both in Rio and São Paulo, among numerous other events, series of lectures on 'Shakespeare and his time' were given with massive attendances.

In 1965 another professional production of the Millor Fernandes *Shrew* was presented in São Paulo and ran for eight months, winning any number of prizes, and again driving some people to think that after all Shakespeare might be a good box-office name. (See Plate XI.)

In 1965, when Rio was celebrating its own quatercentenary, a young producer asked Mr Carlos Lacerda, then governor of the city-state of Guanabara (Rio) and a highly controversial political figure, to translate *Julius Caesar*. Unfortunately Mr Lacerda's good knowledge of

English proved an inadequate basis for a Shakespearian attempt. The whole play is done in prose, and not very attractive prose at that, which is surprising coming from a man whose worst enemies will acknowledge that he is a first-rate political orator. The translation, actually, was not staged until early 1966 in São Paulo. Antunes Filho, who had directed the highly successful *Shrew* of 1965, was not as felicitous with *Julius Caesar*, and the production turned out to be both an artistic and a commercial failure.

In spite of all this, Shakespeare is not unknown in Brazil; and theatre people discuss him so often that one might think, by listening to them, that he was very frequently performed on the Brazilian stage.

New translations will necessarily appear, as the profession and its training mature, and as larger audiences are formed. And while he waits for his cue to go on stage Shakespeare will be carrying on as patron saint.

RECENT SHAKESPEARE PERFORMANCES IN ROMANIA

BY

ALEXANDRU DUŢU

The celebration of the 400th anniversary of Shakespeare's birth and of the 350 years from his death occasioned various manifestations in Romania which showed the great interest of audiences and readers for the creations of the dramatist who continues to speak profoundly to mankind. The plays performed reveal, at the same time, interesting new ways to comprehend and to evaluate the work of 'the only Shake-scene' so vividly present in our age.

The Shakespearian productions of the last two years (1964–6) cannot be looked upon as an exceptional moment in Shakespeare's destiny in our country; his plays have been performed, almost without interruption, for the last hundred years, and in 1912 our great poet, Tudor Arghezi, could write, with great reason—at the end of a captivating competition between three interpreters of the past—'Hamlet is indeed an old friend of the Bucharest playgoer'.[1] But the present is of special interest because it reveals a tendency manifested, especially in the last two decades: that of working towards an entire and deep knowledge of Shakespeare's plays and, also, of increasing their popularity with the large mass of spectators. Certainly, the modern mass media—the channel of the radio and above all TV—assure the performances an audience that Shakespeare did not dream of, but I am referring especially to performances in conditions intended by Shakespeare: within the 'wooden O', in a theatre that allows the playgoer intimate contact with the living personage 'that struts and frets his hour upon the stage'. The last two years carried on the process of spreading the knowledge of Shakespeare through the intermediary of a large network of National and State Theatres.

Without giving boring statistics, I should like to set forth some important facts. In 1964–6, *Twelfth Night* was performed at the National Theatre in Craiova, the old capital of the 'Oltenian Bani', at the State Theatre of the beautiful town of Banat, Timişoara, at the National Theatre of the old capital of Moldavia (Iassy), at the State Theatre in the same region, Bacău, at the State Theatre of the town situated in the centre of Transylvania, Turda, and at the State Theatre of the miners' centre in the Jiu Valley, Petroşani.

The audience at our great harbour, Constantza, those of Craiova, as well as the Maghyar audience, who have at their disposal Maghyar State Theatres at Cluj and at Satu Mare, were equally delighted with *The Taming of the Shrew*.

A very special success was obtained by the production of *The Comedy of Errors* at Lucia Sturza Bulandra Theatre[2] in Bucharest, a play performed also at the State Theatre in Baia Mare, a town in the north of Transylvania, and at the German State Theatre of the old walled city of Sibiu.

The Two Gentlemen of Verona was performed at Craiova, in the Moldavian town Bîrlad, and in the big industrial centre of Banat, Reşiţa, and *Much Ado about Nothing* was performed at the State Theatre of the Danube harbour, Galatz.

As You Like It in a Liviu Ciulei stage production at Lucia Sturza Bulandra Theatre was a brilliant success and so, too, was *The Merry Wives of Windsor* in Lucian Giurchescu's stage production at the National Theatre 'I. L. Caragiale' in Bucharest; attended by tens of thousands of spectators, the two plays were amply commented on by dramatic critics. *The Winter's Tale* was also performed in Bucharest at Barbu Delavrancea Theatre, while *Measure for Measure* was produced in Petroşani.

The immortal love story *Romeo and Juliet* could not be omitted during this time, and, differently interpreted by the producers, it was performed at Galatz, in the big oil city, Ploieşti, in Baia Mare and in Timişoara at the German State Theatre.

Richard III was first presented on the stage at the National Theatre 'V. Alecsandri' in Iassy. Then the character was played at the Theatre 'C. I. Nottara' in Bucharest, by the veteran actor George Vraca, who realized in this role 'a school-interpretation'—as a dramatic critic remarked;[3] the great actor expressed in that role, which was his 'swan-song', the whole tragic destiny of the hero.

Othello appeared again on the Romanian stage, this time at Craiova, a performance highly commended, and at the Maghyar State Theatre in Sf. Gheorghe.

Of particular interest is the fact that, during that time, there were presented plays which had not previously been produced in our country, and which are not too often performed even in others: *Pericles* at the State Theatre in Braşov, *Cymbeline* at the State Theatre in Sibiu and *Troilus and Cressida* at the Comedy Theatre in Bucharest.

If we take into consideration that the majority of theatres attempted tours in numerous small towns lacking theatre companies, we may conclude, at the end of this short list, that during these theatrical seasons the plays of the great dramatist were presented to spectators all over our country, from the North of Transylvania to the Black Sea, from Oltenia to the far end of Moldavia.

The list I have given could suggest a special preference for Shakespeare's comedies and such a conclusion would not be inaccurate, but we must remember that during the previous years *King Lear* was performed in Bucharest, for a long time, in the very impressive interpretation of the octogenarian actor Gheorghe Storin, while *Hamlet* has been a favourite part with actors, being performed by G. Cozorici at Craiova, by Fory Etterle in Bucharest, by Constantin Anatol at Cluj, and, in a suggestive and original way, by Dan Nasta at Timişoara.[4] It is true that 'the Chronicles' were not presented on the stage, and only a few 'Histories', which require a particular setting and a special familiarity with the history of England; but, as for some years *Henry IV* has attracted many producers, it may be that this play (which was gorgeously staged by the talented director Soare Z. Soare in 1935) will lead to more productions of 'Chronicles'.

The presentations of the last two festival years show a continual progress: the repertory of the touring companies included plays less often performed, among them *Troilus and Cressida* and *Pericles*, and producers and actors experimented in new types of production, so as to appeal to a wider public.

Shakespeare addressed himself to spectators of different social classes, and directors who seek to appeal to the masses are following his intention. A correct evaluation of the circumstances which favoured the creation of Shakespeare's plays must recognize the role of those 'groundlings' who prevented Shakespeare from writing 'the academic plays which were the pride of those poets whose work was never clapper-clawed by the palms of the vulgar';[5] but this does not mean that the 'reactualization' of the popular character of his plays facilitates the actor's task.

In a certain sense it is easier to represent a play by Goldoni or Molière than one by Shakespeare who, addressing himself to the apparently unsophisticated public, shook them by the amplitude and profusion of human experience contained in the plays; this fact raises a lot of problems for the producer who tries to render the dramatist's intentions, the more so as each play has an individual complexity. On the other hand, it is not easy to 're-establish' the popular character of the plays, as the taste of the public has changed, and in our country, for example, a different ideological level has been reached, corresponding to a very rapid social progress.

It is not enough for actors to be 'the abstracts and brief chronicles of the time', rebuilding a museum-piece; but a good director will not adapt the plays so that they mean something different from the dramatist's intentions.

The desire to 'suit the action to the word, the word to the action' and to satisfy the needs of a public that would not allow actors to 'out-herod Herod' was the basis of all productions that obtained a resounding success in our country.

The recent performances in Romania have been accompanied by a series of publications which should be mentioned, especially as there has been fuller collaboration among translators, exegetists and theatre-managers, the work of the writers favourably influencing the activity of producers, scene-designers and actors.

First, we must record the publication of all Shakespeare's plays by a group of writers who translated directly from the original. The great dramatist's plays are nowadays assembled in an elegant edition that fulfils the aspirations of those who, years ago, started publishing volumes with the indication 'works' without succeeding in reaching the end of their work. Then, in 1964, was published a selection of his work, including *The Sonnets* in the translation of Ion Frunzetti, many other versions being published in literary periodicals.

Other poets—as: Tudor Arghezi, Alexandru Philippide, Victor Eftimiu—have been influenced by Shakespeare's poetry; the *Bilingual Anthology*, by Dan Duțescu and L. Levițchi, which gives representative fragments in English and Romanian, with ample commentaries, has helped in the understanding of the text, and there is a bilingual *Hamlet*, by Vladimir Streinu, with a full introductory study. Of equal importance is Mihnea Gheorghiu's biographical volume, *Scenes from Shakespeare's Life*, as well as *Studies of World and Comparative Literature* (II, 1963) in which are gathered the Shakespearian contributions of the late Professor Tudor Vianu. An important event was the publishing of the volume *Shakespeare and his Work. A Selection of Critical Texts* (World Literature Publishing House), in which are assembled (in 763 pages) representative fragments signed by critics of eighteen countries, including H. Granville-Barker, J. Dover Wilson, Henri Fluchère, F. Gundolf, Benedetto Croce, Caroline Spurgeon, Irving Ribner, I. S. Turgheniev, A. Anikst and many others (including the best Romanian interpreters). In the autumn of 1964 there was an interesting Shakespeare Exhibition —a display of recent writings on Shakespeare arranged by the British Council.

I made this somewhat ample digression because the correct and poetical text which is nowadays at the actors' disposal, as well as the critical studies that interpret the Shakespearian world, represent important contributions to the progress achieved by the theatre movement in our country. By establishing an organic bond between the translation, the performance and the critical study, our theatrical movement enables the Shakespearian creation to display itself in the right place: on the stage.

Hence those 'commentaries' which precede or are interwoven with the performances, aiming to introduce the playgoer into the atmosphere and world of the play, where the attitude of the characters, the tune of their voices, and their manner of speaking are different from ours; for it is certain that 'when we read or hear a play of Shakespeare's we are, up to a point, consciously or unconsciously translating it, and what we get from it will depend, *inter alia*, on our ability to translate in the widest possible sense of the word, from Elizabethan into modern English'.[6] The director Vlad Mugur preceded the performance of *Twelfth Night* at Bacău, by a recital of some of the Sonnets; to underline the idea of the play within the play, Biondello in Miron Niculescu's production of *The Taming of the Shrew* recited excerpts from the Commedia dell'Arte; at Petroșani Theatre, the atmosphere of *Measure for Measure*, produced by Marieta Sadova, was evoked by music played in the lobby.

For *Cymbeline* the director Iannis Veakis and the designer Elena Veakis created a plastic shape out of a fixed framework, suggesting the scenical box of the baroque theatre, and a large proscenium, intended for neutral commentaries; so that the comic epilogue here added to the play (in which the queen was brought to life again by Cornelius' medicines, Cloten retrieved his head, and Cymbeline his lost sons) could play down melodramatic tendencies and underline the Shakespearian serenity. More prominent deviations from the original aroused criticism, as in the case of *Much Ado about Nothing*, staged at Galatz, where the protagonists amused themselves at the expense of the play. In the majority of recent productions, the actors have helped to change the scenery; and in Mircea Marosin's production of *The Two Gentlemen of Verona*, at Bîrlad, two harlequins were introduced. The scene in Silvia's garden was evoked by the flowers pushed by the harlequins on to the stage.

The attempt to bring out significant elements succeeded, in general, by creating a specific atmosphere in every play. In *The Merry Wives of Windsor*, directed by Lucian Giurchescu, the characters were acted like simple 'humours' of comportment and thought; they were reduced to characteristic profiles. The performance was intended, as the translator of the play, Florian Nicolau, emphasized in the programme, to illustrate 'the essence of realistic art: typical characters in typical circumstances'. Some critics observed that the philosophical and poetical intentions of the dramatist[7] were ignored, but the reception of the comedy indicated that the producer and the actors had succeeded in presenting an entertaining and modern satire.

Nor was *As You Like It*, directed by Liviu Ciulei at the Lucia Sturza Bulandra Theatre in Bucharest, a museum reconstruction, but the play met contemporary needs in another way. Helped, evidently, by the stuff of the comedy, the director underlined its popular features by a subtle irony. By extending the stage into the hall, endowing it with an orchestra placed above, with a small ballet ensemble which appeared in the forest scenes, and by making distinctions in the characters' costumes—the usurper's courtiers displayed flashy garments and a gross, deeply outlined make up, while Rosalind and Celia went bare-footed—the stage-manager suggested that two worlds stood face to face: that of the court, noisy, ostentatious and empty, and that of the exiles, integrated with the sublimity and beauty of nature. This confrontation was expressed also on the ideological plane, especially by the moods of Jaques as impersonated by the director himself. It has been remarked with great reason that Ciulei made a synthesis 'in an artistical piece of work, of its great qualities, of the achievements of some valuable talents, under the sign of poetry and intelligence, respecting the essential law of Shakespearian comedy which urges the audience to think, to feel and to laugh'.[8]

Both by intensifying the satirical element and by creating an atmosphere of subtle irony, these performances realized Shakespeare's comic intention, in which the stress falls less on the evolution of some characters, and more on the intrigue which sharpens men's 'sense of humour, of the differences between what man is and what he vainly pretends himself to be'.[9] In this respect, the publication of the integral Romanian version and especially of the *Sonnets* makes us believe that what Liviu Ciulei achieved will be further developed.

Special attention was given to the delivery of the verse in the performances of *Othello* at Craiova. The director Călin Florian did not seek new significances but wanted to explore the question: how does Othello become a murderer? Iago becomes, thus, the personage who 'pulls the strings', his moral littleness characterizing all his actions. Desdemona appeared as a young woman fond of life, agile, a coquette but virtuous. The trajectory traversed by Othello imposed a simplification on the staging and the director achieved a picturesque beauty, which permanently accompanied the hero's torment: sliding panels, coloured differently by the light of reflectors, localized the action, and suggested dramatic tension. A white-red tone coloured the last scene, the fatal bed appearing as a podium on which the sacrifice is performed, among red torches; an immense white veil moved across the stage and covered Desdemona's body.[10] Mihai Tofan's designs thus seconded the intentions of the producer who left out classical typology in order to stress a general human significance.

A series of articles of great interest has been published in relation to the staging of *Troilus and Cressida*. Appreciated by specialists as 'disconcerting',[11] the play attracted the director David Esrig, who, while still in the period of preparations, outlined his own vision:

The amplitude of the debate is marvellous. There are discussions about peace and war, there are discussions about the price of every human gesture, in principle...The Trojan chivalric desuetude, facing the mercantile brutality and vulgarity of the Greeks, leaves no place for choice...I would like the scenic setting to be very fluid, the twenty scenes flowing one from another with the consequence and easiness of a tale, the changing of the place of action to present no difficulty, but having the flowing structure of an old chivalrous novel.[12]

By the help of the scene-designer I. Popescu Udriște, the director presented a broken field battle which during the performance was not hidden from the spectators by the curtain. Close to it in zones, circumscribed by scenery propelled from below the stage, were represented the indoor scenes; the Trojan knights started the fight on chariots pulled from the wings, giving the impression of statues posted on mobile sockets; the legendary heroes, Ajax and Achilles, dressed in sheepskin, had the necessary space to manoeuvre. It was a rude, false world in which Troilus blundered and Cressida flaunted herself.

The performance started with a stroke on an immense gong with a ridiculous big broom, handled by Thersites, who remained all the time the commentator on the spectacle; affronting Achilles, deriding Ajax and commenting on the scene between Diomedes, Cressida, Troilus and Ulysses, this character, who assumed the function of a classical chorus, made clear the sense of the great 'heroic' battle: 'Wars and lechery; nothing else holds fashion. A burning devil take them!' In an evident way, the producer tried to present first and foremost the shape of the warrior hero whom he then deflated and deprived of glory. The production was compared to that of Luigi Squarzina at Genoa;[13] and to the interpretations given to Shakespeare's plays by Peter Brook. (The fact was underlined that the Romanian director did not attain the simplicity of the English director.)[14] The performance was unanimously praised for its originality.[15]

In the summer of 1965, the Comedy Theatre in Bucharest was awarded the prize for the best national entry, with a special mention for *Troilus and Cressida*. Moreover, Albert Botbol, the director of the University of the Nation Theatre, considered that the 'performance proposed a clear insight into the universe of ideas of the dramatic work and especially an original point of view, deriving from the text itself'. Danish, Hungarian, French and English reviewers praised the performance either for its 'Aristophanic, if not Rabelaisian verve' or for its 'sharp satirical commentary' (*The Times*, 9 June 1965). As a general conclusion, the theatre chronicler of the newspaper *France Soir*, Jacqueline Cartier, wrote these pertinent words:

The surprising scenical apparatus of *Troilus* that accelerates the transformation of the play into a farce (in that sense Esrig goes further, much further, than Planchon, who presented the play last season), the combinations of trap-doors, screens, chariots, absorbing or throwing the characters in accordance with their destiny on a zodiacal background, is not a common success...To act the comedy, the great comedy which punishes, strikes and whips, that one which the Comedy Theatre of Bucharest considers its duty to perform, is a clear theatrical achievement.[16]

This may be considered the dominant feature of the performances produced recently. Bringing forward the ingenuous comical situation, as in *The Merry Wives*, or the lyrical-philosophical atmosphere, as in *As You Like It*, or a clear opposition to the warrior and his mentality, as in *Troilus*, the recent performances have tended to emphasize the humanistic values of the dramatist's work. In the comedies, as well as in the tragedies, special attention has been given to the confrontation of ideas present in the dramatist's work; the conflict between the comic characters or the torment of the great tragic personalities showed significantly the place the dramatist gave to 'fair judgement, without the which we are pictures, or mere beasts'. The profound study and wide dissemination of Shakespeare's works implied quite naturally the stressing of his human understanding which may be recognized in his patterns, motives and artistic technique. In this sense, the directors paid special attention to the artistic unity of their performances and to the free outburst of Shakespearian energy which is sometimes choked by the fatal 'Überinterpretation' condemned with good reason by specialists like W. Clemen.[17] Thus the comedies and the tragedies were presented as theatre plays and not as mere illustrations of psychological 'cases'.[18]

It would be difficult to draw final conclusions on the basis of the recent performances, because the process of deeper understanding of Shakespeare's work goes on. We may recall the significant fact that Shakespeare's plays are often performed by the new generation of actors. Moreover, in 1966, a young director, Andrei Şerban, who had not finished his studies, put on a pre-Shakespearian play, *Arden of Feversham*. Performed at Piatra Neamţ and afterwards in Bucharest, the production was widely commended.

At the same time, we must record the particular impression made by the English actors of the Royal Shakespeare Company, who visited our country in March 1965.[19]

RECENT SHAKESPEARE PERFORMANCES IN ROMANIA

The interest in the great dramatist's work continues beyond the dates appointed for his commemoration. This interest has grown continually during a century and a half and it will naturally continue to grow now when we are able to appreciate even more the answers he gave to the vital questions of mankind and his concept of human dignity.

© ALEXANDRU DUŢU 1967

NOTES

1. Cf. my article 'Primele spectacole cu piese de Shakespeare pe scenele române' ('The first Shakespeare performances on the Romanian stage'), *Studii şi cercetări de istoria artei-Seria teatru* (1964), I, 103–7. For the general aspect see my book *Shakespeare in Romania* (Bucharest, 1964).

2. I should like to note that the late artiste attended the International Theatrical Festival at Edinburgh in August 1957, where she gave an address on Shakespeare in Romania.

3. Florin Tornea, 'Richard III pe scena Teatrului "C.I. Nottara"' ('*Richard III* on the stage of "C.I. Nottara Theatre"'), *Teatrul* (1964), III, 28–36.

4. An index of the plays performed in 1944–63 is to be found at the end of my book mentioned above.

5. Kenneth Muir, 'Changing Interpretations of Shakespeare.' In: *The Age of Shakespeare. A Guide to English Literature* (1961), p. 274.

6. James Sutherland, 'How the Characters Talk.' In: *Shakespeare's World*, ed. James Sutherland and Joel Hurstfield (1964), p. 116.

7. Florin Tornea, 'Anglia lui Falstaff, măşti şi oameni' ('Falstaff's England, masks and men'), *Teatrul* (1964), I, 50–8.

8. Mihnea Gheorghiu, 'Cum vă place' ('*As You Like It*'), *Contemporanul* (1962), I, 4.

9. H. B. Charlton, 'Romanticism in Shakespearian Comedy.' In: *Shakespeare Criticism, 1919–1935* (1956), p. 269.

10. Ion Cazaban, 'Othello', *Contemporanul* (1965), XX, 4–5. Other reviews in *Scînteia*, 8 June 1965, p. 2 (Ileana Popovici); *Teatrul* (1965), VII, 36–40 (Călin Căliman).

11. Cf. Henri Fluchère in *Shakespeare, Poèmes. Suivis d'essais critiques sur l'œuvre dramatique* (Paris, 1959), p. 475: 'Cette pièce déconcertante est le fruit d'une maturité d'esprit agressive qui s'embarasse moins que jamais des précautions à prendre envers les mythes établis. L'exubérance et l'agilité des images et du style en font une des plus brillantes de cette période "engagée", où se poursuit le drame impersonnel d'un poète aux prises avec ses créatures.'

12. Interview published in *Teatrul* (1964), IX, 46–7.

13. V. Silvestru, 'Troilus şi Cressida', *Contemporanul*, 2 April 1965, p. 4.

14. Ana Maria Narti, 'Dialog cu şi despre Shakespeare' ('Dialogue with and about Shakespeare'), *Teatrul* (1965), V, 32–40.

15. Andrei Băleanu, 'Troilus şi Cressida', *Scînteia*, 18 April 1965, p. 2.

16. Fragment reproduced in *Contemporanul*, 4 June 1965, p. 4.

17. Wolfgang Clemen, 'Wo stehen wir in der Shakespeare-Forschung?', *Shakespeare Jahrbuch*, C(1964), 135–48.

18. We refer to interpretations against which Robert Merle humorously protested in 'La procrastination d'Hamlet', *Bulletin de la Faculté de Lettres de Strasbourg* (mai–juin 1965), 891: 'Depuis des générations, nous nous penchons sur le cas de notre tante Gertrude, de tonton Claudius, de grand-papa Polonius et de notre pauvre cousine Ophèlie, vous savez bien, qui s'est noyée.'

19. Mihnea Gheorghiu, 'Teatrul Shakespeare la Bucureşti' ('Shakespeare Company in Bucharest'), *Scînteia*, 12 March 1965, p. 2.

IA (Vienna, Nationalbibliothek MS 122, fol. 44ᵛ): the Thyestean banquet (title-page for the play)

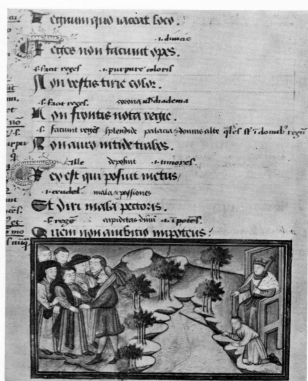

IB (Vienna Nationalbibliothek MS 122, fol. 55ᵛ): *Thyestes*, chorus II (ll. 343 ff.): the Chorus describes the pains of greatness and the pleasures of humility

IC (Vienna, Nationalbibliothek MS 122, fol. 185): *Troades*, ll. 371 ff.: the Chorus wonders if men live on after their bodies have been buried

IIA (Vienna, Nationalbibliothek MS 122, fol. 190): *Troades*, ll. 519 ff.: Andromache hides Astyanax in Hectors tomb, while Ulysees enters

IIB (Vienna, Nationalbibliothek MS 122, fol. 96): *Thebais*, ll. 443 ff.: Jocasta kneels between the armies, outside the walls of Thebes. The gateway is said to be that of Guyenne

III Prospero's Cave. Design by J. H. Grieve for *The Tempest*, Covent Garden, 1806

IVa Hotspur's Camp near Shrewsbury

IVb King's Tent

DESIGNS BY THE GRIEVES FOR 'I HENRY IV', COVENT GARDEN, 1824

VA *Cymbeline*, Covent Garden, 1827

VB Shylock's House. *The Merchant of Venice*, probably for Covent Garden, 1830

VC Garden at Belmont. *The Merchant of Venice*, Act v, Princess's Theatre, 1857

VIA Masque of Robin Goodfellow. *All's Well That Ends Well*, Covent Garden, 1832

VIB Hamlet's Castle. Probably for Drury Lane, 1835

VIC Herne's Oak. *The Merry Wives of Windsor*, Covent Garden, 1840

VII 'HAMLET', DEUTSCHES THEATER, BERLIN, 1964–7. Directed by Wolfgang Heinz settings by Heinrich Kilger. Hamlet (Horst Drinda) and the Ghost (Bruno Trotsch)

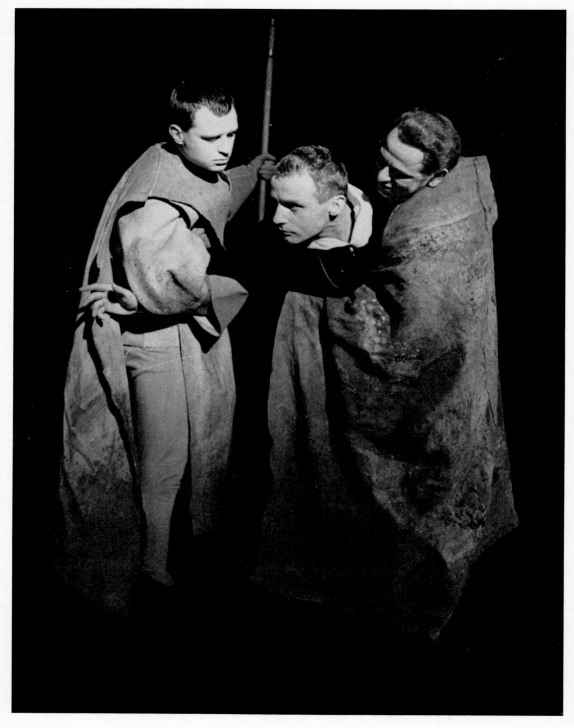

VIII 'HAMLET', STÄDTISCHE THEATER, KARL-MARX-STADT, 1964–6. Directed by Hans Dieter Mäde settings by Peter Frilde. Hamlet (Jürgen Hentsch with Horatio (Eugen P. Herden) and Marcello (Horst Junghänel)

IX 'CORIOLANUS' (BRECHT/SHAKESPEARE), BERLINER ENSEMBLE, 1964–. Directed by Wekwerth/ Tenschert, settings by Karl von Appen. Helene Weigel as Volumnia and Ekkehard Schall as Coriolanus

X A 'KING LEAR', DEUTSCHES THEATER, BERLIN, 1957–65. Directed by the late Wolfgang Langhoff.
Lear (Wolfgang Heinz) and Gloucester (Friederich Richter) in IV, vi

X B 'THE TWO GENTLEMEN OF VERONA', KAMMERSPIELE, BERLIN, 1964–5. Directed
by Benno Besson. Fred Düren as Launce (II, iii)

XIA Armando Bogus as
Petruchio and Eva
Wilma as Katherina

'THE TAMING OF THE SHREW', SÃO PAULO, 1965. Directed by Antunes Filho, settings and costumes by Maria
Bonomi

XIB The Banquet (v, ii)

XII 'TWELFTH NIGHT', ROYAL SHAKESPEARE THEATRE, 1966. Directed by
Clifford Williams, settings by Sally Jacobs. Alan Howard as Orsino and Diana
Rigg as Viola

SHAKESPEARE, THE TWENTIETH CENTURY AND 'BEHAVIOURISM'

BY

GARETH LLOYD EVANS

The ravages executed on Shakespeare by Restoration and eighteenth-century adaptors have become a source of academic speculation and amused commentary. But Peter Hall, the most distinguished and articulate begetter of contemporary adaptation, would, one is convinced, dissociate himself from Dryden and Tate. His position is simply that producers should 'try to express Shakespeare's intentions in terms that modern audiences can understand'. It is important to emphasize the distance in attitude between Hall and the early adaptors. The sharpest critic, unnerved by what seems extraneous sensationalism in a Hall production, must often accept that it is possible to detect a reason which goes beyond a mere desire for effect in what is presented. Hall gives the impression, in many of his statements, of having a potent, grave and reverent conception of the value of the plays, and a wish to relate their profundity to the realities of the contemporary world. Whereas Sir Tyrone Guthrie seems nearer in theory to the Restoration mode, and demonstrates it in practice by his ruthless cuts and interpolations, Hall is, by contrast, cautious. He has stated that 'any cutting which alters or affects the theme of the play must be immoral' and that 'cuts should be made within speeches'.

If Hall's statements are examined and placed beside the evidence of the productions under his directorship, it is clear that there is a deep socio-philososophical purpose behind his attitude. Sociologically, Hall's tendency is to 'democratize' the social strata of the plays. This is a projection of the nature of the organization which he has created in the Royal Shakespeare Theatre. The most creative feature of this company is its insistence upon a democratic ideal of ensemble playing and direction. The results of Peter Hall's determination can be seen in the growth of recognizably individual characteristics in interpretation and design particularly and, to some extent, in acting.

The Royal Shakespeare Theatre has a strong sense of community; mutual criticism and advice is both encouraged and given. In a very real sense this theatre is a world within a world. All the directors, and many of the actors, believe they are justifying a notion that a civilized society cannot exist without theatre by themselves creating a kind of society within their own theatre. In that society acting becomes a part of living, interpretation can be a comment on the values of contemporary life, and a production is often regarded as achieving the best and most valid results when what it communicates can make a statement to this century. The philosophy, democratic in spirit, governing this theatre, is one which takes its strength from the belief that drama is life, that theatre can be a microcosm of society at large, and that it must speak directly to its own age. It is essential to emphasize that, for the Royal Shakespeare Theatre, the word 'democracy' should not be equated with 'left-wing'. Nor should it be assumed that the productions and interpretations are 'committee-created'. The word is used, of the organization, to suggest that there is a healthy freedom of speech, a 'classless' but non-politically aligned ethos. But the buck of responsibility stops at Peter Hall, and his associate directors.

The interacting talents of directors like Hall, Barton and Clifford Williams have had the effect of creating a dialogue, as it were, around this proposition that Shakespeare must speak to the twentieth century. This is not to say that all three are in unargumentative agreement about the proposition or about the ways in which it can be translated into actual terms. Indeed one might suspect that Barton is the most cautious of the three. He bases his justifications for adaptation upon a belief, strongly supported by many scholars, that cutting, transposition of scenes, elimination of minor characters or their reduction, is a perpetuation of Elizabethan theatre practice. He is very concerned to 'maintain the spirit' of the text. His stated belief is that cutting, in the widest sense of the term, should be minimal. If Hall gives the impression of being the philosophical theorist, Barton is the imaginative technician, but, in the end, it is the overall conception of the theorist that seems to dominate the tone and shape and drive of the finished products. Let us look at some of these.

The 'democratization' of the plays is best revealed by an examination of two general methods employed in interpretation and production. The first is to reduce, as it were, from the habitual context of high-flown language, manners, social status and attitude, those upper class characters who most obviously display this context. The most notable example of this was in Hall's production of *A Midsummer Night's Dream* (1959 and 1962). John Russell Brown described Hall's presentation of the young lovers as emphasizing youth, foolishness and clumsiness. He found, too, that their verse was 'absurdly guyed, with exaggerated, unmusical stresses' (*Shakespeare Survey 13*, p. 143). Brown's diagnosis is true, but the effect of extraneous burlesque which he emphasizes was matched by a feeling that these lovers were firmly put outside the vein in which Shakespeare had created them—self-indulgent, spoilt, playful, not over-intelligent, but spiritedly genteel—because Hall felt that this would bore his audience and be out of key with our contemporary world.

The second method is to attempt the same result by an opposite method. Here, the audience's rooted expectations of how the upper class speak and behave are increased by overstressing haughty gentility, languor through lack of occupation, wealth without productivity, and affected phraseology. The character then becomes ludicrously, not to say distastefully, comic, while the 'democratic' principle is negatively asserted in the audience's mind. Orsino in the 1966 *Twelfth Night* is a clear example of this method. He appears in the first scene surrounded by courtiers who form an arc about him, formally posed. In this enveloping human opulence he speaks 'If music be the food of love' with a rough impatience, as if Love were not doing enough for his high-bred sensibilities. The effect almost achieves the ludicrous because of the unmusical pitch of the voice and the illogical phrasing. It is impossible to decide whether this last is due to faulty acting or to deliberate intent. There is no doubt, however, about the total impression made by Orsino—that of high-class petulance, inbred stupidity and self-indulgence. Such an interpretation would not, in itself, be hard to justify, except that this Orsino has few redeeming features. Viola's love, therefore, seems a surprising and disappointing error in one who, as played by Diana Rigg, has such charm of movement and music of voice, romanticism of spirit and intelligence. On the whole, women, in this sociology, are allowed, at least visually, to retain more of unridiculous high breeding than are the men. Portia (Janet Suzman) in 1965 had more 'class' than Bassanio (Peter McEnery), who was boorish, ill-spoken and untidy in movement. Juliet (Dorothy Tutin) in 1961 shone with aristocratic splendour compared with the almost oafish classlessness of her Romeo (Brian Murray). Recently the visual grandeur which high-born women have been allowed to maintain has been ironically negatived by the verbal roughness with which they have expressed themselves. There is a startling example this season (i.e. 1966), in the wooing scene in *Henry V*. Henry wears a dull brown tunic, giving the effect of being merely his best battle-dress, and though he wears a crown, it seems out of place, not only with the rest of the costume, but, more particularly, with the rough, bluff style of Ian Holm's acting. Katharine of France is a beautifully costumed, charmingly shaped creature, and the first visual impression is that it is to be down-to-earth Englishness taming and winning and 'democratizing' Gallic snobbery. But when Katharine speaks, it is quickly noticeable that she lost her pure vowels somewhere on the journey from a French court to an English King's heart. The democratic spirit has confronted the aristocratic and has conquered it, but the French Princess is already half way to being like Henry—and the rest of us—before the victory has been won. She has merely been rescued from the ivory tower to take her place on Henry's factory floor. It is with *Henry V* that the urge towards 'democratization' seems to have reached its ultimate in the Royal Shakespeare Theatre. It is with this production, too, that the fundamental philosophy governing this theatre's approach to Shakespeare becomes clearly apparent. It is at this point that it is possible to see clearly the nature of the new form of adaptation.

In the last two seasons we have had *1* and *2 Henry IV*, *Henry V* and *Hamlet*, and this season *Twelfth Night* has been added, and it becomes important now to examine Barton's statement that 'we would certainly not rehandle a major play of Shakespeare's as we have rehandled the three *Henry VI*'s'.

The textual cuts this season are by no means excessive. All producers are always able to find theoretically cogent reasons for cutting, and it becomes profitless to engage in disputation about the disappearance of single lines. More serious this season at Stratford, however, is the ellipsis caused, for example, by the reduction of the traitors in *Henry V* to one, and by the division into two large chunks, followed later by a third segment, of the Chorus's speech in Act v. What can be claimed is gained is theatrical neatness—what the Chorus refers to verbally then follows in action, first the French scene, then the English. But what is lost is a sense of simultaneous contrast, a quality of rhetorical unity. The music breaks, therefore the emotional rhythm breaks, and therefore the Chorus's function of being more than a reporter. The breaks disabuse him of his almost magical function as scenic and atmospheric artist.

These are but two examples of rehandling of a major play, but they are both admittedly arguable. What is more to the point is the sense that not only the histories but also *Hamlet* and *Twelfth Night* have been subjected to a reshaping whose result is sometimes subtle, sometimes crude, to meet the demands of contemporaneity. This reshaping has contrary results—some completely acceptable, others which run counter, often in an obvious sense, to the spirit of the original. With each production it is possible therefore to draw up a very clear debit and credit account in a manner which is not always possible with theatrical productions. Usually in Shakespearian productions the dark and the light shade into one another, the shadows have no crispness, the problem of assessment becomes even more a matter of individual sensitivity. But with the Royal Shakespeare Theatre what is good is vividly apparent, what is bad is implacably unavoidable.

Over all it is *Hamlet* which comes out best. Peter Hall's Elsinore is a place of power politics, a place where the naïve go to the wall, and the sensitive find frustration and despair. Thus Ophelia is, from the beginning, in a state of young bewilderment, and Hamlet grows into a wry dark despondency as his sensitivity struggles to find in the political world of Elsinore a logic, a creative dynamic, a meaning, that is more than based on expediency. Warner's Hamlet is one who has no sense of God, and to whom his society offers nothing trustworthy. Given Warner's appearance—long, lean, suffering in face—and his acting—lank in movement and gesture, thin-voiced, touched with a malaise of spirit—it is easy to see the modern late-teenager, pathetic in his lack of grip, strangely poignant in his angular helplessness. The interpretation's strength lies precisely in this context—it does speak to a young generation and no more proof of this is required than the evidence of its popularity with young audiences.

The production achieves its unity from this centre. Polonius is a shrewd, sniffingly suspicious politician nearing the end of his corridor of power, a repository of that unwanted stuffy authority which makes youth cavil at age and increases its sense of frustration and defeat, but still with enough status to seem to both youngsters, Ophelia and Hamlet, a threat. The play can accommodate this particularity of interpretation which is given a final cogency by its Claudius (political power unmatched by moral strength), and its Gertrude (sexual potency unmatched by intelligence). The total effect—a kind of cancelling out—is one of ultimate apathy, which does not preclude action or violence, but makes them pointless—it might almost be said Absurd.

Yet the very positive strength of direction which achieves this world on stage sometimes slinks away at those very points where the text itself asserts an inevitable destination. Thus, if Hamlet is to be accepted as apathetic, the verbal communication of that apathy must be positive.

Weakness and negativeness need as much rightly directed strength and positive acting as anything else—perhaps even more—and an actor must not only be 'weak' on stage but must be seen to be deliberately so. Warner seems to overlook this. Rhythm and music are at a discount, the voice often seems roughly *sotto voce*, the pausing *ad hoc*. At once it is noticeable that two of the play's most potent realities are shied away from. The first is a quality of Princeliness in the protagonist, the second is that almost indefinable quality by which Hamlet is archetypal as well as individual. One can nowadays, perhaps with impunity, democratize the prince, but the archetypal Hamlet exists outside the confines of any fashionable or individual interpretation (although it can contain them) mainly through the poetry he speaks. To denude him and the play of the associative power of poetic utterance is to take away the timeless dimension.

The history plays have lost little of that power to excite theatrically which marked the Royal Shakespeare Theatre's exploration of the *Henry VI* plays two years ago. Amidst the comment, both favourable and adverse, which has been expended liberally on these productions, it has been forgotten that they have represented a shrewd theatrical justification for the scholarly theory of their original serial conception by Shakespeare. Despite all the adaptation and cutting which has been indulged in, an inherently epic quality is present; if Shakespeare had a grand design the Royal Shakespeare Theatre's productions have done much to emphasize its presence if not, perhaps, its quality. This determination to present a flow of history has undoubtedly given the *Henry IV* and *Henry V* productions an immediacy of visual effect, a naturalistic depth, both in the scenes of private and public confrontation, and a clarity of narrative line. This theatre is unmatched in its ability to handle large scenes—of battle, of conference, of grave and gay assembly—and some of the most memorable parts are the battle scenes in *Part One* and in

Henry V; the French camp before Agincourt; the Boar's Head—particularly in *Part Two* where the comic-pathetic descent of Falstaff into a state of senescence is illuminated by a superbly realized performance by Elizabeth Spriggs as Mistress Quickly. Indeed one might speculate that this season directors and players seem most confident when they have to deal with multiple performances rather than with the single consistent individual one.

Yet within a framework of excellence of theatrical realization there lie disturbing mutations on Shakespeare's original. Scholarly knowledge (with which this theatre is well-endowed) can sometimes attempt cogent justifications of cutting on the grounds that it was customary in the Elizabethan theatre. It can confound the purist with the question: 'How much of any given text is Shakespeare's?' Yet, granted the doubts about individual authorship in certain speeches and scenes, the simple fact remains that the texts are Elizabethan, and that it is not a logical but fatal step to assume that we may dismiss the cohesiveness of the play's Elizabethan reality as cavalierly as we accept doubts about individual authorship.

Simply, in the Royal Shakespeare Theatre productions this season, a strong impression emerges that the 'Elizabethanism' of the history plays has been not so much sacrificed as put in the position of handmaid to modernism. The most specific example of it in the history plays is to be found in the treatment of the Prince and, by association, of other characters, particularly Hotspur.

Ian Holm (Hal) is a clever actor—his gifts are fine timing, clear enunciation, and an ability to hold the attention of an audience, sometimes, however, in expectation that he will provide an unusual gloss on a line or an unexpected emotional context to a speech. It is an irrelevance to speak of his small stature as a disadvantage. He is capable, at best, of turning it into distinct virtue, especially in modern plays (*The Homecoming*, for example), and in moments of reflectiveness. His main weakness is to impersonate rather than interpret (or, at least, to give an impression of it). He tends, that is, to act from the outside of a character, and to engage in tricksiness of speech and gesture. Diligent preparation for a role (and it is certain that Mr Holm is diligent) does not seem to compensate, in him, for an occasional demonstration of a playfulness of spirit. This never lets him down in a strictly theatrical sense, but prevents him from a final engagement with the character. His Hal is restless, occasionally querulous in tone (particularly in *Part One* where his relationship with Falstaff is curiously personally disengaged). This Hal is a young man of some conceit, quickness of wit, and impatient of those issues which are implicit in the play— political and physical combat. At times (as in 'I know you all' and the first Boar's Head scene) he gives the impression of being an onlooker, not from another area of society, but from another time (ours). He is fretful at the effeteness and stupidities of his surroundings, he sees little point in war, though he is prepared to go through with it with a tight-lipped tough resignation. He becomes, in effect, a contemporary commentary on what is happening around him. What he sees, and seems to react to, is—power corrupts, leadership corrodes, war, as a solution, is wasteful, filthy, noisome and pointless. Hal seems to embody these notions in this production. They are unexceptionable notions to hold, but their presence, as I see it, in these productions, while it may reflect the undertone of Shakespeare's own belief, distorts the dramatic subtleties and tensions of the plays. With Hal as the chief agency, other characters are yanked away from the play's inherent dramatic pattern. Hotspur is played with the traditional aura of roguishness, tactlessness and robust physicalness—a sort of butch Mercutio—but his thematic status in the play is reduced. The traditional appearance of the character is allowed to stand for the whole reality. Hotspur's role as a positive alternative to Hal is not emphasized. His reality as a vital representative (in contrast with Hal) of an outworn world of medieval political convention is made petty to the point of the ridiculous, particularly in the manner of his death, and in the offhand quasi-pathetic way with which Hal speaks the encomium over his dead body.

It is one thing to hold that war is a dirty humiliating affair, that outmoded political concepts verge on the ridiculous in action—yet it is another to blur the dramatic line of a play and to reduce the particular tensions between character and opposing political or psychological attitudes which are the play's *raison d'être*.

In this context of thematic and dramatic reduction emanating from the conception of Hal, both Henry IV and Falstaff suffer diminution and change. The King, played with conscientious attention to detail by Tony Church, has no vestiges of Bolingbroke in him. It is impossible to believe that here is the man who, with excited reluctance, took Richard's crown. The text clearly allows more than vestiges of Bolingbroke to emerge, but Mr Church's Henry is sick in mind and body almost to senility. One suspects that, true to an overall conception, the intention is to convey corrupted power, cankered conscience. Yet, once again, implicit dramatic tensions in the play are driven away. Thus, it is difficult to believe, literally, that this King would have the physical strength to appear at Shrewsbury. But, more pertinently, there is little suggestion of that agonizing tension between Henry's estimation of Hal's character and behaviour and our own knowledge of the precise purposes that Hal clutches behind his madcap disguises. This tension, in the play, is both political and personal but, in this production, the political is submerged by the personal. In itself this is superbly achieved, particularly in *Part Two*, but there is a feeling of isolation in its effects. Its moving pathos becomes merely a way of endearing Hal to us rather than being a rich element in the overall complexities of their relationship—son is at odds with father, certainly, but more than that, old worlds are at odds with new.

There is, too, a sense of isolation about Falstaff. He does not hold a place in this production as King of the world of commodity, with a wealth of sly experience to bequeath to the political predator who has descended into his kingdom to learn. There is a logic about Falstaff's rejection which may offend the heart while making sense as a political necessity. Falstaff's isolated status at the Royal Shakespeare Theatre makes the rejection merely emotionally stirring as an act of itself. With so much concentration on Hal as a representation of a set of attitudes towards what lies about him, Falstaff becomes an observed character in a play. The gigantic wit is reduced to comic self-indulgence, and although there is an incisive efficiency of timing, a lingering pathos (well realized in *Part Two* by Paul Rogers) in the acting, the status of Falstaff is basically that of yet another victim of Hal's predominant view of his world, and of his half-reluctant progress towards kingship.

The kingship which is achieved in Shakespeare's *Henry V* is total, encompassing a necessary ceremonial, a rigorous but just application of law, a patriotic insistence on the validity of national aspirations, a natural flow of responsibility to the community, and a reciprocal flow of duty in return, martial power and bravery, severe magnanimity. This is the ideal and idealized totality to which Shakespeare's history plays have moved. Yet, within this, there are richer, personal qualities whose presence in this particular king justify the whole action of the two plays of *Henry IV*. There is the 'common touch', given a validity by Hal's active experience of the commonalty; there is the sense of actual communication between king and subjects, even of the meaner sort, given reality by that same experience. There are the vestiges of that other Hal—the one who, though taking upon himself a madcap disguise, found his own disposition to playfulness, to practical joking, to young prankishness, one of the hurdles to overcome in his progress to the throne.

The Royal Shakespeare Theatre production of *Henry V* has encapsuled many of these qualities, indeed most of them, but, yet again, the impression is that they have been reduced to serve a particular and twentieth-century end. Henry V is workmanlike. It appears in his garb; he is, like those retired military men turned politician, given to wearing the beret of action and the battledress of combat, attired in the rough-hewn and serviceable. It appears, too, in his manner, which is businesslike, particularly in the first scene, in the French capitulation scene, and (with more than a slight suggestion of Olivier) in the wooing scene. These manifestations of honest, down-to-earth purpose have their source, it would seem, in a conception of the play which underemphasizes its ceremonial aura and its position as an English 'epic'. The martial events leading up to and including the battle of Agincourt are presented as bloody, clobbering, and unpleasant. There are no traditional heroics in the speeches of the king to his troops. This is a ragged army led by a leader at times almost desperate with fatigue. The heroism, where it exists, is found almost entirely in sheer dogged pugnaciousness. It is the heroism of the First World War trenches, of attrition, of unsung deeds done as a matter of course, and of men following a leader, not because he is a king but because he is as tired and as stubbornly determined as they are. It is, in short, democratic twentieth-century heroism.

This creates, in terms of theatrical effect, some scenes of emotional impact, and the production is fortunate in its Fluellen (David Waller) and its common soldiery in having actors who minister to this typically twentieth-century response.

Yet, what is won in terms of emotional rapport by placing the play in a modern context is lost from its dramatic entity. The thematic loss, which has been noted in *Henry IV*, is duplicated here. There is little sense of a growth into total kingship; there is little sense of a nation, both secular and non-secular, girded for greatness. The Archbishop of Canterbury is a mummerset cleric, not *au fait* with the workings of politicians, happening to be an unexpected expert on the Salic Law, good, honest. He is significantly un-notable as the representative of the Church's place in the confident acceptance of Henry V by the kingdom. The French are almost all presented in ridiculous colours, their 'classy' effeteness shown in ridiculous contrast to the raw-boned English. The princess, alone, seems prepared in voice, as has been noted, to be amenable to reformation by the no-nonsense English king. What is lacking is a balance between naturalism and ritual and rhetoric (though Ian Richardson's Chorus is finely spoken). It may be argued that there is no place in the twentieth century for ritual and rhetoric and that, indeed, beneath the play's ceremonial movement the voice of the realist (of Shakespeare himself) can be heard. This argument, however, ignores the self-evident fact of the nature of Shakespeare's dramatic uniqueness. It is that whatever debatable cases can be made for Shakespeare's own personal 'attitude', or for a basic realism being the true measure of his histories, there is an 'acceptance' quality in his manipulation of historical action and meaning. He may, privately, have believed honour is to him 'who died o' Wednesday'; he may, secretly, have believed the concept of divine right to be a barrier to human reality; he may, like Northumberland, have felt 'crafty sick' at the thought of rebellion. Yet he also knew that honour had its ritual, divine right its mystery, and that lust for power, if corrupt, also had its glamour. He knew, in short, that drama gleaned from history was a subtle, rich mixture of realism and ritual, of natural and rhetorical—and that, in a sense, in so being, it mirrored the true nature of the human scene, not for one age, but for all. The Royal Shakespeare Theatre, with infinite care and skill, has taken one-half of Shakespeare's vision of history, and one-half of Shakespeare's dramatic subtlety, and made him very right for 1966 without any suggestion that what they have found in him will be right for 1967.

It would be wrong to state or to imply that there is a wilful attempt to bring Shakespeare up to date merely for the sake of it by the Royal Shakespeare Theatre. It would perhaps be nearer the truth to say that Peter Hall, in particular, and some of his associates, in varying degrees, are conscious, perhaps sometimes over-conscious, of the fact that if the director, the actor, the designer of a play is a twentieth-century man, then the result is bound to 'speak' to some extent with a twentieth-century voice. It may also be added that the spirit of experimentation which exists in this company would accept that it is valid to relate a production to a very particular time-space (say 1966), and that 1967 might demand a re-thinking of the same play. It is surely not beyond the bounds of possibility, though the mind boggles, that we should have a series of *Hamlets* from the Royal Shakespeare Theatre.

If my assessment of the spirit and belief and substance of this theatre is correct, then it is only right to say that it has succeeded in its intentions. There is, now, the fact that a Royal Shakespeare Theatre production is instantly recognizable in several ways. Casting is often unusual, surprising, seeming at times to be done in a spirit of risky not to say dangerous experiment (Warner as Hamlet, Holm as Henry V).

Character interpretation is often surprising, unusual (Warner's Hamlet, Holm's Malvolio, Church's Polonius and Archbishop of Canterbury). Stage design and setting have, at best, forceful economy about them. Mechanical ingenuity and artistic effect are, again at best, completely unified (the sets for *The Jew of Malta* (1964–5), the periaktoi for *Henry IV*, the mechanics for the ghost in *Hamlet*).

Materials used both for sets and costumes are the result of painstaking experiment and detailed design. Costumes, in particular, have a startlingly realistic quality in terms of texture, though the material used is often, though not always, synthetic. By comparison, costumes for Shakespeare used in other theatres sometimes have a stagey, skimped quality. In fairness to them, however, it may be that their budget in this respect is smaller than that of the Royal Shakespeare Theatre. A Royal Shakespeare Theatre version is often recognizable by the amount of modernization, sometimes in the replacement of Elizabethan words by modern, but especially in the giving of modern associations by emphasis and colouring to the Elizabethan words. For example in *The Taming of the Shrew* (1962) the expletive 'You nit' was given a contemporaneity by the hard spitting pronunciation which is characteristic of its present-day usage. More recently contemporaneity can be observed in the occasional 'in-references' which are forced from the lines, the most glaring example being in Ian Richardson's speaking of the lines

> Henry the Sixth in infant bands crowned King
> Of France and England, did this King succeed;
> Whose state so many had the managing,
> That they lost France, and made his England bleed:
> Which oft our stage hath shown.

The speaking is accompanied with a knowing look on the last line, which gives the impression of a mixture of self-pride and confidence that the audience will get the message—the Royal Shakespeare Theatre strikes again. One does not object to this particular example so much as wonder why the effect achieved is thought worth doing. It diminishes the Chorus at the final point of the play to the position of a coy cabaret announcer.

The new adaptation of Shakespeare characteristic of the Royal Shakespeare Theatre carries with it its own virtues which I have tried to describe. However, quite apart from the debatable assumption that, in essence, the adaptations are part of the contemporary retreat from the values of the past, they have, in practical terms, their own vices. It has been noticeable, this season, how often an overt modernity has spilled over the productions. It appears in several ways. In the giving of modern tonal associations to words; in the unnecessary striving for the contemporary response ('Coopey la Georgie', 'Piss-tool' for Pistol, in *Henry V*); in the insertion of confidential glances and words addressed to the audience (Falstaff, before wetting his eyes with sack to make false tears, asks the audience to 'excuse me'). These examples may be multiplied and indeed vary in number and intensity in different performances of the same play.

In all they add up to a kind of behaviourism—unrelated responses which sometimes suggest a fear that, without them, the audience will be bored. Sometimes, too, they suggest a desperate, even *ad hoc*, attempt to support the principle of speaking to the twentieth century. In more important terms this 'behaviourism' can be seen intermittently in acting and interpretation. There are certain moments in *Hamlet* when the attention is drawn more to the player than to the character—he becomes, as it were, Hamlet playing David Warner. Again, the brilliantly original and superbly executed Malvolio of Ian Holm is disquieting since, in accent and phrasing, it bears a strong resemblance to a well-known, though now defunct, television comedy character. In appearance this Malvolio appears to guy the bust of Shakespeare at Holy Trinity. The interpretation is, so to speak, over self-consciously 'with it'. To respond to present-tense reality alone perhaps inevitably involves the exercise of behaviourism in interpretation, acting and speaking.

This behaviourism is often starkly apparent in comic scenes of a strong visual intensity that almost always has an immediate theatrical effect, but often seems to be external to the text. The most notable examples are to be seen in this season's *Twelfth Night*, particularly in Aguecheek's appearance after the encounter with Sebastian, where a comic effect is created, not out of the fact that Aguecheek has had his head broken across, but from his wearing of a grotesquely huge arm-splint. It should be noted, too, that recently the Royal Shakespeare Theatre is given to creating comic moments at quite inappropriate times with the effect of distorting first the dramatic atmosphere of a scene and, second, character. When Antonio leaves Sebastian with his purse with a promise to meet him at the Elephant, this would hardly seem an occasion for comedy, but, incredibly, the stolid, bluff sea-salt, Antonio, having spoken the words 'To th' Elephant', wraps his cloak over his face, produces a firearm, and lopes off with a slow motion indicative of dark deeds to be done which is more worthy of the Red Barn than of Illyria. There are many details which mark out a Royal Shakespeare Theatre production, and, in each case, the effect achieved is sometimes good, sometimes bad. This mixture is perhaps inevitable in a theatre which seems to have such a sense of unity of community—family enthusiasm is sometimes to be admired, sometimes to be embarrassedly dismissed.

But acceptance or dismissal on this level is so often a matter of subjective judgment. What is more amenable, perhaps, to objective appraisal, is the whole question of whether the Royal Shakespeare Theatre in its policy of making Shakespeare speak for the twentieth century 'tragically, comically, historically' is not unconsciously abrogating one of the primary functions of art in a civilized society. We live in an age in which, in so many respects, judgment of value is placed upon the proposition that to live in the present-tense must involve a rejection of the past. Inventiveness and originality of form are minority results of this prevailing notion; superficiality of meaning is a majority result. The sense of the past as an artery for thought, feeling and civilized activity is diminished. Nowadays it is old to be twenty, and youth looks at the generation which bore it with uncomprehending cynical eyes. Thus, of Shakespeare, this age is inclined to say that there is so much in him that is meaningless in terms of modern social reality, that he must be changed. Divine right; honour, as a concept; the sin of usurpation; baronial warfare; royal complexities; the interaction of responsibility and duty in society, have no relevance, it is said, for us. Yet some might think that the rejection of what the past has to give in every facet of art and culture cannot, without great risk, be undertaken without knowing what it is that is to be rejected. Or again, some might believe that the great themes of, say, Shakespeare's history plays might, of themselves, in their own realities, have something to tell us. To believe that they can speak directly to us does not presuppose that Shakespeare's plays must be done 'plain', or 'Elizabethanized', or as antiquated repositories of home truths.

Quite plainly the Royal Shakespeare Theatre has done much to excite the responses of modern audiences to Shakespeare. It has, in particular productions, achieved great distinction in interpretation, in setting, and in acting. It is a virile and exciting organization. In this context experimentation is inevitable and necessary and the onlooker must be prepared to consider, when conscious of failure, how much of success would be lost if the Royal Shakespeare Theatre was not as it is.

Yet it must also be considered that the form of adaptation nurtured by the Royal Shakespeare Theatre may set a standard which could map the course of Shakespeare production for decades to come. In hands less skilful than those of the Royal Shakespeare Theatre the adaptation, and the resultant behaviourism which is its main flaw, would become unbearable. The long process of re-discovering Shakespeare and, through Shakespeare, the values of the past, undertaken by previous centuries, would have to begin again. Already there are many people who believe Shakespeare wrote a play called *Edward IV*. It is only a short step from this to a situation in which people might never have the opportunity to recognize or to experience the innate reality of plays called *Hamlet* or *Henry IV*—or what you will.

THE YEAR'S CONTRIBUTIONS TO
SHAKESPEARIAN STUDY

1. CRITICAL STUDIES

reviewed by NORMAN SANDERS

While there is much in recent Shakespeare studies to suggest that the damaging division between 'historical' and 'critical' approaches is still being preserved, there are also some signs that a synthesis of these attitudes is being attempted; and many authors, while firmly bent on defining the totality of a play, or determining its special relevance to our age, nevertheless make skilful use of the ever-growing knowledge of the playwright's own time. As one might expect, L. C. Knights in his *Further Explorations*[1] has a good deal to say on the critical/historical dichotomy; and in one essay[2] tackles the subject head-on. He restates his well-known position rather less stridently than in his earlier explorings:

The meanings of a poem are not exhausted by the meanings it may have had for its original readers...
The meanings that it had for the original audience cannot in any case be identified with the meanings of which they were fully conscious;

and expresses his distrust of historical scholarship's tendency to 'substitute accumulated "knowledge about" for living responsiveness' thereby obscuring the essential nature of art and missing its 'personal vibrancy'. Knights is so attractively and seriously concerned with what is important in literature and life that it is difficult to take issue with him while reading his hard-thought-out articulations; and this is specially true when he admits the value of what scholarly research can supply in terms of such things as the habits of mind and ear of Renaissance man or the 'life-bearing ideas of Shakespeare's age'. However, for all his native critical sensitivity (and his justifiable great faith in it), he perhaps should be aware of one important limitation—one that is implied in these words:

There are many preliminaries to criticism that only scholarship can provide: information about stage conditions, dramatic conventions...

While Knights continues to believe that stage conditions and conventions (and all that they imply about Shakespeare's art) are merely 'preliminaries' to criticism, as opposed to those more central matters of 'traditional moral philosophy', so long will his criticism of the drama fall short of the complex and total response he seeks; so long too will the important epithet in his famous phrase 'the play as a dramatic poem' appear to some of his readers to be all too often an unnoticed modification.

One volume, entitled *Shakespeare in a Changing World*,[3] attempts a critical synthesis by

[1] Chatto and Windus, 1965.
[2] 'Historical Scholarship and the Interpretation of Shakespeare', pp. 138–54.
[3] Edited by Arnold Kettle (Lawrence and Wishart, 1964).

eschewing the extremes of the two approaches which Knights discusses. Its editor tells us that the twelve essays it contains are connected by

a rejection of...mystical, purely impressionist, anti-rational, anti-historical approaches, and...of the kind of pedantic academism which, losing sight of the whole in its concern for the parts,...ignores the living and not infrequently disturbing content of great literature.

A further unifying factor is the common belief in the 'relevance of Marxist thinking' to the contributors' approaches. Each of these beliefs brings with it its own strengths and weaknesses, as well as its own vocabulary. One is struck, on the one hand, by the ready references to the brotherhood of man, implicit democratic sentiment, the coarse vocabulary of the bourgeois ethic, or the cheerful self-deception of the capitalist individualist; and, on the other hand, by the real insight into what one writer[1] calls the connexions between the vast range of conflicting values and standards within the Elizabethan situation, and its incorporation by the dramatist in his poetic vision of society.

The individual essays vary in quality, though most combine genuine fresh observation and irritating oversimplification. Many stress the social content of the plays they discuss. For example, J. K. Walton[2] sees *Macbeth* as embodying the conflict between feudal and bourgeois man in relation to society, the tragedy having relevance to the historical development of Britain as a whole; and Arnold Kettle[3] locates the central issue in *Hamlet* as a man in conflict with a rotten society, rather than a prince with a personal or psychological problem. Shakespeare's concern with social morals are emphasized by Charles Barber[4] in his discussion of *The Winter's Tale* as a play dealing with the country/court dichotomy in Jacobean times; and also by David Craig[5] in an illuminating comparison between the handling of problems of passion within a social organization in *Measure for Measure* and in some modern writers, particularly D. H. Lawrence.

Other contributors to the volume range more widely: Kenneth Muir[6] looks again at the dramatist's implied judgments on order, wealth, the class conflict, and democracy, in an essay in which the suggestiveness of the individual observations is far more exciting than the somewhat watery conclusion he draws from them. V. G. Kiernan,[7] with a useful display of classified statistics, attempts with some success an assessment of the vast topic of human relationships in the plays, though his opinion that the conspirators in *Julius Caesar* constitute an heroic band of brothers tends to shake one's faith in his other conclusions. Two essays in particular carry their Marxist burden rather heavily. Zdeněk Stříbrný[8] takes issue with Henry V's eulogists, and contends that the king's soul and face are saved from the effects of his 'new' self-destructive ways by his coming to accept (*sic*) the standpoint of the common soldiers whom he then leads

[1] Robert Weimann, 'The Soul of the Age: Towards a Historical Approach to Shakespeare', pp. 17–42.
[2] '*Macbeth*', pp. 102–22.
[3] 'From *Hamlet* to *Lear*', pp. 146–71.
[4] '*The Winter's Tale* and Jacobean Society', pp. 233–52.
[5] 'Love and Society: *Measure for Measure* and Our Own Time', pp. 195–216.
[6] 'Shakespeare and Politics', pp. 65–83.
[7] 'Human Relationships in Shakespeare', pp. 43–64.
[8] '*Henry V* and History', pp. 84–101.

as a brother and father. Raymond Southall[1] sees Shakespeare as giving a fine implicit lambasting to the spirit of capitalism in *Troilus and Cressida* as it finds its expression in love and war. Some of his incidental analysis is very good indeed, but he tends to become dazzled by his own opinions, and is thus led into making statements which have some strange implications; for example, if it is true that the love in the play is coarse because it finds its 'natural expression in the vocabulary of trade', does not this make love in a number of other works (including *The Merchant of Venice* and some of the Sonnets) very coarse indeed?

The very real results that can ensue from a strongly social approach to the plays are exemplified in an essay on *Othello* by G. M. Matthews.[2] His broadly racial view of the play is of great interest, with its stress on the isolated attempts by Othello and Desdemona to create human dignity in an antagonistic society, and its original analysis of Iago's irrationality and barbarism. I think Matthews weakens his case, however, with his super-subtle reading of the hero's final speech. In the two weakest pieces in the volume, Dipak Nandy[3] gives a fairly routine rehearsal of the worlds of *Antony and Cleopatra* to point out the opposition between love and 'policie'; and Alick West[4] offers some not fully worked-out observations on Jan Kott's work in particular and the changed significance of Shakespeare in general. Altogether an interesting book; but one from which one remembers rather longer than one would wish such irritating items as Kettle's silly footnote on the Fool in *King Lear* on p. 169, or his grossly oversimplified account of the issues of the play, or his and West's surely unsupportable belief that the revolt of Cornwall's servant against his master is the turning point of the tragedy.

It is *King Lear* that is selected by Maynard Mack[5] for a book-length study to determine the play's special appeal for our time. The core of this volume is his important essay which was discussed in *Survey 19* when it appeared in *The Yale Review*. This is given a context by, first, a discussion of aspects of the play's stage history. After describing the travesties of Tate and the nineteenth-century actor-managers, Mack remarks that 'our stage, for all its advantages...has worked out ways of altering the effect of Shakespeare's text which are quite as misleading as any our ancestors used', and he proceeds to condemn the 'directors' theatre' and modern sub-textual productions. While one would go along with much that Mack says, many of his observations on modern productions carry less weight than they might owing to his apparent reliance on written accounts of recent performances. For example, he asserts that the Noguchi *Lear* was 'disastrous', citing Gielgud's testimony to this effect. Now, this production may have appeared so to Sir John, but surely it is well-known that participating actors are notoriously unreliable witnesses about the overall effect of a play. In fact, while many pejorative adjectives could be applied to this production, 'disastrous' is not one of them; its unique qualities and distinctive imaginativeness only just missed making it one of the most impressive mountings of the play in recent years. In the second section of the book, Mack considers the tradition of thought and feeling in which Shakespeare shaped his source material. He well defines the blend of natural homeliness and archetype, of realism and artifice in the play, and is illuminating on what he calls:

[1] '*Troilus and Cressida* and the Spirit of Capitalism', pp. 217–32.
[2] '*Othello* and the Dignity of Man', pp. 123–45.
[3] 'The Realism of *Antony and Cleopatra*', pp. 172–94.
[4] 'Some Current Uses of "Shakespearian"', pp. 253–66.
[5] '*King Lear*' in Our Time (Methuen, 1965).

the presentation of characters, all of whom have at some time, and some of whom have most of the time, a mode of being determined by what they are and represent in the total scheme of the play rather than by any form of psychic 'life' fluctuating among 'motives'.

A somewhat similar point, in his discussion of the general inadequacy of the traditional concept of character,[1] is made by L. C. Knights, who also examines the play as a non-naturalistic drama in the light of the metaphorical process in general, and provides some brilliant close analysis of the idea of Justice in the play, which he claims offers the audience not a novel concept but rather the question of Justice 'lifted to a plane transcending that of our everyday conceptions', thus providing a new direction for imaginative thought.[2]

Other papers deal with various aspects of the same play. Hildegard Schumann[3] sees two basic concepts of Nature in the play, which may roughly be equated with those of Hobbes and Hooker, and argues against some of the recent nihilistic views of the ending. Two groups of images, those of division relating to public evil and of confinement connected with private evil, are related to the moral structure of the play by John W. Velz,[4] who claims that Shakespeare demonstrates two moral truths: that evils multiply when the head of state makes a wrong decision, and that the function of evil is to teach man by suffering. The important character of Albany receives some close attention from Warren Stevenson,[5] who argues that he is the transformed soul of the British people and of humanity, and from Peter Mortensen,[6] who stresses his 'ordinary' qualities of caution, patience, and calmness, without which neither goodness nor order nor justice can long survive. In a scholarly piece Dean Frye[7] provides a context for Lear's 'unbuttoning', which leads him to some interesting conclusions about the moral content of the play, among which is that the good in the play is

man-made, not sent by the ambiguous gods. It is far different from ceremonial attempts to create something better than unaccommodated man. It is an art which draws on nature, like the art of the physician who is Cordelia's agent, which somehow taps the resources of natural order through music.

Among the tragedies it is, of course, *Hamlet* which claims the bulk of critical attention, being the subject of three books and numerous essays. Salvador de Madariaga[8] has issued a second edition of his celebrated essay, to which he adds an epilogue replying to the points made by J. Dover Wilson. He claims to 'have shown that Hamlet has a self-centred nature, and an attitude to life resembling the Borgias', and depicts a barbarous, intellectually subtle, and egotistical Prince in opposition to what he regards as the sentimental hero-worship of most commentators. The play is also used as the basis for an important study by Morris Weitz[9] of the philosophy

[1] 'The Question of Character in Shakespeare', *Further Explorations*, pp. 186–204.

[2] '*King Lear* as Metaphor', *ibid*. pp. 169–85.

[3] '*König Lear*', *Shakespeare Jahrbuch*, C/CI (1965), 192–207. (This is the first essay to be noticed in this review which appears in a new annual of this name, published in Weimar. To avoid the bibliographical confusion thus caused, the already existing *Shakespeare Jahrbuch* has renamed itself *Deutsche Shakespeare-Gesellschaft West Jahrbuch*.)

[4] 'Division, Confinement, and the Moral Structure of *King Lear*', *Rice University Studies*, LI (1965), 97–108.

[5] 'Albany as Archetype in *King Lear*', *Modern Language Quarterly*, XXVI (1965), 257–64.

[6] 'The Role of Albany', *Shakespeare Quarterly*, XVI (1965), 217–26.

[7] 'The Context of Lear's Unbuttoning', *ELH*, XXXII (1965), 17–31.

[8] *On Hamlet* (Frank Cass, 1965).

[9] '*Hamlet*' and the Philosophy of Literary Criticism (University of Chicago Press, 1964).

of literary criticism. Weitz attempts to define what criticism is by taking instances of what critics of *Hamlet* have actually done, so that the first part of the book constitutes as valuable an analysis of the major positions taken about the play as any yet written. Central to Weitz's attitude is a belief in 'the logical multiplicity of *Hamlet* criticism, and, consequently, the falsity of the assumption, pervasive in this criticism, that all its discourse is true or false statement'; and he proceeds to isolate the four functions of criticism: to describe (Does Hamlet delay?), to explain (Why does Hamlet delay?), to evaluate (Is *Hamlet* a great play?), to theorize about poetics (Why is *Hamlet* tragic?), noting that only one of these processes—the first—involves answers that are true or false. In the second half of the book, Weitz groups the principal issues that criticism deals with under one or other of the four functions he has defined, and tests the validity of particular criticisms, chosen as representative specimens. It is here that many critics of the play come in for some harsh handling: for example, Lily B. Campbell is castigated for offering as description what is really explanation; Ernest Jones's views are rejected as having an untenable hypothesis which ignores Hamlet's love of his father which Weitz sees a *datum* of the text; and, perhaps most surprisingly, G. Wilson Knight is dismissed because 'his entire criticism, both in theory and practice, is not true'. While it is very useful to have Weitz's detailed analyses, it appears to me that his position can be challenged on several grounds: basically that the difference between 'explanation' and 'description' in a dramatic work is not always as clearly defined as he would suggest, and specifically that it is surely true that there lies behind much of the criticism Weitz discusses the tacit understanding that 'there is no true, best, correct, or right explanation, reading, interpretation or understanding of *Hamlet*'. Three articles deal with specialized aspects of Weitz's subject: Neille Shoemaker[1] surveys the aesthetic criticism of the play from 1692 to 1699; Walter Muschg[2] examines critically the influence of the play on German writers; and Harold Jenkins[3] supplies as clear a marking through the wood of *Hamlet* writings as one could wish for in a small compass.

The third book-length study of the play[4] is a surprising performance for the year 1965. Its author, Arthur G. Davis, develops at repetitious length what is virtually a Bradleian-type character study. Davis's scrutiny is directed to such matters as the question of Hamlet's insanity, his procrastination, his personal relationship with Horatio, his personal reasons for his attitude to his mother's remarriage, and the nature of the Ghost, etc. All this and much more is achieved by an exclusive concentration on motive, personality, and explained behaviour; and by an almost total lack of reference to the poetic and verbal effects of the play, and an apparent ignoring of almost everything written on the play since 1935. For Davis, Hamlet is 'the good man...at the opposite extreme from a moral depravity that can assimilate many wrongs' and one whose faults arise 'basically from a spirituality and the weakness that accompanies it in man'. Hermann J. Weigand,[5] taking a similar approach to Davis's, comes to a quite different conclusion about the Prince, whom he views as a pitiful adolescent whose incarceration in a mental institution would be required by society if death did not intervene.

[1] 'The Aesthetic Criticism of *Hamlet* from 1692 to 1699', *Shakespeare Quarterly*, XVI (1965), 99–104.
[2] 'Deutschland ist Hamlet', *Deutsche Shakespeare-Gesellschaft West Jahrbuch* (1965), pp. 32–58.
[3] '*Hamlet* Then Till Now', *Shakespeare Survey 18* (1965), 34–45.
[4] *Hamlet and the Eternal Problem of Man* (St John's University Press, New York, 1964).
[5] 'Hamlet's Consistent Inconsistency', *The Persistence of Shakespeare Idolatry*, ed. H. M. Schueller (Wayne State University Press, Detroit, 1964), pp. 135–72.

Other writers stress different aspects of the play, with Gunnar Boklund[1] noting the various kinds of despair the hero passes through before asserting his *virtu* at the end; Matthew N. Proser[2] reading the play as pre-eminently one about knowledge and Hamlet's coming to a recognition of his human limitations in order to act as best he can; and Robert Hapgood[3] likening it to the absurdist drama in its rhythm of arrested actions and its critique of human deeds and communication. A far more aggressively modern reading is offered by Stanley Cooperman,[4] who rather long-windedly compares Hamlet with Dostoyevski's Underground Man as a victim of existentialist disgust and despair, who is able to achieve consciousness through suffering, and thus emerges as the true anti-hero. Two writers draw on historical scholarship to illuminate the play. Ruth M. Levitsky[5] argues that Hamlet's problem of what constitutes true nobility was a living issue for the sixteenth century, which saw the alternatives as Aristotelianism, Stoicism, and Christian Ethic; the Prince, however, avoids a clear-cut choice and manages a *mélange* of 'Passion combined with Reason, sensitivity combined with circumspection, faith in Divine Providence combined with faith in oneself'. Renaissance writings on medicine and psychology are used by Burton R. Pollin[6] to suggest a death-wish in Hamlet, and his impulse to suicide as a dominant theme of the play. The three articles just mentioned appear in the first issue of a new annual, *Shakespeare Studies*, edited by J. Leeds Barroll and published by the University of Cincinnati. It is a beautifully bound and printed volume of substantial critical essays and long reviews, which would appear to aim at being thoroughly academic in its policy. Altogether it is a promising addition to the yearly Shakespeare output, spoiled for me only by its lack of an index and the hideously 'pop' portrait of the bard on its cover.

Among the more limited aspects of *Hamlet* considered are Francis R. Olley's[7] analysis of Hamlet's action in not killing Claudius at prayer, by which he both avoids the dreaded act of revenge and yet fulfils the evil demands of the revenge code; and Alex Newall's[8] contention that the 'To be, or not to be' soliloquy is not a meditation on suicide but an expression of Hamlet's central problems at that time. George W. Williams[9] has an interesting note on the connotations of sleep in the play, which he sees as being those of inattention, inactivity, and evasion of responsibility; Dorothy Hockey[10] illuminates the phrase 'Wormwood! Wormwood!' by reference to the herbal lore which would have been known to the Elizabethan audience; and B. L. Reid[11] gives a reading of v, i as the prelude to Hamlet's Passion, where the purger of Denmark accepts God's will and sees his own role in its proper perspective.

[1] 'Judgment in *Hamlet*', *Essays on Shakespeare*, ed. G. W. Chapman (Princeton University Press, 1965), pp. 116–37.
[2] 'Hamlet and the Name of Action', *Essays on Shakespeare*, ed. Gordon Ross Smith (Pennsylvania State University Press, 1965), pp. 84–114.
[3] 'Hamlet Nearly Absurd: The Dramaturgy of Delay', *Tulane Drama Review*, IX (1965), 132–45.
[4] 'Shakespeare's Anti-Hero: Hamlet and the Underground Man', *Shakespeare Studies*, I (1965), 37–63.
[5] 'Rightly to be Great', *ibid.* pp. 142–67.
[6] 'Hamlet, a Successful Suicide', *ibid.* pp. 240–60.
[7] 'Claudius at Prayer: The Problem of Motivation in *Hamlet*', *Drama Critique*, VII (1964), 22–5.
[8] 'The Dramatic Context and Meaning of Hamlet's "To be or not to be" Soliloquy', *PMLA*, LXXX (1965), 38–50.
[9] 'Sleep in *Hamlet*', *Renaissance Papers 1964* (Southeastern Renaissance Conference, 1965), pp. 17–21.
[10] '"Wormwood, wormwood!"', *English Language Notes*, II (1965), 174–7.
[11] 'The Last Act and the Action of *Hamlet*', *Yale Review*, LIV (1964), 51–80.

Five of the major tragedies are linked by Matthew Proser[1] who, in a good book, sees their heroes as victims of a common tragic discrepancy

between the main character's self-conception and his full humanity as it is displayed in action. Briefly, my idea is this: although in each tragedy we find a major character who is confronted by a critical situation, the action the hero takes is as much determined by his conception of himself, his 'heroic image', as by exterior circumstances.

While this approach is not revolutionary, the author's unpretentious reading of the plays he discusses enables him to provide genuine illumination of some of the characters' problems. For example, to the more or less accepted view of Brutus as a man who brings catastrophe to Rome and himself by his acting out the role of self-appointed saviour in the face of a quite different political reality, he adds some perceptive analysis of the language Brutus uses as a vehicle for his own preconceptions and fears which he construes as 'reason'. Novel too is the opinion that Brutus's dilemma is endemic to all human action:

For civilized man, at the heart of action is the chosen self which reflects the chosen ideal, and even the necessity of choice is a form of tyranny.

The essay on *Macbeth* is superior to that on *Caesar*; and Proser works out with considerable virtuosity the way in which the false image of manliness (of which the crown is the symbolic proof, while murder is its means of expression) struggles with and finally dominates the hero's humane tendencies. Among the many fine things in this piece are the discussion of the functions of Banquo's Ghost and of the degree to which the hero is the source of his own fate, and a subtle account of Shakespeare's management of the final Act.

Coriolanus and *Othello* are taken together as explorations of the limitations of the noble-soldier hero on the public and personal levels. Rightly, Proser's discussion of the love drama centres on the way the hero's mind works in symbolic terms, and on the dramatic form given to Othello's and Iago's rhetorical impulses. In the later play, however, the dramatic juxta-positions of characters and the impact of the key scenes are given more emphasis, with excellent results in the discussion of Virgilia's importance, and of the impact of the 'gown of humility' scene. Antony, also, attempts to live by the image of himself as the noble soldier he conceives himself to have been; but by means of his own sensuality and Cleopatra's manipulation of it, his image is destroyed, only to be reasserted by the Egyptian queen in her final vision of him as soldier, hero, and husband. This is a book which is well worth every student's attention; but there are indications throughout that it is but an interim report on a discussion of Shake-spearian tragedy as a whole which the author has not yet fully worked out.

Elias Schwartz[2] also focuses attention on the characters of the tragic heroes and attempts to define their reality, which he locates in the Christian concept of the person that could not have existed before the Incarnation, 'the very ground of the super-eminent dignity of the human person'. John W. Draper[3] also contrasts Attic with Shakespearian tragedy, and sees Shakespeare as being hardly conscious of ὕβρις in his earlier tragedies, creating 'a great protagonist in the Sophoclean mould' only in Coriolanus.

[1] *The Heroic Image in Shakespeare's Tragedies* (Princeton University Press, 1965).
[2] 'The Idea of the Person in Shakespearian Tragedy', *Shakespeare Quarterly*, XVI (1965), 39–48.
[3] '"Hybris" in Shakespeare's Tragic Heroes', *Etudes Anglaises*, XVIII (1965), 228–34.

There has been a varying amount of work on the other tragedies. *Romeo and Juliet* receives attention in two good essays: Gordon R. Smith,[1] in a very well-written piece, performs a valuable service in surveying the main interpretations of the play and providing a balanced account both of its modern appeal and of its themes as they work on various levels; and Norman Holland[2] delightfully demonstrates, by means of an analysis of the character of Mercutio, how 'a character...can be both realistic and, as Wilson Knight would have him, "purely symbol[ic] of a poetic vision"'. It would appear that *Timon of Athens* has a special appeal for Marxist critics: for Walter Martin[3] sets himself to examine how Shakespeare's brilliant insight into the monetary system can be explained from the social development of the seventeenth century, viewing the play as essentially concerned with the downfall of a class. Armin-Gerd Kuckhoff[4] also stresses the theme of money, notes Marx's own observation of it, and suggests that only on the stage of the Socialist world can the play's richness, realism, and prodigious unity be realized. A context for both of these articles, and indeed for all criticism of the play, is provided by a well-printed and illustrated book on the literary history of *Timon* by Francelia Butler,[5] who has read and critically digested apparently all significant work on the piece. She arranges the studies in two main groups: those dealing with structure and those with meaning; and provides a conclusion which suggests the possibility of a synthesis between these two main streams of critical activity.

Two quite different views of *Macbeth* are offered by B. L. Reid[6] and Elizabeth Nielsen.[7] The former argues that the compact form of the play 'is a form of hope for the central meanings of the play', which deals with moral absolutes and the loss and recovery of grace; the latter, however, reads the play in the light of the law of tanistry, and sees Macbeth as being motivated by a sense of injustice rather than ambition. Two illuminating notes are provided by Grover Smith[8] on the justification supplied by Renaissance iconography for Shakespeare's linking of the 'naked new-born babe' and 'heaven's cherubim'; and by Dennis Biggins[9] on the association of scorpions with flattering treachery.

Among the Roman heroes, the character of Coriolanus has received some analysis. The presence of an internal conflict, generated by Coriolanus's recognition of the concept of selfless honour and his awareness of conscience, is detected by Charles Mitchell,[10] who lays stress on the lack of feeling and desire for the reward of honour. However, Dean Frye[11] finds Coriolanus rather less culpable than Mitchell does, noting that the comments on the man provided by other characters which carry greatest weight with the audience are those which see more to praise

---

[1] 'The Balance of Themes in *Romeo and Juliet*', *Essays on Shakespeare*, ed. Smith, pp. 15–66.

[2] 'Mercutio, Mine Own Son the Dentist', *ibid.* pp. 3–14.

[3] 'Shakespeare's *Timon von Athen* im Lichte der Widerspiegelungstheorie', *Shakespeare Jahrbuch*, C/CI (1965), 227–52.

[4] '*Timon von Athen*—Konzeption und Afführungspraxis', *ibid.* pp. 135–59.

[5] *The Strange Critical Fortunes of Shakespeare's 'Timon of Athens'* (Iowa State University Press, 1966).

[6] '*Macbeth* and the Play of Absolutes', *Sewanee Review*, LXXIII (1965), 19–47.

[7] '*Macbeth*: The Nemesis of the Post-Shakespearian Actor', *Shakespeare Quarterly*, XVI (1965), 193–200.

[8] 'The Naked New-Born Babe in *Macbeth*: Some Iconographical Evidence', *Renaissance Papers 1964*, pp. 21–8.

[9] 'Scorpions, Serpents, and Treachery in *Macbeth*', *Shakespeare Studies*, I (1965), 29–36.

[10] 'Coriolanus: Power as Honor', *ibid.* pp. 199–226.

[11] 'Commentary in Shakespeare: The Case of Coriolanus', *ibid.* pp. 105–17.

than to blame. As usual the criticism of *Antony and Cleopatra* tends to be concerned with the nature of its tragedy and the impact of its style. Working from Shakespeare's deviations from North and other contemporary plays with similar themes, Paul A. Jorgensen[1] locates two plays rather than one: the first in the tradition of a soldier's relation with a seductress, the other exemplifying the triumph of Love. The tragic element is believed by Anthony Caputi[2] to be different from that in the other tragedies because of its want of terror and its capacity to convey an experience we think of as peculiarly metaphysical, in that it concerns two characters who evade conventional moral judgments. The part played by the language in the effect of the play is examined by Edith M. Roerecke,[3] who suggestively isolates its Baroque elements which are exhilarating to the senses but not wholly convincing to the mind; and by Madeleine Doran,[4] who sees a contrast between the Elizabethan ideal of excellence, which dominates the poetic frame of the play, and the 'complex, unsentimental relationship between two richly endowed but very imperfect people'. Among shorter notes on the Roman plays: David L. Carson[5] argues that the Casca–Cinna dispute in *Caesar*, II, i, links Brutus's decision to kill Caesar with the prodigies; John Long[6] displays how the drinking scene in *Antony and Cleopatra* is a composite of two bacchanals described by Plutarch; and Peter Seng[7] suggests that the song in II, vii of the same play is a parody of a Latin hymn, *Veni sancte spiritus*.

One of the features of recent Shakespeare criticism has been the increase of interest in the comedies, and here one strong influence has been the work of Northrop Frye. During the past year this critic has published one of the best books[8] on Shakespeare's comic art yet to appear. Frye, who is in his own terminology an *Odyssey* rather than *Iliad* critic, has no doubt that tragedy is but a phase rather than the climax of excellence in Shakespeare's work, in which 'there is a logical evolution towards romance...and consequently no anti–climax, whether technical or spiritual, in passing from *King Lear* through *Pericles* to *The Tempest*'. The book proceeds to present a complex theory of Shakespearian comedy, the essence of which is seen to lie in structure rather than in any special illumination of reality. In eschewing realistic conventions, and adopting stylization or distortion, the dramatist allows 'the story [to seek] its own end instead of holding the mirror up to nature'. Frye makes his distinction between that kind of comedy which demands imaginative faith in a self-contained unrealistic world (the dramatic experience) and that which involves the critical capacity (the dramatic construct), by means of an incisive comparison between Shakespeare's and Jonson's art and the directions in which they developed. The second section of the book deals with the importance of convention, particularly by reference to *Pericles* and *Cymbeline*, and argues that, because 'literary conven-

---

[1] 'Antony and the Protesting Soldiers: A Renaissance Tradition for the Structure of *Antony and Cleopatra*', *Essays on Shakespeare*, ed. Smith, pp. 163–81.

[2] 'Shakespeare's *Antony and Cleopatra*: Tragedy Without Terror', *Shakespeare Quarterly*, XVI (1965), 183–92.

[3] 'Baroque Aspects of *Antony and Cleopatra*', *Essays on Shakespeare*, ed. Smith, pp. 182–95.

[4] '"High Events as These": The Language of Hyperbole in *Antony and Cleopatra*', *Queen's Quarterly*, LXXII (1965), 26–51.

[5] 'The Dramatic Importance of Prodigies in *Julius Caesar*, Act II, i', *English Language Notes*, II (1965), 177–80.

[6] '*Antony and Cleopatra*: A Double Critical Reversal', *Renaissance Papers 1964*, pp. 28–35.

[7] 'Shakespearean Hymn-Parody', *Renaissance News*, XVIII (1965), 4–7.

[8] *A Natural Perspective: The Development of Shakespearean Comedy and Romance* (Columbia University Press, New York and London, 1965).

tions are descended from myths', then they enable the poet 'to recapture something of the pure and primitive identity of myth'.

The typical comic structure of Shakespeare Frye takes to be the Lent–Saturnalia–*komos* pattern which tends to draw the audience into participation by offering a model of impossible desire in the festive conclusion, and a drive to find personal and social identity. However, there is always in any well-constructed comedy the *idiotes* figure who stands outside the comic action and is often paired with the clown. The comic point lies in the tension between the two worlds thus created:

Participation and detachment, sympathy and ridicule, sociability and isolation, are inseparable in the complex we call comedy, a complex that is begotten by the paradox of life itself, in which merely to exist is both to be a part of something else and yet never to be a part of it, and in which all freedom and joy are inseparably a belonging and an escape.

The final section of the book is devoted to a discussion of Shakespeare's use of the myth of nature and his incorporation within the comic structure of chaos, rebirth, and renewal. This brief outline does not do justice to Frye's brilliant critical performance, nor does it indicate the many fine discussions it contains on individual plays, and on such topics as the problem of character in comedy, or the role of the Fools, or comic marriage, or the theme of identity. This is a book which no one interested in Shakespeare can afford not to read. A group of other studies examine various aspects of the comedies generally. John S. Baxter[1] stresses their festive mood and the common search of the main characters for fulfilment; A. Colby Sprague[2] discusses the moments of emotional change in various plays; and Dean Frye[3] questions the sophisticated attempts to read the low comic plots as realistic *exposés* of the main plots in the early romantic plays.

Since Harold Brooks laid bare the graver matters contained in *The Comedy of Errors*, the earliest plays are getting more attention than formerly. A book was being prepared on these plays by E. M. W. Tillyard just before his death, and the parts he had completed have now been published by his son.[4] It is divided into two parts: one being on the background and range of Shakespearian comedy, the other containing discussions of *The Comedy of Errors*, *The Taming of the Shrew*, *The Two Gentlemen of Verona*, *Love's Labour's Lost*, and *The Merchant of Venice*. It was to have been completed by an essay on *A Midsummer Night's Dream* and a general conclusion. In seeking for a point of view from which these comedies may be criticized with justice, Tillyard rejects as old-fashioned the division of literature into genres, and suggests that one should approach the plays by viewing them in terms of their psychological content. Thus comedy contains 'a variety of mental states', which cut across traditional type-divisions, and include both the drive to be part of one's society, the urge to opt out of its regulated patterns, as well as the desire for escape and laughter. The special appeal made by Shakespeare's comedy is to those mental reaches which find their expression in romance materials, whether they derive from oral or literary originals. However, although Tillyard allows the influence of the

[1] 'Present Mirth: Shakespeare's Romantic Comedies', *Queen's Quarterly*, LXXII (1965), 52–77.
[2] 'Moments of Seriousness in Shakespearian Comedy', *Deutsche Shakespeare-Gesellschaft West Jahrbuch* (1965), pp. 240–7.
[3] 'The Question of Shakespearean Parody', *Essays in Criticism*, XV (1965), 22–6.
[4] *Shakespeare's Early Comedies* (Chatto and Windus, 1965).

Italian novella, or of the plays of the University Wits, or medieval narratives on Shakespeare, he is dubious about those 'festive' elements which are so prominent a part of the criticism of Frye or C. L. Barber. The chapters on the individual plays contain a good deal of illuminating incidental comment. Among other papers on these early plays, *Love's Labour's Lost* receives most attention, with J. V. Cunningham[1] demonstrating Shakespeare's facility by examining three key cruxes in the light of some theories of composition of the period; and Anselm Schlösser[2] and James L. Calderwood[3] throwing light on Shakespeare's attitude to taffeta phrases and the true purpose of language. The theme of alienation is detected in *The Comedy of Errors* by Schlösser;[4] and William O. Scott[5] illustrates how Proteus in *The Two Gentlemen of Verona* incorporates many of the qualities of mythic figures.

The fourth Shakespeare volume to be included in Arnold's *Studies in English Literature* series is devoted to *Much Ado About Nothing*. In it J. R. Mulryne[6] stresses how the comic experience of the play is 'as much that of a world in motion as of a world verbalized', and gives a sensitive commentary on the action which shows an admirable theatrical awareness. In other chapters he considers the part played by character in the play and its moral content, the key to his attitude perhaps being found in his dictum 'we must expect no more than a moral paradigm; and accord it proportional place in the total literary and theatrical experience'. The essay on what Mulryne calls the 'intricate texture' and the suggestive final comparison with *The Winter's Tale* are characterized by imagination and a fine consciousness of the limits of criticism. On the other plays of this period, Pinchas Blumenthal[7] stresses the importance of the Jewishness of Shylock; Barbara K. Lewalski[8] discusses the involvement of the Epiphany and the spirit of Christmas in *Twelfth Night*; and Leonard Goldstein[9] comments on the treatment of the child–parent relationship in *The Merry Wives of Windsor*.

Measure for Measure continues to provoke interesting essays about its problems. Howard C. Cole[10] faces up well to the major difficulties and concludes that it is St Paul who lies behind much of the Duke's behaviour rather than Christ; while Herbert Howarth[11] makes good use of the *Basilikon Doron* to prove that Shakespeare was blending flattery with criticism of James I. Two passages in the play are taken up by Nevill Coghill,[12] whose contention that Lucio penetrates the Duke's disguise is denied on thematic grounds by Christopher Spencer.[13] The character-

---

[1] '"With That Facility": False Starts and Revisions in *Love's Labour's Lost*', *Essays on Shakespeare*, ed. Chapman, pp. 91–115.

[2] '*Love's Labour's Lost*. Shakespeares Jahrmarkt der Eitelkeit', *Zeitschrift für Anglistik und Amerikanistik*, XIII (1965), 25–34.

[3] '*Love's Labour's Lost*: A Wantoning with Words', *Studies in English Literature*, V (1965), 317–22.

[4] 'Das Motiv der Entfremdung in der *Komödie der Irrungen*', *Shakespeare Jahrbuch*, C/CI (1965), 57–71.

[5] 'Proteus in Spenser and Shakespeare: The Lover's Identity', *Shakespeare Studies*, I (1965), 283–93.

[6] *Shakespeare: 'Much Ado About Nothing'* (Studies in English Literature, 16; Edward Arnold, 1965).

[7] 'Shylock, der Jude', *Deutsche Shakespeare-Gesellschaft West Jahrbuch* (1965), pp. 279–304.

[8] 'Thematic Patterns in *Twelfth Night*', *Shakespeare Studies*, I (1965), 168–81.

[9] 'Some Aspects of Marriage and Inheritance in Shakespeare's *The Merry Wives of Windsor* and Chapman's *All Fools*', *Zeitschrift für Anglistik und Amerikanistik*, XII (1964), 375–86.

[10] 'The "Christian" Context of *Measure for Measure*', *JEGP*, LXIV (1965), 425–51.

[11] 'Shakespeare's Flattery in *Measure for Measure*', *Shakespeare Quarterly*, XVI (1965), 29–38.

[12] 'Two Small Points in *Measure for Measure*', *Review of English Studies*, n.s., XVI (1965), 393–6.

[13] 'Lucio and the Friar's Hood', *English Language Notes*, III (1965), 17–21.

ization of *All's Well that Ends Well* receives some defence from Robert H. Hethmon,[1] who sees the play as a good theatre script and 'a complex of realistic character'; and also from Robert Hapgood,[2] who is pleasantly unorthodox in his sympathy with Parolles's vitality and decision to cling to life, shame notwithstanding. It is, however, *Troilus and Cressida* among the Problem Plays which appears to be stimulating the hardest thinking and all five studies concerning it have something of value to offer. The best of them attempts to answer the question 'What kind of play is it?' To this R. J. Kaufmann[3] replies, in a brilliant examination of the play's position in Shakespeare's development:

Shakespeare's strangest contribution to [the] literature of preliminary devaluation...It is a pre-tragic dramatization of human need for ceremonial participation, appropriately stressing the imagery and practice of self-consumption, and technically devised to permit complex scrutiny of suspension in multiplicity.

Part of the complexity noted by Kaufmann lies for D. R. C. Marsh[4] in the simultaneous assertion of and challenge to human integrity; and its technical devising has importance for Norman Rabkin[5] in the way the themes are expressed by rather than through the double plot structure. The ideas of honour and love are explored respectively by Alice Shalvi[6] and David E. Jones.[7] Aspects of *The Tempest* which are examined are the play's refutation of Montaigne's cultural primitivism, by Dean Ebnor;[8] the symbolism of Prospero's punishments and rewards, by Mary Rickey;[9] and the use of metalanguage and the difference between speech and communication, by W. T. Jewkes.[10]

Shakespeare's ability to include both the wide perspective and the personal close-up in his history plays encourages critics to concentrate on one or other of these aspects of the plays. Some take a single important figure for examination: for example, Adrien Bonjour[11] defends the Bastard's indomitable spirit and his valuable advice to King John; Samuel M. Pratt[12] notes the differences between Shakespeare's and the Chronicles' treatment of the mythic status of Humphrey, Duke of Gloucester; William C. Morris[13] uses the character of Derby to illustrate the dangers of cutting *Richard III* for stage performance; and Larry S. Champion[14] traces the

[1] 'The Case for *All's Well*', *Drama Critique*, VII (1964), 26–31.
[2] 'The Life of Shame: Parolles and *All's Well*', *Essays in Criticism*, XV (1965), 269–78.
[3] 'Ceremonies for Chaos: The Status of *Troilus and Cressida*', ELH, XXXII (1965), 139–59.
[4] 'Interpretation and Misinterpretation: The Problem of *Troilus and Cressida*', *Shakespeare Studies*, I (1965), 182–98.
[5] '*Troilus and Cressida*: The Uses of the Double Plot', *ibid.* pp. 264–82.
[6] '"Honor" in *Troilus and Cressida*', *Studies in English Literature*, V (1965), 283–302.
[7] '"Mad Idolatry": Love in *Troilus and Cressida*', *Drama Critique*, VII (1964), 8–12.
[8] '*The Tempest*: Rebellion and the Ideal State', *Shakespeare Quarterly*, XVI (1965), 161–74.
[9] 'Prospero's Living Drolleries', *Renaissance Papers 1964*, pp. 35–43.
[10] '"Excellent Dumb Discourse": The Limits of the Language in *The Tempest*', *Essays on Shakespeare*, ed. Smith, pp. 196–210.
[11] 'Bastinado for the Bastard?', *English Studies*, XLV (1964), 169–76.
[12] 'Shakespeare and Humphrey Duke of Gloucester: A Study in Myth', *Shakespeare Quarterly*, XVI (1965), 201–16.
[13] 'Consistency in *Richard III*', *Drama Critique*, VII (1964), 40–6.
[14] 'The Evolution of Mistress Quickly', *Papers on English Language and Literature*, I (1965), 99–108.

growth and changes in the character of Mistress Quickly in the plays in which she appears. Ranging rather more widely, A. L. Morton[1] links the tension in the history plays with that between the feudal and bourgeois 'worlds' which existed in Shakespeare's own day, and traces the playwright's changing attitudes to kingship, war, and man's control over his political destiny. A rather different dichotomy—that between the epic and the pastoral—is seen to lie behind Shakespeare's organization of 'his system of contrasts and parallels in the histories' by Charles R. Forker.[2] On individual early plays, or certain aspects of them, there are two essays of value. A fresh and thought-provoking treatment of Shakespeare's utilization of the two images of King John which existed at the time is supplied by John R. Elliott;[3] and Nicholas Brooke[4] argues that *Richard III*'s stature as tragedy is derived in part from the delicate structural contrast between characterization and moral history.

Naturally, it is the second tetralogy that attracts most interest. Ronald Berman[5] examines, through an analysis of the motifs of disease, imposture, and inhumanity, the nature of guilt in the *Henry IV* plays, and Hal's attempts to deal with it. Hal's behaviour as prince and king is examined by Peter G. Phialas,[6] who sees him as the monarch that achieves the reconciliation between the demands of public function and the claims of individual nature which had eluded his predecessors. Jonas Barish[7] stresses the element of self-rejection in the Prince and in an original way compares the character with Antony; and Anselm Schlösser[8] unconvincingly argues for the juxtaposition of two opposing views of France in *Henry V* and for a strong vein of irony in the patriotic picture of Agincourt. It is, however, Hal's relationship with Falstaff which brings out the best in three critics. One of the most suggestive considerations of the topic to appear for some time is Harold E. Toliver's [9] balanced discussion of the nature of the history play which draws on character, ritual, and mythological approaches. Falstaff and Hal are both viewed in the context of the theme of theft at high and low social levels by Robert Hapgood,[10] who makes good use of contemporary rogue pamphlets. The initial confrontation scene in the tavern in *1 Henry IV* is sensitively dissected by Waldo F. McNeir,[11] who shows how its miniature five-act structure contains both the 'balance and symmetry of Renaissance art and the involute multiplicity of Baroque art'. Francelia Butler's[12] note on the relationship between old age and moral competence in the second tetralogy, and Anselm Schlösser's[13] argument that the arrange-

[1] 'Shakespeare's Historical Outlook', *Zeitschrift für Anglistik und Amerikanistik*, XII (1964), 229–43.

[2] 'Shakespeare's Chronicle Plays as Historical-Pastoral', *Shakespeare Studies*, I (1965), 85–104.

[3] 'Shakespeare and the Double Image of King John', *ibid*. pp. 64–84.

[4] 'Reflecting Gems and Dead Bones: Tragedy Versus History in *Richard III*', *Critical Quarterly*, VII (1965), 123–34.

[5] 'The Nature of Guilt in the *Henry IV* Plays', *Shakespeare Studies*, I (1965), 18–28.

[6] 'Shakespeare's *Henry V* and the Second Tetralogy', *Studies in Philology*, LXII (1965), 155–75.

[7] 'The Turning Away of Prince Hal', *Shakespeare Studies*, I (1965), 9–17.

[8] 'Der Widerstreit von Patriotismus und Humanismus in *Heinrich V*', *Zeitschrift für Anglistik und Amerikanistik*, XII (1964), 244–56.

[9] 'Falstaff, the Prince, and the History Play', *Shakespeare Quarterly*, XVI (1965), 63–80.

[10] 'Falstaff's Vocation', *ibid*. pp. 91–8.

[11] 'Structure and Theme in the First Tavern Scene of *Henry IV, Part One*', *Essays on Shakespeare*, ed. Smith, pp. 67–83.

[12] 'The Relationship Between Moral Competence and Old Age in *Richard II, 2 Henry IV*, and *Henry V*', *Shakespeare Quarterly*, XVI (1965), 236–8.

[13] 'Konturen unter der Oberfläche in *Heinrich VIII*', *Zeitschrift für Anglistik und Amerikanistik*, XII (1964), 257–65.

ment of diverse elements in *Henry VIII* reveals the essence of despotism, each has points of interest.

The quatercentenary aftermath continues to produce a number of general books on Shakespeare aimed at various classes of readers. Three are directed to 'the intelligent general reader', and all have something of value to offer that imaginary being. Norman Holland's *The Shakespeare Imagination*[1] is based on what must have been a very good series of television programmes. The various chapters are brightly written, preserving the tone of the medium for which they were designed: and the whole volume, with its well-chosen illustrations and excellent good sense, does exactly what the author hopes—namely, provides general introductions to thirteen major plays and offers 'largely the coin of current Shakespeare teaching'. Rather less lavishly, though with a similar cogency, K. R. S. Iyengar's *Shakespeare: His World and his Art*[2] covers the same ground as Holland, and in addition interestingly finds parallels between the plays and Indian life and literature. A rather less academic and more personal guide to the works is John Wain's *The Living World of Shakespeare*.[3] Wain tends to look on his writing of the book as something of a God-ordained duty in order to rescue the general reader from the clutches of the historical scholars. However, once he has got his Foreword off his chest, he settles down to giving his chosen audience a most readable account of the poet's work which is full of perceptive judgments and insights.

Two other books assume a rather more expert knowledge of the plays and their critics. John Arthos's *The Art of Shakespeare*,[4] a wide-ranging though sometimes vaguely written study, attempts an exploration of Shakespeare's philosophy of the individual human character. He traces this topic through three groups of plays selected from the tragedies, the serious comedies, and the romances. The great excellence of Shakespeare in this sphere Arthos sees as the ability to hold all things in a balance similar to Nature itself of which his art is thus a reflexion. The tragic heroes Arthos chooses to discuss are viewed as three manifestations of men's differing inability to reconcile their inner lives to the outer reality of the world. Macbeth, 'the tragic subject *par excellence*', exemplifies the man who enters on a path of evil and whose lack of imagination forces him to live so inwardly that he is unable to reconcile himself to the world's truth. Othello, though equally damned in not being able to accept qualities like love, trust, order, and faithfulness, is a superior character to Macbeth because of his conception of honour as an absolute thing; but it is also a quality without grace. In their excessive imaginations Antony and Cleopatra escape tragic judgment because in the last resort they are able to deny mortality. The trilogy of comedies provide comments on human aspiration that only that genre can provide: *The Merchant of Venice* offers a vision of a possible though unbelievable happy existence in its final Act; *All's Well that Ends Well* points to 'the central morality...that love is noble and that the ignoble are unworthy of it'; and *Troilus and Cressida* finds its note of hope in the fact that Troilus survives.

The final section of the book, on *Pericles* and *The Winter's Tale*, really follows on from the conclusions Arthos reached about *Antony and Cleopatra*, though one can see that he felt obliged to interpolate the essay on the comedies, because he argues that the Romances maintain a comic detachment. The issue of personal and natural balance is pursued in the two plays, and *Pericles*

[1] Macmillan, New York, 1964. [2] Asia Publishing House, 1965.
[3] Macmillan, 1964. [4] Barnes and Noble, 1964.

is highly praised for its dramatic sprawl and the visionary response demanded by its hero. *The Winter's Tale* asserts Nature's balance, excellence and powers of renewal in the face of those 'matters in society and in the universe that spoil it'. One gathers that the author's original plan was to include *The Tempest* in this section, but as he decided to postpone discussion of this play to another occasion, presumably it was not really important to his thesis. After a first reading, my opinion of this book was 'woolly', but after a second, when I still found some of the argument hard to follow, perhaps 'difficult' is a more respectful opinion.

David Horowitz's *Shakespeare: An Existentialist View*[1] promises a modern approach. However, the author means by the fashionable term in his title 'a view that proves itself in the reality of lived existence, not in the principles of metaphysic or theological discourse'. He further couples Existentialism with Renaissance humanism as 'a return to the main Western tradition from the divergent stream of neoplatonic (mainly Christian) thought'. The book is divided into two parts: the first of which focuses on the relation between human vision and human realization; and the second on the connexion between human values and human reality. Four plays are used to explore the first of these relationships: *Much Ado About Nothing, Antony and Cleopatra, Lear* and *The Tempest*. *Much Ado* is seen to contain both romantic engagement and satiric detachment, as it projects a conviction, through the empty romance of Claudio and Hero and the imaginative criticism of love's meaning by Beatrice and Benedick, that reality is what men apprehend according to their differing stances. Antony and Cleopatra are a step further on from Beatrice and Benedick in that they realize the fullness of human potential; but Horowitz curiously suggests that the play's answer to the question 'How to give substance to the word "Love"?' is 'Death', in which Antony attains a synthesis of the opposing forces which have dominated his life. *Lear, The Tempest* and *The Winter's Tale* exemplify the regenerative movement out of the tragic abyss with their recognition of how we destroy what we need, a process which brings us self-sense and leads to 'essential reconciliations'. This idea is illuminated by a good exposition of the 'double process' of Nature in the ripening/rotting imagery.

The final section of the book is concerned with what Horowitz calls 'human order' or 'the bonds of human kindness'. *Troilus and Cressida* is analysed to show its ideas on value, and *The Merchant of Venice* as a critique of law as the instrument of 'commodity'. This book certainly conveys a Shakespearian concern with life on this earth; but while it thus emphasizes the 'human' Shakespeare, it tends, because of its pseudo-philosophical and abstracted vocabulary, to intellectualize and rarefy what are often warm human effects.

In shorter general essays, Rudolf Stamm[2] and Wolfgang Clemen[3] wrestle expertly with the difficulties of defining the quintessence of Shakespeare's art; Gustav Kirchner[4] provides a brief run-through of some major problems; Virgil K. Whitaker[5] skilfully traces some few of the poet's personal perceptions and reflexions in his artistic means; A. D. Nuttall[6] resurrects the

---

[1] Hill and Wang, New York, 1965.
[2] 'Wer war Shakespeare?', *Deutsche Shakespeare-Gesellschaft West Jahrbuch* (1965), pp. 80–102.
[3] 'Das Drama Shakespeares', *ibid.* pp. 11–31.
[4] 'Shakespeares Weltgeltung', *Shakespeare Jahrbuch*, c/ci (1965), 160–91.
[5] 'In Search of Shakespeare's Journal', *Studies in English Literature*, v (1965), 303–15.
[6] 'The Argument About Shakespeare's Characters', *Critical Quarterly*, vii (1965), 107–20.

issue of the reality of Shakespeare's characters; Robert B. Heilman[1] gives a fascinating and well-written answer to the question 'What does Shakespeare offer us?'; and Clifford Leech[2] sensitively traces Shakespeare's ability to combine the abstract eloquence and structural juxtaposition of the Elizabethan drama with the sensuous and concrete apprehension of detail and the structural fusion characteristic of the Jacobean drama.

The problem of the Sonnets provokes two opposing approaches: those of G. P. V. Akrigg,[3] who contends that the Q1 order relates an entirely coherent story of spiritual struggle, and of Rudolf Germer,[4] who pleads for a rejection of the cycle as a kind of *roman à clef* and for an examination of the single poems based on artistic rather than biographical principles. Richard Levin[5] gives a close reading of Sonnet CXXIX to display the poem's dramatic rather than logical working-out of the poet's pain. On the other poems, Murray Copland[6] views *The Phoenix and the Turtle* as a conscious contribution to the metaphysical fashion of discussing love in a Platonic vein and as meditation on mortality; and Clifford Leech[7] compares Shakespeare's ability to portray a woman in love in *Venus and Adonis* with Marlowe's in *Hero and Leander*.

There is the usual batch of studies on specialized aspects of the plays. Among those well worth reading on the language are Kenneth Muir's[8] consideration of the attitudes to Shakespeare's imagery during three centuries, which offers some *desiderata* for future study; Harry Levin's[9] quick-witted and learned tour through Shakespeare's nomenclature; C. H. Hobday's[10] tracing of the genesis of the famous 'flattery–dogs–sweets' image cluster; Leslie Hotson's[11] brilliant heraldic exposition of Hotspur's reference to plucking honour from the moon; and J. Copley's[12] discussion of the 'word/ward' and 'fool/fowl/foul' puns. Language's relationship to spectacle in the plays is the subject of a book by Francis Berry,[13] who, in what he hopes is a 'fresh attack on the problem', claims that 'we need a term to express [the] kind of episode... where the imagined spectacle is at odds with the actual spectacle'. He proposes the word 'Inset', which he defines as the dramatist's method of introducing the narrative there-and-then into the dramatic here-and-now. Berry distinguishes five types of Inset: the expository (the narrations of Prospero, Othello, Aegeon, Enobarbus); the interior-plot-required (Falstaff's death, Oliver's escape from the snake in Arden); the voluntary (Mercutio's Queen Mab speech); the songs; the play-within-the-play. A good deal of the commentary in the various chapters on each of these kinds is fairly obvious; but the chapters on the use of the songs is uniformly good and occasionally scintillating, as it is on the subject of the Fool's and Feste's lyrics. The value of the

[1] 'The Role We Give Shakespeare', *Essays on Shakespeare*, ed. Chapman, pp. 3–34.

[2] 'Shakespeare, Elizabethan and Jacobean', *Queen's Quarterly*, LXXII (1965), 5–25.

[3] 'The Shakespeare of the Sonnets', *ibid.* pp. 78–90.

[4] 'Shakespeares Sonette als Sprachkunstwerke', *Deutsche Shakespeare-Gesellschaft West Jahrbuch* (1965), pp. 248–63.   [5] 'Sonnet CXXIX as a "Dramatic Poem"', *Shakespeare Quarterly*, XVI (1965), 175–82.

[6] 'The Dead Phoenix', *Essays in Criticism*, XV (1965), 279–87.

[7] 'Venus and her Nun: Portraits of Women in Love by Shakespeare and Marlowe', *Studies in English Literature*, V (1965), 247–68.

[8] 'Shakespeare's Imagery—Then and Now', *Shakespeare Survey 18* (1965), 46–57.

[9] 'Shakespeare's Nomenclature', *Essays on Shakespeare*, ed. Chapman, pp. 59–90.

[10] 'Why the Sweets Melted: A Study in Shakespeare's Imagery', *Shakespeare Quarterly*, XVI (1965), 3–18.

[11] 'Taking Shakespeare at his Word', *Shakespeare Studies*, I (1965), 137–41.

[12] 'Two Shakespearean Puns', *English Studies*, XLVI (1965), 250–2.

[13] *The Shakespeare Inset* (Routledge and Kegan Paul, 1965).

categories is also demonstrated in a revealing analysis of the Insets of *Hamlet*, which are unusually numerous for the good reason that the play is a revenge tragedy and the mood of revenge

is prospective—the revenger's sights are set on a target that will only show itself as suitable for attack at some point in the future. But the revenger is dedicated to that point in the future and so cannot accept the present.

In a suggestive chapter on the Romances, Berry moves his consideration, of what has been seen up to this point as a dramatic technique, on to the conceptual plane to view these plays as 'entities moving in time and *space*—which is exactly what they are during actual performance on the stage'.

It is rare these days to find writers on Shakespeare able to tackle fruitfully in a small compass the poet's handling of a large issue. However, the proportion is higher than usual this year. Northrop Frye[1] steers a course halfway between the general history of an idea and specific commentary as he dwells on the latent dialectic expressed in the words 'nature' and 'nothing' in the histories, comedies, and Romances. Harold E. Toliver[2] considers Shakespeare's 'Time' as a vital dimension of things conceived as continually lapsing; and Max Lüthi[3] stresses the importance of the motif of losing and finding oneself. Using Renaissance views of their subjects, John Draper[4] and C. A. Patrides[5] consider respectively Shakespeare's ladies-in-waiting and his treatment of the mob.

As writings about Shakespeare become more numerous, it is increasingly the task of the specialist to provide the student with guides to criticism and scholarship. Certain areas are well covered in a recent book, *The Persistence of Shakespeare Idolatry*.[6] In it Henri Peyre[7] wittily laments the barrier which appears to exist between Shakespeare and the French, and provides some fascinating observations on the opinions of nineteenth-century authors and on those aspects of the plays with which the French find fault. The same task is performed more optimistically by Hermann J. Weigand[8] for German appreciation of the playwright; and elsewhere Robert Falk[9] supplies an excellent guide to Shakespeare's influence in America up to 1900, being particularly interesting on the poet's influence on Melville. J. D. Levin[10] and Stanisław Helstýnski[11] discuss Russian and Polish translations of the plays. From the Institute of Russian Literature of the USSR Academy of Sciences comes a very full study (in Russian) of *Shakespeare and Russian Culture*, edited by M. P. Alekseev.[12] So far as English criticism is concerned, S. H.

[1] 'Nature and Nothing', *Essays on Shakespeare*, ed. Chapman, pp. 35–58.
[2] 'Shakespeare and the Abyss of Time', *JEGP*, LXIV (1965), 234–54.
[3] 'Selbstverlust und Selbstverwirklichung bei Shakespeare', *Deutsche Shakespeare-Gesellschaft West Jahrbuch* (1965), pp. 205–28.
[4] 'Shakespeare's Ladies-in-Waiting', *Neophilologus*, XL (1965), 255–62.
[5] '"The Beast With Many Heads": Renaissance Views on the Multitude', *Shakespeare Quarterly*, XVI (1965), 241–6.
[6] Ed. H. M. Schueller, (Wayne State University Press, Detroit, 1964).
[7] 'Shakespeare and Modern French Criticism', pp. 1–46.
[8] 'Shakespeare in German Criticism', pp. 105–33.
[9] 'Shakespeare in America: A Survey to 1900', *Shakespeare Survey 18* (1965), 102–18.
[10] 'Die Westeuropäische Shakespeare-Forschung in Russland und ihre Popularisierung durch V. P. Botkin', *Zeitschrift für Anglistik und Amerikanistik*, XII (1964), 278–96.
[11] 'Polish Translations of Shakespeare in the Past and To-day', *Shakespeare Jahrbuch*, C/CI (1965), 274–93.
[12] Navka Publishing House, Moscow and Leningrad, 1965.

Monk[1] has a good brief study of Dryden's attitudes; Earl R. Wasserman[2] answers the question 'Did Shakespeare's plays, among the Romantics, ever pass beyond idolatry to become a source of archetypes?'; and Anne Paolucci[3] corrects Bradley's wrong notion of Hegel's view of Shakespearian tragedy to suggest future avenues of research. It is manner rather than age or nation that Charles R. Crow[4] concentrates on in his pleasantly written paper on the enduring practice of finding fault with the Bard.

The subject of Christianity in the plays has, during the year, occasioned a good deal of unusually vigorous scholarly discussion, an example of which is G. Wilson Knight's 'private protest'[5] against the injustices done to him in Roland M. Frye's book, *Shakespeare and Christian Doctrine*. On the same subject, Wolfgang Wicht[6] contends that religion plays only a minor role in Shakespeare's work generally; while Robert West[7] suggests that to anyone who respects the Renaissance origin and background of the tragedies they display both man and the cosmos in a dignity that spares us desperation and ultimate rebellion. One book is devoted to Shakespeare's Christianity, R. W. S. Mendl's *Revelation in Shakespeare*.[8] This will not cause any controversy since it is devoted chiefly to proving that there are religious, spiritual, and supernatural elements in Shakespeare's art (which is generally admitted), and that the plays are 'essentially those of an English Christian of his time', a proposition demonstrated by simple statement ('Enobarbus repents like a Christian', 'God is in the background by implication, even if He is not specifically mentioned') and the recording of obvious biblical echoes.

© NORMAN SANDERS 1967

2. SHAKESPEARE'S LIFE, TIMES AND STAGE

reviewed by STANLEY WELLS

The quatercentenary occasioned a spate of books retelling Shakespeare's life story, and attempting to create an image of the elusive personality that should be more accurate, or more glamorous, or more exciting, or more 'contemporary' than the others that were available. We could run the gamut from Burgess, through Rowse, to Bentley. The spate has now dwindled, and the main recent offering is a reprint of a book first printed in 1928. John S. Smart's *Shakespeare: Truth and Tradition*[9] has an excellent 'Memoir of the Author' by W. Macneile Dixon in which he remarks that 'To Smart's friend and successor in the Queen Margaret College Lectureship, Mr Peter Alexander, we owe the transcription of the pencilled chapters and notes, a labour of

---

[1] 'Dryden and the Beginnings of Shakespeare Criticism in the Augustan Age', *The Persistence of Shakespeare Idolatry*, pp. 47–75.

[2] 'Shakespeare and the English Romantic Movement', *ibid*. pp. 77–103.

[3] 'Bradley and Hegel on Shakespeare', *Comparative Literature*, XVI (1964), 211–25.

[4] 'Chiding the Plays: Then Till Now', *Shakespeare Survey 18* (1965), 1–10.

[5] 'Shakespeare and Theology: A Private Protest', *Essays in Criticism*, XV (1965), 95–105.

[6] 'Christliches in Shakespeares Dramen. Zu einigen Fragen der Verwendung und Wiederspiegelung zeitbedingter christlich-religiöser Vorstellungen', *Zeitschrift für Anglistik und Amerikanistik*, XII (1964), 350–74.

[7] 'Morality and its Ground in Shakespeare's Tragedies', *Renaissance Papers 1964*, pp. 43–8.

[8] John Calder, 1964.   [9] Clarendon Press, Oxford, 1966.

love, which made it possible to send this book to the press'. Professor Alexander has been constant in his loyalty. In his own *Shakespeare*, itself one of the offerings of 1964, he wrote: 'of modern works, the best brief introduction to a study of Shakespeare's Life and Times' is Smart's book, and pointed out that it had long been out of print. Now for its reissue he has written a Preface setting Smart's achievement in context. Such a Preface was necessary; for if the book deserves to be regarded as a little classic, it has some of the disadvantages implied by such status. Progress in the study of Shakespeare's life since it was published has not, it must be confessed, been so remarkable as to render the book seriously out of date on matters of fact. But Smart's method was to tilt, with a gentlemanly but tough and wholly admirable reason-ableness, at many of the traditional fallacies current about Shakespeare at the time he was writing. False traditions are still rife; but emphases have changed. A writer of the present day, for instance, would hardly devote so much space to the Baconian lunacies. As far as it goes, Smart's is a work of literary art. It has something of the quality of the best writing in the literary periodicals of his time: an ability to be lucid and agreeable without making any sacri-fices of scholarship or condescending limitations of reference. But the fact remains that his book is unfinished, and is thus both less satisfying and less comprehensive than it might have been. Its reissue is to be welcomed; but, as Professor Alexander's Preface recognizes, it needs to be seen in relation to the state of scholarship at the time of its composition. It is not really a 'modern work' on Shakespeare, even though it makes better and sounder reading than many more recent studies.

One of the problems of Shakespeare's life which Smart does not consider is the identity of Mr W.H., the dedicatee of the sonnets. J. M. Nosworthy[1] has revived and re-argued the entertaining theory that 'W.H.' is a misprint for 'W.S.' or 'W.SH.', and that the book is dedicated by the publisher to Shakespeare himself. As he says, if this is right 'we can bid fare-well for ever to "Mr W.H." and to what is, perhaps, the most fatuous proliferation of unverifi-able conjecture that has ever bedevilled Shakespearian scholarship'. This is a consummation devoutly to be wished; but unless Mr Nosworthy can discover a copy of the sonnets with a dedication in the appropriately corrected state, his suggestion must itself remain an unverifiable conjecture. A. L. Rowse, who believes that the sonnets were addressed to the Earl of South-ampton but dedicated to Sir William Harvey, has written *Shakespeare's Southampton: Patron of Virginia*,[2] an admirable biography which will appeal to those concerned with Shakespeare, but which differs little in its treatment of the direct relationship between poet and patron from Dr Rowse's earlier biography of Shakespeare.

An essay that concerns itself largely with Shakespeare's inner life rather than his day-to-day existence is J. F. Kermode's 'On Shakespeare's Learning'.[3] This characteristically learned and thoughtful piece culminates in a discussion of *The Phoenix and the Turtle*, which Professor Kermode finds 'learned, but not so learned that only a scholar could possess the materials of which it is made; its language, though wrought from a technical vocabulary, is free-standing, the language of a poet and not of a scholar, the language of a man whose craft is learned but not scholarly'. And this he describes as the centre of his argument. A somewhat similar approach

[1] 'Shakespeare and Mr W.H.', *The Library*, 5th ser., XVIII (1963), 294–8.
[2] Macmillan, 1965.
[3] *Bulletin of the John Rylands Library, Manchester*, XLVIII (1965), 207–26.

is adopted by Geoffrey Bullough in his British Academy lecture, *Shakespeare the Elizabethan*,[1] in which he suggests that a great deal of Shakespeare's 'worldly success may have been due to the ordinariness of his views, his acceptance of the Establishment, and his ability to embody in his plays commonsense ideas which most people in his audience could accept without question'. He also surveys the increasing richness and profundity with which Shakespeare's plays explore concerns that were common to many of his contemporaries.

An entirely fictional treatment of episodes of Shakespeare's life is offered by Harold Rubinstein in his trilogy of one-act plays, *Unearthly Gentleman*.[2] These do not offer anything essentially new, and they suffer from a certain stiffness in the presentation of expository matter; but they include some lively episodes, and are written in straightforward and unpretentious prose that would make them quite suitable for amateur performance.

A particular aspect of Shakespeare's early career is treated by G. C. Harlow. In the second part of his excellent two-part article 'A Source for Nashe's *Terrors of the Night*, and the Authorship of *1 Henry VI*'[3] he argues that the resemblances between *1 Henry VI* and *The Terrors of the Night* are more likely to be the result of Nashe's recollections of the play than of his having had any hand in its composition, and in the process suggests that *A Defensative Against the Poison of Supposed Prophecies* (1583), by Henry Howard, was among the books that Shakespeare read. A related problem is tackled by Macdonald P. Jackson in '*Edward III*, Shakespeare, and Pembroke's Men',[4] in which he seeks to show that passages from *Edward III* are echoed in *The Contention* and *The True Tragedy*, and thus that it is likely to have been in the repertory of Pembroke's Men and that it was written 'about 1590'. He believes that this hypothesis confirms the arguments for Shakespeare's authorship of *Edward III*. Karl P. Wentersdorf[5] finds references in *Edward III* to the Armada, and suggests that it was written about 1589–90. This play, which still hovers uneasily on the borders of the Shakespeare canon, can now be conveniently read in William A. Armstrong's useful collection, *Elizabethan History Plays*,[6] which reprints it along with another play of exceptional interest in relation to Shakespeare, the anonymous *Woodstock*, as well as Bale's *King John*, Ford's *Perkin Warbeck*, and Robert Davenport's *King John and Matilda*.

Shakespeare's working methods are touched on by Roland Mushat Frye in 'Shakespeare's Composition of *Lucrece*: New Evidence'.[7] Pointing to the existence in the third edition (1633) of *The Philosophers Banquet* 'compiled by W.B., Esquire' of four stanzas from *Lucrece* in the sesta rima form, he suggests that 'coming fresh from the publication of *Venus and Adonis*, Shakespeare at first vacillated between the stanzaic form he had used so successfully there and the form he eventually adopted for *Lucrece*'.

At the other end of Shakespeare's career, J. Leeds Barroll has investigated 'The Chronology of Shakespeare's Jacobean Plays and the Dating of *Antony and Cleopatra*'.[8] This is a closely and comprehensively argued essay which, though it centres on *Antony and Cleopatra*, is useful as a reminder of the uncertainty of the foundations underlying many of the orthodox opinions

[1] From the *Proceedings of the British Academy*, L, 121–41. [2] Gollancz, 1965.
[3] *Studies in English Literature*, V (1965), 31–47 and 269–81.
[4] *Notes and Queries*, n.s., XII (1965), 329–31.
[5] 'The Date of *Edward III*', *Shakespeare Quarterly*, XVI (1965), 227–31.
[6] The World's Classics (Oxford University Press, 1965).
[7] *Shakespeare Quarterly*, XVI (1965), 289–96.
[8] In *Essays on Shakespeare*, edited by Gordon Ross Smith (Pennsylvania State University Press, 1965), pp. 115–62.

about the chronology of Shakespeare's plays in general. Though his article is much concerned with the endeavour to establish fact, Mr Barroll ends with a fascinating conjecture. Having worked out the frequency of plague in London during the five years following James's accession, he asks if we are not 'faced with the possibility that court or other private performances were, for long periods of time, the only legitimate outlets for plays in or about London'. And he proceeds to the speculation that at times Shakespeare, writing plays that would be first performed at Court, might have felt the need for 'an increasing emphasis on artistic achievement and on complexity of effect', that the tragedies of this period may have been for him not simply 'items in the casual commercialism of a stage career, but vigorous and ambitious responses to the kinds of ideological and literary sophistication for which Jonson also wrote his masques'.

'Shakespeare's Head', by Mary Hyde,[1] describes a painting of Shakespeare which may have been Tonson's shop sign; and in 'The Real Bowdler' Noel Perrin[2] demonstrates that the first, anonymous edition of the *Family Shakespeare* (1807), which included twenty plays, was edited not by Thomas Bowdler but by his sister, Miss Henrietta Maria Bowdler. Alwin Thaler is partly concerned with Shakespeare's posthumous impact in *Shakespeare and Our World*,[3] a collection of essays and addresses, some of which are revisions of earlier publications. Some are particularly concerned with the impact of Shakespeare on the modern world; others examine aspects of his dramatic technique; and the longest piece is 'Shakespearean Recollection in Milton: A Summing-Up', which re-shapes material previously printed in *Shakspere's Silences* and elsewhere. It is a bit of a mixed bag, and some of the pieces are of local rather than general interest; but all of them are informed by true scholarship and a generous humanity.

An early influence of Shakespeare is suggested by Charles R. Forker in 'Shakespeare's Histories and Heywood's *If You Know Not Me, You Know Nobody*'.[4] Also concerned with a history play is Joan Rees in 'Richard II in 1615',[5] in which she shows from a speech of Bacon's that *Richard II*'s 'political explosiveness was still remembered and even feared in the context of a new situation'. A much later influence is discussed in Robert F. Fleissner's *Dickens and Shakespeare*,[6] a photographed dissertation which assembles a good deal of material on the relationship between the two writers but needs to be used with care, as it is by no means free from error.

Ronald Berman's *A Reader's Guide to Shakespeare's Plays*[7] is described as a 'discursive bibliography', and fills a real need. It lists about three thousand items, and thus provides a critical bibliography larger in scope and more informative than for instance those in the 'Writers and their Work' series, but more selective than the full bibliographies. Each play has a separate section, and a wide range of material is covered.

As usual, there have been a number of notes on particular passages in the plays, and on Shakespeare's linguistic usages. H. M. Hulme has written on '*Malice* and *Malicious* in Shakespearean Usage'.[8] Comments on particular plays include Anthony Baker's 'Mistress Quickly's Bawdy',[9] Leslie E. F. Pearsall's 'Pike and Jacks in *Henry IV, Part 2*',[10] 'The Owl and the Baker's

[1] *Shakespeare Quarterly*, XVI (1965), 139–43.
[3] The University of Tennessee Press, Knoxville, 1966.
[5] *Notes and Queries*, n.s., XIII (1966), 130–1.
[7] Scott, Foreman and Co., Chicago, etc., 1965.
[9] *Notes and Queries*, n.s., XIII (1966), 132.

[2] *Notes and Queries*, n.s., XIII (1966), 141–2.
[4] *Neuphilologische Mitteilungen*, LXVI (1965), 166–78.
[6] Haskell House, New York, 1965.
[8] *English Studies*, XLVII (1966), 190–9.
[10] Ibid. pp. 132–3.

Daughter: A Note on *Hamlet*, IV, v, 42–43' by Robert Tracy,[1] and '"Addition" (*Troilus and Cressida*, IV, v, 141)' by Peter Ure.[2] In '"Get thee to a Nunnery"—a Comment'[3] D. S. Bland cites from the *Gesta Grayorum* an example of 'nunnery' used in the sense of 'brothel'. (It is only fair to remark, however, that it occurs in a lengthy analogy between a nunnery and a brothel, and does not prove that the word would have been likely to carry a double-entendre when used on its own.) In '"Fillet of a Fenny Snake"' James O. Wood[4] suggests by reference to Golding's Ovid that in this phrase from *Macbeth* 'fillet' means 'not a slice of the snake but the ribbon of its cast scarf-skin', and that it is 'fenny' because fen-bred. G. N. Murphy in 'A Note on Iago's Name'[5] draws attention to the fact that Santiago (or St Iago) was the patron saint of England's traditional enemy Spain, and was especially known as Santiago Matamoros—St James the Moor-killer.

Helen Phelps Bailey's *Hamlet in France from Voltaire to Laforgue*[6] is a comprehensive, scholarly, and readable study of the fortunes of *Hamlet* in France, from the asperities of Voltaire till 'with the emergence of Symbolism, Hamlet may be said to have come into his own'. She studies the translations and adaptations of the play, such as those of Ducis, Guizot, François-Victor Hugo, and Dumas-Meurice; its influence on other creative artists, such as de Vigny (in *Chatterton*), Berlioz (in *Lélio*), Ambroise Thomas (in his operatic version), and Delacroix (in his drawings, paintings, and lithographs). She comments on critical writings about the play, some of them (Hugo's, for instance) based on a comparison between the first and second quartos in the belief that the first quarto represents Shakespeare's unrevised version of the play; and she remarks on the impact of performances such as those given in Paris by Kemble and Harriet Smithson, and those of native performers such as Talma and Mounet-Sully. An Epilogue sketches the history of the play during the present century. This book is a useful contribution to the history of Shakespeare's posthumous reputation.

Moving further afield, *William Shakespeare No Brasil: Bibliografia das Comemorações do 4º Centenário 1964*[7] is a very detailed, illustrated record of the celebrations in Brazil. Stanisław Helstyński edited *Poland's Homage to Shakespeare*,[8] which includes a series of articles tracing Shakespeare's influence in Poland. There are also some more specialized contributions. Witold Chwalewik suggests a possible Polish source of *Hamlet*, and perhaps the most generally useful article is Margaret Schlauch's 'The Social Background of Shakespeare's Malapropisms'. The book is entirely in English. O. Vočadlo, in 'Shakespeare and the Slavs' (*The Slavonic and East European Review*, XLIV [1966], 36–50), has an interesting comment on the mock-Russian spoken in *All's Well that Ends Well*. He also suggests that we may imagine 'Feste singing his melancholy songs to the accompaniment of a gusle to please his love-sick *gospar knez*'.

Studies in Shakespeare's sources proceed apace. Indeed there have in recent years been so many suggestions of minor sources for particular passages in the plays as distinct from the overall narrative and dramatic sources that are being collected by Geoffrey Bullough, that the time

---

[1] *Shakespeare Quarterly*, XVII (1966), 83–6. [2] *Notes and Queries*, n.s., XIII (1966), 135.
[3] *Notes and Queries*, n.s., XII (1965), 332. [4] *Ibid.* pp. 332–3.
[5] In Germaine Brée *et al.*, *Literature and Society*, edited by Bernice Slote (University of Nebraska Press, Lincoln, 1964). [6] Droz, Genève, 1964.
[7] Celuta Moreira Gomes and Thereza da Silva Aguiar (Divisão de Publicações e Divulgação, Rio de Janeiro, 1965). [8] Warsaw, 1965; PWN—Polish Scientific Publishers.

may soon be ripe for a comprehensive survey of the claims that have been made for Shakespeare's reading.

In his British Academy lecture, referred to earlier, Professor Bullough writes of *The Orator* (1596), translated from the French of Alexander Silvayn. He points to the bearing of two of the declamations on the situation of Isabella in *Measure for Measure*, 'not because I think Shakespeare was necessarily influenced by that particular book but because it indicates the kinds of problem in which his characters became more and more involved as his ethical sense deepened and his comedy discussed grave issues more confidently'. The possible influence of *The Orator* on *The Merchant of Venice* has often been suggested. Now Winifred Nowottny, in 'Shakespeare and *The Orator*',[1] suggests that it had a much more extensive influence on Shakespeare, and that in several of his plays he was indebted to it both for details of the speeches and for stimulus of a larger kind. Mrs Nowottny presents her case—it seems strong—with characteristic subtlety and intellectual rigour. This is no simple piling up of parallels; the writer's concern with larger issues than mere verbal correspondences stimulates her to some deeply thoughtful criticism, especially of *Coriolanus*. Also concerned with a writer who may have influenced Shakespeare in a number of plays is Gareth Lloyd Evans, whose 'Shakespeare, Seneca, and the Kingdom of Violence'[2] includes an examination of the treatment by Shakespeare and Seneca of analogous situations, and is particularly interesting on the theatrical realization of them in modern productions.

Other source studies have been concerned with single plays. The most massive and intricate is T. W. Baldwin's *On the Compositional Genetics of 'The Comedy of Errors'*,[3] which demonstrates the extent of Professor Baldwin's reading with more certainty than it demonstrates Shakespeare's. *The Comedy of Errors* deserves to be taken more seriously than it often has been; whether it should be taken with this sort of seriousness is open to question. E. M. W. Tillyard, in an appendix ('The Fairytale Element in *The Taming of the Shrew*') to his posthumously published *Shakespeare's Early Comedies*,[4] pleads that 'more should be made of the story of King Thrushbeard as an analogue of *The Taming of the Shrew*'. The story, which appears to have had wide currency, stresses the educative rather than the humiliating aspects of the heroine's experience. The ballad of Chevy Chase has been suggested[5] as a source for the single combat of Prince Hal and Hotspur. In 'Caesar's Just Cause' G. A. Starr[6] suggests a source in Cicero for the phrase that Shakespeare may have written. A. P. Stabler in 'Elective Monarchy in the Sources of *Hamlet*'[7] 'seeks to present a fuller and more accurate picture of the Danish constitutional situation as portrayed in the sources, and hence possibly aid in the solution of any dramatic "ambiguities" derived from them'. A related essay is Gunnar Sjögren's '*Hamlet* and the Coronation of Christian IV',[8] in which he describes the elective nature of the Danish monarchy in the sixteenth century, points out the frequency of the names Rosencrantz and Gyldenstiern at the coronation in 1596 of Christian IV, tells us that during the festivities the King's Guard paraded dressed up in imitation of the Pope's own Swiss guard, and remarks on the presence of a troupe

[1] In *Hommage à Shakespeare*, *Bulletin de la Faculté des Lettres de Strasbourg* (Mai–Juin 1965), pp. 25–45.
[2] In *Roman Drama*, ed. by T. A. Dorey and Donald R. Dudley (Routledge and Kegan Paul, 1965), pp. 123–59.
[3] University of Illinois Press, Urbana, 1965. [4] Chatto and Windus, 1965.
[5] Truman W. Camp, 'Shakespeare's *Henry IV*, *Part 1* and the Ballad "Chevy Chase"', *Notes and Queries*, n.s., XIII (1966), 131–2. [6] *Shakespeare Quarterly*, XVI (1966), 77–9.
[7] *Studies in Philology*, LXII (1965), 654–61. [8] *Shakespeare Quarterly*, XVI (1965), 155–60.

of English actors, from one of whom, he suggests, Shakespeare may have got information on Denmark and the ways of the Danish court. He also reproduces an interesting drawing of the festivities.

There are three notes on *Macbeth*. William Leigh Godshalk, in 'Livy's Tullia: A Classical Prototype of Lady Macbeth',[1] points to an analogue to Lady Macbeth, and a possible source for some aspects of her character, in Livy's *History*. John Orrell[2] notes the parallel association of owl and bellman in *Macbeth* and *Blurt, Master Constable* (1602), and James O. Wood in 'Lady Macbeth's Suckling'[3] suggests a source in Golding's Ovid for Lady Macbeth's image at I, vii, 54–9.

The extent of Shakespeare's reading in foreign languages is a special problem, of which one aspect is tackled by E. A. J. Honigmann in '*Othello*, Chappuys and Cinthio'.[4] He discerns in *Othello* the influence of both Cinthio's Italian and the French version by Chappuys, and concludes 'either that Shakespeare read up the story of *Othello* in both Italian and French, or that there was an English version based on the two foreign ones which, though now lost, served as Shakespeare's source'. The suggestion that Novella I, 4 of Fenton's *Certaine Tragicall Discourses* (1567) was a source for the same play is supported in '*Othello* and Fenton: An Addendum' by William E. McCarron,[5] who also feels that the names of Bianca, Cassio, and Roderigo may derive from the same volume. E. E. Duncan-Jones,[6] too, is concerned with a name: Hermione's, she suggests, derives from Ovid's *Heroides*. Finally among the plays, *The Tempest*: Eleanor Prosser[7] convincingly suggests a source in Montaigne's essay 'Of crueltie' in Florio's translation for a speech of Prospero, and David R. Clark writes on '*Ecclesiasticus* and Prospero's Epilogue'.[8]

Two pointers to literary rather than autobiographical aspects of the Sonnets are John F. Reichert's 'Sonnet XX and Erasmus' "Epistle to Perswade a Yong Gentleman to Mariage"'[9] and John M. Steadman's 'Shakespeare's Sonnet 130 and Aretino's "Ragionamenti"'[10] which draws an analogy between Shakespeare's 'My mistress' eyes...' and a burlesque serenade of Aretino, suggesting that they both belong 'in essentially the same subspecies of burlesque verse'.

An important book concerned with both Shakespeare and the dramatic works of his contemporaries is S. Schoenbaum's *Internal Evidence and Elizabethan Dramatic Authorship*.[11] It is more enthralling than its title might suggest, partly because it is a historical as well as a theoretical study. Professor Schoenbaum provides a lucid and attractively written survey of the development of investigations into the authorship of Elizabethan plays, and has much to tell about the men who pursued the investigations as well as about the methods they employed. To place the work of scholars such as Furnivall, Fleay, Oliphant, and Robertson in a context is itself a valuable service. One function that this book may usefully fulfil is to remind us of the uncertain foundations on which much that we regard as orthodoxy has been built. Professor Schoenbaum demonstrates the illogicalities, the follies, the sheer muddleheadedness of many of the attempts to establish authorship by the use of internal evidence. He has naturally much to say about the

[1] *Shakespeare Quarterly*, XVI (1965), 240–1.
[2] 'The Bellman in *Macbeth*, II, ii, 3', *Notes and Queries*, n.s., XIII (1966), 138.
[3] *Notes and Queries*, n.s., XIII (1966), 138. [4] *Notes and Queries*, n.s., XIII (1966), 136–7.
[5] *Notes and Queries*, n.s., XIII (1966), 137–8. [6] 'Hermione in Ovid and Shakespeare', *ibid.* pp. 138–9.
[7] 'Shakespeare, Montaigne, and the Rarer Action', *Shakespeare Studies*, I (1965), 261–4.
[8] *Shakespeare Quarterly*, XVII (1966), 79–81. [9] *Shakespeare Quarterly*, XVI (1965), 238–40.
[10] *Notes and Queries*, n.s., XIII (1966), 134–5. [11] Edward Arnold, 1966.

disintegrators of the Shakespeare canon and of the efforts to prove multiple authorship of some of the plays. Outside Shakespeare, he singles out *The Revenger's Tragedy* as a case-study of peculiar complexity and interest. Taking as he does a bird's eye view of the various battlefields, he may well make us feel that no final victory is possible in any of them. But he is not without his own opinions, and succeeds in maintaining at least a qualified optimism in spite of all the follies that he chronicles and all the nonsense that he must have had to read during the composition of his book. His final section is called 'Avoiding Disaster', and offers constructive advice to those concerned with attribution, warning them of possible pitfalls and offering a number of basic principles. No one who investigates such problems can afford to neglect this book, and anyone with a scholarly interest in Shakespeare and his contemporaries is likely to find in it much that will be instructive and not a little that will be entertaining.

Shakespeare's predecessors in the drama are surveyed by Zdeněk Stříbrný in *Shakespearovi předchůdci*,[1] which is written in Czech but includes a fairly full summary in English, from which it is clear that Professor Stříbrný offers a new and scholarly study of the development of secular drama in England from Medwall to Marlowe.

Students of the Renaissance mind are likely to learn much from Frances A. Yates's *The Art of Memory*,[2] which studies the development of the art of memory, invented by the Greeks, in the European tradition. Giordano Bruno figures largely in the book; and so does Robert Fludd, an English Hermetic philosopher whose major work, *Utriusque Cosmi Maioris Scilicet et Minoris, Metaphysica, Physica atque Technica Historia*, was published in two parts, one in 1617 and the other two years later. Miss Yates believes that in his illustration of a theatre which was to serve as a guide to memory, Fludd was influenced by the Globe. She is reviving a theory that was propounded by Richard Bernheimer, but in which he had little confidence. Miss Yates's learning commands respect, but the logic of her argument is open to question. Any association between Fludd and the Globe is purely speculative, and Miss Yates does not convincingly demonstrate its existence.

Shakespeare's other playhouse, the Blackfriars, has tended to receive less attention than the Globe. Irwin Smith's large-scale study *Shakespeare's Blackfriars Playhouse*[3] does a good deal to restore the balance. There are times when one feels that it is on too large a scale; that the author has done too little to order his material and to determine its significance. He includes, for instance, a great deal of information about the history of the order of the Black Friars, their place in society, the design of their buildings, and the history of that particular building which became a playhouse. It is true that the attempt to understand the design of the theatre—even indeed to decide in which room of the friary it was located—requires a study of the whole purpose and function of the building. But the reader who is mainly interested in learning about its use as a playhouse may sometimes wonder whether Mr Smith might not have spared him some of the details, or at least have so told the story that the connexion between the background and the foreground was more easily apparent. Readers interested mainly in Shakespeare may feel too that Mr Smith is a little reactionary in his views on the authenticity of, for example, the vision scene in *Cymbeline*, and, especially, the text of *The Tempest* 'which so clearly has

---

[1] Universita Karlova, Praha, 1965. [2] Routledge and Kegan Paul, 1966.
[3] Peter Owen, 1966. There is an extended and authoritative review by Charles Shattuck in *JEGP*, LXV (1966), 178–82.

12-2

been disfigured by other hands'. They might also wish to object that music 'as an enrichment of the drama' was not 'contrary to the usages of the public playhouses', even if it was more common in plays written for private houses; and they could probably think of more dances in Shakespeare's pre-Blackfriars plays than those mentioned on p. 234. Nevertheless this book is an impressive achievement, displaying a wide range of learning and displaying it on the whole to good advantage. Mr Smith has studied all the available evidence, including that provided by the plays written for the theatre, and though inevitably much still remains conjectural, he makes a reasoned and convincing case for the building as he would reconstruct it. He is interesting on, for instance, the use of act-intervals in the private theatres, and the likelihood that these were necessitated mainly by the need to tend the candles used for illumination. He does not neglect the periods either before the occupancy of the theatre by Shakespeare's company or after Shakespeare's death. He provides many useful photographs and drawings; and reprints (in modern spelling) all the relevant documents. This is a necessary book both for those who are interested in the physical structure of the Blackfriars, and also for those with an interest in the details of plays presented there.

Also concerned with the Blackfriars is Herbert Berry in 'The Stage and Boxes at Blackfriars',[1] in which a document describing a brawl at the theatre in 1632 is used as the basis of some speculations about its design. In 'The Swan Theatre in the 16th Century'[2] Joyce I. Whalley offers a facsimile and transcript of the well-known drawing of the Swan and the Latin description of it. This copy of the de Witt drawing is, of course, commonly used in attempts to envisage other theatres, especially the Globe. Richard Hosley now uses it in the attempt to reconstruct the Swan itself, which he suggests had twenty-four sides. His article ('Reconstitution du Théâtre du Swan') is one in a splendidly produced and illustrated collection, *Le Lieu théâtral à la Renaissance*,[3] the fruit of a 'Colloque International' held at Royaumont in 1963, which includes many significant articles on the theatre in Italy and elsewhere. Contributions that are also of particular relevance to the Elizabethan theatre are Glynne Wickham's 'Emblème et Image; quelques remarques sur la manière de figurer et de représenter le lieu sur la scène anglaise au xvie siècle' and Jean Jacquot's summing-up, 'Les Types du lieu théâtral et leurs transformations de la fin du Moyen Age au milieu du xviie siècle'.

Other theatre studies include T. J. King's 'Staging of Plays at the Phoenix in Drury Lane, 1617–42'[4] in which he investigates the texts of plays performed at the Phoenix and concludes that on the whole those who wrote for this private theatre 'were following the conventions of the earlier Elizabethan "open stage" rather than anticipating the modes of presentation usually associated with the Restoration period'. In 'A Picture of the Salisbury Court Theatre'[5] Edward A. Langhams reproduces and discusses a puzzling theatre illustration from a map of 1706. Andrew Gurr's 'Elizabethan Action'[6] is partly concerned with a linguistic investigation of the Elizabethan terminology of acting, and stresses that 'the criterion of acting on the stage was, from 1602 at least, much more the convincing portrayal of character than the quality of the player's Action and Pronunciation'.

[1] *Studies in Philology*, LXIII (1966), 163–86. [2] *Theatre Notebook*, XX (Winter 1965/6), 73.
[3] Edited by Jean Jacquot (Editions du Centre National de la Recherche Scientifique, Paris, 1964); Professor Hosley's article is on pp. 295–316. [4] *Theatre Notebook*, XIX (1965), 146–66.
[5] *Ibid.* pp. 100–1. [6] *Studies in Philology*, LXIII (1966), 144–56.

168

From the press of the University of Illinois comes a major new reference book. Charles H. Shattuck in *The Shakespeare Promptbooks: A Descriptive Catalogue*[1] catalogues promptbooks of Shakespeare from the Dering manuscript of *1 Henry IV*, dating from the 1620s, to those of 1961. Most of them are in England or America—many of the English ones, such as those for Granville-Barker's Savoy Theatre productions of *A Midsummer Night's Dream* and *Twelfth Night*, in America. Of course, many promptbooks have not survived and there must also be many whose whereabouts is not recorded. Professor Shattuck invites corrections and additions for publication in *Theatre Notebook*. What he provides is an immediately indispensable tool of reference for research into the history of Shakespeare's plays on the stage. All the more important books are described, so that the reader has a chance to assess their value to him before seeing them. The introduction provides a concise but authoritative and immensely helpful survey of the material, and there is also an invaluable account of 'Symbols and Abbreviations in the Older Promptbooks'.

Many of the promptbooks described by Professor Shattuck are of course based on adaptations of Shakespeare's plays. The longest-lasting of these were some of those made in the late seventeenth century; in our times they have been much described but rarely reprinted. Montague Summers's *Shakespeare Adaptations* (1922), which includes the Dryden–Davenant *Tempest* and Nahum Tate's *King Lear* along with Thomas Duffett's burlesque of *The Tempest*, is difficult to obtain and in various ways unsatisfactory. Christopher Spencer's *Five Restoration Adaptations of Shakespeare*[2] fills a notable gap. He provides carefully edited and well-printed texts of Davenant's *Macbeth*, the Shadwell–Dryden–Davenant version of *The Tempest*, Nahum Tate's *King Lear*, Colley Cibber's *Richard III*, and George Granville's *The Jew of Venice*. His introduction has none of the scorn and flippancy with which these versions are often treated. It is an earnest and scholarly attempt to see them as their makers saw them, to appreciate what is good in them, and to justify their study. Perhaps Professor Spencer is a little too earnest. It may be as well to admit that there are mirth-provoking discrepancies between some of the adapters' work and their great originals. But the adaptations are significant documents in the history of taste, and no one should quarrel with Professor Spencer's wish to see them seriously studied, or feel anything but gratitude for the skill and thoroughness which he has brought to the preparation of the texts and notes.

Restoration adaptations are also the subject of W. Moelwyn Merchant's 'Shakespeare "Made Fit"'[3] in which with his inimitable discursiveness he discusses some of them, not making excessive claims on their behalf, but pointing out that 'it is an exercise of critical decency to recognise their *genre* and to assess the temper and ideals against which their failure must be judged'. Martin Lehnert has written about a later version of Shakespeare in 'Arthur Murphys *Hamlet* Parodie (1772) auf David Garrick'.[4] He reprints and very thoroughly annotates a playlet by Murphy based on *Hamlet*. It is not a specially distinguished piece, but is interesting particularly in relation to Garrick and his adaptations of Shakespeare. Shakespeare's Ghost complains that he is

> Doom'd for a certain term to leave my works
> Obscure and uncorrected; to endure

[1] Urbana and London, 1965.   [2] University of Illinois Press, Urbana, 1965.
[3] In *Restoration Theatre: Stratford-upon-Avon Studies*, VI (Edward Arnold, 1965).
[4] *Shakespeare Jahrbuch* (East), CII (1966), 97–167.

The ignorance of players; the barbarous hand
Of Gothic editors; the ponderous weight
Of leaden commentator; fast confin'd
In critic fires, till errors, not my own,
Are done away, and sorely I the while
Wish'd I had blotted for myself before.

A good deal of light relief is also offered by Winton Dean in his delightful essay 'Shakespeare in the Opera House'[1] which is closely related to his fuller treatment of the same subject in *Shakespeare in Music* (reviewed in *Shakespeare Survey 19*). He includes a useful check-list of operas based on the plays. D. S. Hoffman's 'Some Shakespearian Music, 1660–1900'[2] is a brief survey.

Shakespeare on the foreign stage is the main subject of *La Revue d'Histoire du Théâtre*, vol. XVI, no. 1 (Janvier–Mars 1965). There are articles on France, Russia, Hungary, and Italy. John Russell Brown's 'The Study and Practice of Shakespeare Production'[3] claims that 'the study of Shakespeare production from then to now in England has too little acquaintance with the professional practice of Shakespearian production today', and pleads that 'scholars should work with, and in, the professional theatre'. The same writer has a distinguished review of some notable Shakespeare performances, including Sir Laurence Olivier's Othello.[4] Laurence Kitchin writes about this and other important productions in *Drama in the Sixties: Form and Interpretation*,[5] which includes, too, some longer pieces considering attitudes to Shakespeare prevalent in the modern theatre and cinema. He has also published 'Shakespeare on the Screen',[6] a brief survey. Two other thoughtful reviews of recent productions are Robert Speaight's 'Shakespeare in Britain'[7] and Bernard Beckerman's 'The 1965 Season at Stratford, Connecticut'.[8]

© STANLEY WELLS 1967

3. TEXTUAL STUDIES

reviewed by J. K. WALTON

John Dover Wilson's edition of *The Sonnets*[9] gives us an admirable conclusion of his contribution to the New Cambridge Shakespeare, in the editing of which he has played by far the major part. Here we have a comprehensive and judicious discussion of the many problems involved. In *The Sonnets* textual problems are closely related to others, such as the identity of Mr W.H., and in keeping to the more strictly textual aspects of the edition, it is not possible to do justice to the full force of his arguments.

Dover Wilson believes that the printer's copy for the 1609 edition, published by Thorpe, may have been Shakespeare's manuscript, but 'if not an autograph it must have been a tolerably

---

[1] *Shakespeare Survey 18* (1965), 75–93.
[2] *Ibid.* pp. 94–101.
[3] *Ibid.* pp. 58–69.
[4] *Ibid.* pp. 147–55.
[5] Faber and Faber, 1966.
[6] *Shakespeare Survey 18* (1965), 70–4.
[7] *Shakespeare Quarterly*, XVI (1965), 313–24.
[8] *Ibid.* pp. 329–39.
[9] *The Sonnets* (Cambridge, 1966).

competent transcript, perhaps copied out by more than one transcriber' (p. xxvi). It is unthink-able, however, that the copy, with its many sonnets referring to the private affairs of Shake-speare and the Friend, should have been sent to the press by either of them, and there remains only the Dark Woman herself, 'unless some pirate unknown had been at work' (p. xl). Dover Wilson's text is, as he says, conservative: 'that is to say it very rarely departs from Malone's' (p. cxxiii), who was the first to bring about a genuine resurrection of the 1609 text, and whom he sees as 'the prince of Sonnet editors and commentators' (p. xi). Unlike Malone, however, he follows the punctuation of the 1609 quarto very closely, since 'the chances are that in a poem and particularly poetry of a highly emotional character like a love sonnet, Shakespeare might have used punctuation to make the meaning quite clear if otherwise in doubt, to bring out the rhythm, and that on the other hand when he wished to be ironical or ambiguous, as he often is in the *Sonnets*, the pointing might be very scanty indeed' (pp. cxxiii–cxxiv).

What constitutes the main innovation in Dover Wilson's edition is his interpretation of the order of the sonnets, though he prints the original order unchanged. He agrees with the commonly accepted division of the 1609 order into two main sections, 1–126 being written to or about a young man, and most of those in 127–54 to or about a dark woman. Dover Wilson, however, questions the order in which the sonnets are given within each of these two groups. He feels bound to assume that 'Thorpe or some other person had originally procured them on separate leaves or in separate bundles which he was unable to sort out correctly' (p. xxvii). The absence of an ordered arrangement is especially notable in 127–54, and Dover Wilson here follows Brent Stirling's view that the sonnets in this group were originally well arranged and that this arrangment becomes clear if we assume that 'sonnets were inserted two to a leaf, recto-verso'. Thus 'a leaf accidentally turned over would keep the two sonnets together but transpose the authentic order', while 'disruption of sequence would occur by displacement of leaves'.[1] The disruption of order in Section 2 is all the greater, because 'it looks, indeed, as if Thorpe or someone else simply threw together into this section sonnets he could find no place for in the other' (p. xxviii).

For Dover Wilson, the main problem of order is presented by Section 1.[2] Here there exists 'a general framework, embracing in particular the initial sequence 1–17 upon marriage, together with traces of several other sequences which appear at different parts of Thorpe's collection: for example, the group concerning the Rival Poet and, perhaps most obvious of all, the group (97–126) that concludes Section 1 as a whole' (p. xxix). In Section 1, he suggests, Thorpe

had to deal with two distinct classes of sonnets: (*a*) what we may call framework sonnets, namely the 'sugred sonnets' known in part to Meres by 1598, and probably including many written later; and (*b*) what we may call secret or private sonnets, namely those connected with the young man's sexual adventures, presumably sent to him but which we can feel confident Shakespeare did not release for circulation among his friends, however 'private' these friends might be. But Thorpe's real problem was to keep the framework intact with its concluding Envoy, while inserting the secret sonnets at convenient places within it. (p. xxxv)

[1] Brents Stirling, cited by Dover Wilson, p. 243. Dover Wilson points out that Stirling's evidence 'for the whole arrangement is based on the fact that most of the sonnets fall into pairs and sequences'. He notes that 'Stirling claims that these clear pairs and clear sequences account for eighteen out of the twenty-eight sonnets in the series' (p. 244).

[2] Dover Wilson inclines to believe 'that sonnets in Section 1 were written two to a side' (p. 243).

In this way, Dover Wilson is able to solve what he calls 'the chief puzzle of the 1609 text': the fact that sonnets 33–5, charging the Friend with paying court to the poet's mistress, precede sonnet 70, which credits him with 'a pure unstained prime' (pp. xxxiii–xxxiv). There are, in Dover Wilson's view, in all, nine or ten 'secret' sonnets.[1] The principal example of the interpolation of 'secret' sonnets is provided by 33–5 and 40–2, which precede and follow a stylistically connected group, 36–9, sonnet 36 having a superficial resemblance to 35, and 39 to 40. Dover Wilson considers that the group 36–9 was itself misplaced by Thorpe to suit his purposes; it should follow sonnet 25, where we first hear 'Shakespeare complaining against fortune and his low condition' (p. xxxii). Dover Wilson also finds misplacement within the rival poet framework, and also in the last group in Section 1, though in both of these groups the misplacement was owing simply to Thorpe's inability to discover the right order. Dover Wilson's arguments are impressive, even after we allow for the possibility of dramatic juxtaposition.

Related to the question of the order of the sonnets is the problem of dating and the attendant problem of the identity of Mr W.H., whom he takes to be William Herbert, Earl of Pembroke, and of the Rival Poet, whom he believes to be Chapman. He rejects the hypothesis that the main body of the sonnets was written in 1593 or 1594. Following H. C. Beeching, he assigns their beginning, largely on the evidence of verbal parallels from *Henry IV*, to 1597–8. This dating supports and is supported by his arguments for taking Chapman to be the rival poet. So too it rules out Southampton as the Friend. As Dover Wilson observes, 'if we accept 1597–8 as the year in which Shakespeare began the *Sonnets*, he was at that date too old, being then twenty-four or twenty-five, while he must have been thirty or more when Shakespeare was writing his Envoy to his "lovely boy"' (p. xci). The whole question of the identity of Mr W.H. and the Rival Poet, as well as that of the dating, is too large to be discussed here. What is certain is that Dover Wilson's detailed and closely interlinked arguments about the order of the *Sonnets* will have to be considered with the greatest care by all future editors. His edition represents an important landmark which may come to be seen as comparable with that represented by the edition of Edmond Malone.

J. C. Maxwell provides us with an excellent text of *Venus and Adonis, The Rape of Lucrece, The Passionate Pilgrim, The Phoenix and the Turtle,* and *A Lover's Complaint*.[2] The authoritative text of *Venus and Adonis* is the single extant copy of the 1593 Quarto. As Maxwell observes, it has very few substantive errors, but he inclines to doubt if we can argue from the fewness of misprints that Shakespeare himself corrected the proofs (pp. 146–7). He finds positive evidence against authorial proof correction in *Lucrece*, where 'the proof-corrector has done rather more harm than good' (p. 148). The most significant of his changes, Maxwell points out, is in line 50, sig. B ('Colatium' uncorr. and 'Colatia' corr.), 'where the form of the name in the uncorrected state is to be preferred—it is that used in the Argument and in l. 4—though the corrected gives the true Latin form' (pp. 147–8). The interference of the press-corrector appears to have been limited to sig. B, and in sig. I Maxwell rightly accepts the corrected readings.

In *The Passionate Pilgrim*, Maxwell finds 'the only real Shakespearian interest' in the text of the first poem ('When my love swears that she is made of truth'), where he considers that Jaggard 'had access to an earlier version of the sonnet than appears in the 1609 collection, and not

---

[1] Nos. 33, 34, 35, 40, 41, 42, 48, 57, 58, 61. Dover Wilson suggests that the autobiographical order is: 48, 57, 58, 61, 40, 41, 42, 33, 34, 35: see p. xxxv.   [2] *The Poems* (Cambridge, 1966).

just an inaccurate transcript' (p. 149). *The Phoenix and the Turtle* presents no textual difficulties. *A Lover's Complaint*, however, which Maxwell accepts as Shakespearian, contains 'about as many errors as one would expect to find in the same number of lines of a reasonably good dramatic text' (p. 150). In addition to substantive errors on which editors are generally agreed, Maxwell with good reason suspects the text in lines 61, 161, 212, and 233.[1] He finds 'some odd spellings and forms, some of which can be paralleled in other Shakespeare texts', and 'there is nothing to rule out a reasonably clear manuscript in Shakespeare's hand, if that is what we are inclined to believe in on other grounds' (p. 150).

A. R. Humphreys in his edition of *2 Henry IV*[2] gives a lucid survey of the main textual problems. He rightly takes the 1600 quarto, which has all the marks of a play printed from the author's autograph, as the primary authority for the text. Of the eight major lacunae in Q, 'four may reflect an attempt to shorten the play for performance': I, i, 166–79, I, iii, 21–4, I, iii, 36–55, and II, iii, 23–45 (p. lxx). Humphreys argues compellingly that the other four— I, i, 189–209, I, iii, 85–108, IV, i, 55–79, and IV, i, 103–39—may result from political censorship (p. lxxi). In approaching the difficult problem of the nature of the copy for F, he makes a careful comparison of the many differences in reading between F and Q. These differences are many, not only in the substantive readings but also in accidentals such as punctuation and spelling, and have led some critics, including Matthias Shaaber, to hold that F was set directly from manuscript and not from a quarto corrected with reference to it. Others, most notably Alice Walker, have argued, from the number of errors and anomalies in spelling common to the two texts, that the copy for F was a quarto corrected with reference to a manuscript. The solution adopted by Humphreys to this apparent conflict of evidence is that proposed by Fredson Bowers, who has suggested that 'for some reason an annotated quarto was transcribed to form a manuscript which was used as printer's copy for the Folio'.[3] But is such a complicated and improbable solution necessary? What we need to know is not only the number of errors and anomalies common to Q and F but also their nature. Greg has remarked that 'what Shakespeare could produce as a draft we may, I believe, see in the famous three pages of *More*, and I imagine that it was something of this sort that he often handed to the company'.[4] In the 147 lines of the three pages there are, in addition to anomalies of spelling and punctuation, eight minim errors, the omission of two contraction marks, one transposition of letters, one e/d confusion, one speech-prefix wrongly placed, one failure to make a necessary deletion. According to this amount of error, Shakespeare's manuscript of *2 Henry IV*, with its 3446 lines, would have had about 23 times as many errors as the 147 lines of *More* D: namely, 184 minim errors; 46 omissions of contraction marks; 23 transpositions of letters; 23 e/d confusions; 23 speech prefixes wrongly placed; and 23 failures to delete. This suggests that the amount of error in Shakespeare's manuscript must have been large, much greater in fact than the number of errors common to Q and F *2 Henry IV*. When we consider the power of survival, as evidenced in later texts, of errors and anomalies common to Q and F, the problem may seem to be why, on the theory of

---

[1] He suggests 'fastly' (line 61) is an error for 'softly' (spelt 'saftly'); 'wits' (line 161) an error for 'wills'; 'invised' (line 212) an error for 'unused'; and 'Or' (line 233) an error for 'A'. He adopts, however, only the second of these, 'wits', in his text.

[2] *The Second Part of King Henry IV* (The Arden Shakespeare, 1966).

[3] Bowers, cited by Humphreys, p. lxxxi.   [4] *Shakespeare Quarterly*, VII (1956), 102.

manuscript copy for F, these errors and anomalies are so few and not why they are so many. *More* D would also lead us to believe that in a Shakespeare manuscript the substantive errors were mainly graphic. The substantive errors common to Q and F are, in fact, mostly of this sort.

But if Humphreys is wrong about the nature of the copy for F, this does not prevent him from producing what is in many ways an admirable text. Bowers's theory, however improbable, gives, in effect, an editor a very free hand, and thus does not prevent a good editor from producing a good text. Humphreys admits about eighty of F's variants, as against about 280 Q variants which are preferred to F's, 'not counting Q's profanities, colloquialisms, and solecisms, refined away from F but retained here' (p. lxxxiii).

In his edition of *Measure for Measure*, J. W. Lever[1] takes an optimistic view of the text. He argues that 'behind some slapdash work in the printing house, and a number of scribal idiosyncrasies, stands Shakespeare's own rough draft, in reasonably good condition' (p. xxxi). He examines in detail what many editors have found to be discrepancies, and concludes that most of these disappear on closer examination. He finds that 'those remaining seem less serious and extensive than had once been supposed', and that they are in themselves evidence 'that the text had its basis in Shakespeare's own papers' (p. xxiv). Lever's arguments are cogent, though he has to allow for some scribal editing, especially in the consistency of the speech-prefixes (p. xxvii), and he sees the end of IV, iii as having been 'hurriedly and rather carelessly revised' (pp. xxx–xxxi). In keeping with his theory of the copy for F, his text is conservative.

Ernst Leisi's 'Old-Spelling and Old-Meaning' edition of *Measure for Measure*[2] is still more conservative. He tells us that 'the readings of F1 have been left unaltered except in the case of such obvious misprints as shifted or inverted letters. All the other doubtful readings, however unconvincing, have been allowed to stand in the text but are of course discussed in the notes' (p. 12). The argument against such a procedure is that we are deprived of the value of a facsimile without being given that of an edited text.

J. M. Nosworthy considers *Macbeth*, *Troilus and Cressida*, and *The Merry Wives of Windsor*, plays which are usually thought to have been written for some special occasion, together with *Hamlet*, which he also includes in this category.[3] *Hamlet*, he holds, was first acted in both Universities before 1603 and possibly as early as 1600, and was specially commissioned and written so as to provide a play 'which sorted with the particular interests of a cultured and discriminating audience' (pp. 170–1). For evidence, he points to the Q1 title-page, which states that it was, among other places, acted in Cambridge and Oxford; to the number of characters in the play who have been to a university; and to the length of the good texts, Q2 and F, which would have been too long for public performance. He argues that Q2 and F represent two stages, 'presumably the penultimate and the final, in the history of the occasional play' (p. 182), F serving as prompt-copy for the performances at the Universities, while a still further abridged version was prepared, probably by Shakespeare himself, for performance at the Globe. Q1, he argues, is a memorially corrupt text of the version given at the Globe. What emerges from Nosworthy's study of the four plays as a whole is a Shakespeare who revised his own work,

---

[1] *Measure for Measure* (The Arden Shakespeare, 1965).
[2] *Measure for Measure: an Old-Spelling and Old-Meaning Edition* (Heidelberg, 1964).
[3] *Shakespeare's Occasional Plays: Their Origin and Transmission* (Edward Arnold, 1965).

or, in *The Merry Wives*, a lost play by Henry Porter. Not everyone will agree with Nosworthy's conclusions, but his closely argued case merits careful attention.

Most critics agree that Shakespeare had some part in *The Two Noble Kinsmen*. Paul Bertram,[1] however, seeks to demonstrate that he wrote it all. Bertram's arguments are many and ingenious, but the fact remains that there are two distinct styles in the play, which are shown not merely by metrical tests but by a different use of imagery. The double authorship is supported by the attribution of the play to Shakespeare and Fletcher in the entry in the Stationers' Register as well as on the title-page of the first edition (1634).

Kenneth Muir[2] examines the complex problems which an editor of *Othello* has to face. Although he accepts Alice Walker's theory that F is based on a copy of Q imperfectly collated with an authoritative manuscript, he rejects her view that there may be fifty or sixty errors common to the two texts and assumes, on account of the number of variable factors involved, that 'there may be hundreds of common errors—or hardly any' (p. 227). He also rejects the view that the readings of Q are necessarily inferior to those of F, and holds that 'a reasoned and controlled eclecticism should be the basis of a modern text' (p. 239). What he gives us is a valuable analysis of 'some representative divergencies between Q and F', ignoring variants which are unanimously preferred. This analysis shows that F possesses no overwhelming superiority. Muir points out that one of the sources of variation is revision by Shakespeare, but even here the quarto variants include 'Shakespeare's first thoughts which are superior to his second thoughts' (p. 229), though he emphasizes 'that it is not always possible to decide in which category the variants fall—whether they are errors of copyists or of compositors, Shakespeare's second thoughts or Folio sophistications' (p. 237). He concludes by giving a list of all the variants in I, i and finds that, out of a total of 45 variants, 21 Q readings are to be preferred.

G. I. Duthie[3] argues convincingly that Q *Henry V* is a memorially corrupt report of F. His evidence consists of the 'anticipations' and 'recollections' which abound in Q. The actors he suspects are those playing the parts of Exeter, Gower, and the Governor of Harfleur, who appear in the best rendered scenes in Q, though two actors only may have been involved, 'for the small part of the Governor could have been taken by one of the others' (p. 117). He finds 'it difficult to accept the claim that the manuscript "parts" of these actors, or authentic copies of them, were available' (p. 117). While he regards it as possible that 'what the reporters were trying to reconstruct was not F but an abridgement of F', he thinks that 'after the memorial reconstruction had been made, it was itself abridged' (p. 119). All this 'points to the theory that the motive for the reconstruction was to produce a prompt-book for provincial performances of the play' (p. 124). Duthie's essay is a telling rejoinder to those critics who still believe that Q represents an early version of F.

Peter Alexander provides a Preface to a reprint of John S. Smart's *Shakespeare: Truth and Tradition*,[4] where he makes clear the importance of Smart's work, not least in its bearing on the segregation of the 'bad' quartos. Alexander points out that 'as well as placing *The Contention* and *The True Tragedy* in the group of "stolne and surreptitious" pieces described by Pollard

[1] *Shakespeare and The Two Noble Kinsmen* (Rutgers University Press, New Brunswick, 1965).
[2] 'The Text of *Othello*', *Shakespeare Studies*, I (1965), 227–39.
[3] 'The Quarto of Shakespeare's *Henry V*', *Papers: Mainly Shakespearian*, collected by G. I. Duthie (Edinburgh, 1964), 106–130.   [4] *Shakespeare: Truth and Tradition* (Clarendon Press, Oxford, 1966; first pub. 1928).

as the "bad" quartos, Smart added yet another'. This was *The Taming of a Shrew*, which 'had long been regarded as an original work which Shakespeare revised and produced as *The Taming of the Shrew*' (p. xi). Although Smart was not the first to advance these views, his arguments are especially cogent when taken in conjunction with the reasons advanced elsewhere in his book for rejecting the conception of Shakespeare as an illiterate from Stratford who, before he began his career as a dramatist by patching other men's work, had held horses' heads outside the theatre.

Alexander[1] has recently pointed out how Richard Hosley's discussion of the sources and analogues of *the Shrew* helps to demonstrate that it was not based on *a Shrew*.[2] There are two sources mentioned by Hosley. The first, published about 1550, is an anonymous verse tale entitled *Here Begynneth a Merry Jest of a Shrewde and Curste Wyfe, Lapped in Morrelles Skin, for Her Good Behavyour*, where the hero marries the elder of two daughters, her mother's favourite, whom he reduces to peaceful domesticity through brutal treatment. The second is a colloquy by Erasmus published in an English translation in 1557, where the shrewish wife is tamed by gentler means. The existence of these sources does not of course rule out *a Shrew*, but Alexander proceeds to show that there are structural features wherein *a Shrew* differs from *the Shrew*, and that these features can be explained only by supposing that the quarto version was derived from that given in F. He points out that 'in Shakespeare's plot, although there are only two sisters, the Shrew and Bianca...the final scene presents us with three married couples; for Shakespeare means to demonstrate the happy outcome of Petruchio's tact in a wager on wifely obedience that could hardly be represented as a triumph for his discernment in choosing Kate, unless she responds in an unusual way; and this requires there to be at least two very different reactions to enforce the exceptional nature of her response'. Shakespeare, therefore, 'has kept Hortensio the third bridegroom in reserve, employing him meanwhile in his un-married state most economically to demonstrate in his encounter with the Shrew something of her force and temper as well as to help to give substance to the intrigue round Bianca; he is then available, married to the widow, to provide the indispensable third party in the final test'. But, as Alexander observes, all this is hopelessly confused in *a Shrew*, where Polidor, the equivalent of Hortensio, has no need of lessons in 'the taming school', since he and Emilia have already expressed their mutual affection. Alexander is surely right in holding that 'Polidor's visit to "the taming school" is...a tell-tale survival from the original situation as presented in *the Shrew*'.

Charlton Hinman[3] makes a distinction between the New Bibliography, which has been chiefly preoccupied 'with the manuscripts, now of course all lost, which necessarily underlie the first printed editions of the plays', and the 'newer' bibliography which determines 'how much and in what specific ways this copy, whatever its nature, suffered modification during the printing process itself' (p. 25). He believes that Q1 *Richard II* and the first quartos of some other Shakespeare plays were set by formes and not seriatim; and he illustrates from *Richard II* how the casting off of copy made necessary by this procedure might lead a compositor deliberately to alter the text when forced to get more into a given type page than it could

---

[1] *The Times Literary Supplement*, 8 July 1965, p. 588.

[2] 'Sources and Analogues of *The Taming of the Shrew*', *Huntington Library Quarterly*, XXVII (1964), 289–308.

[3] 'Shakespeare's Text—Then, Now and Tomorrow', *Shakespeare Survey 18* (1965), 23–33.

accommodate. He points out that what might appear 'anticipation' on the part of a scribe familiar with the text could arise if a compositor, in setting from cast-off copy, had already read the text some pages ahead. Thus an apparent anticipatory error would in fact be only a recollection.

D. F. McKenzie's history of the Cambridge University Press, 1696–1712,[1] has far-reaching implications which demand the most careful consideration by all who are interested in the application of bibliography to the problems of the Shakespeare text. Its importance consists in the fact that the very full press records of the Cambridge University Press, which include workmen's vouchers for composition, correction, and presswork, provide a unique body of detailed evidence of how a small printing-house was actually run in the seventeenth and eighteenth centuries. What bibliographers faced with a Shakespeare text base their theories on is simply the text itself considered as a physical object. Everything else we know about Elizabethan and Jacobean printing-houses, including the physical 'facts', is based on inferences from these printed texts, apart from a few fragmentary references in contemporary documents and the information to be acquired from printers' manuals, the earliest of which in English is Moxon's *Mechanick Exercises* (1683). Part of the great value of the Cambridge records is that they provide us with information of the kind that bibliographers have hitherto had to infer. These records make it clear at once that many theories based on the method of making inferences about the procedures of a printing-house from the evidence of printed texts considered as physical objects may be at variance with the facts. For example, the assumption that it is possible to judge the division of work among compositors by the width of compositors' measures as shown by the type page is seen to be baseless: 'Analysis of a few volumes suggests that it would be impossible to judge how work was divided on any of the Cambridge books simply from this kind of evidence' (I, 116). Again, as McKenzie has elsewhere remarked, 'one of the more delicate exercises in advanced analytical bibliography is tracing the pattern of skeleton formes in order to determine the order of press work and, it might be claimed, the number of presses used'.[2] But an analysis of the skeleton formes employed, for example, in printing the second edition of Newton's *Principia* (1713) shows that 'the number used and their pattern...have no obvious connection with the pattern of presswork on the book' (I, 126). McKenzie's work makes it plain that, again and again, analytical bibliography could not have produced the right answers to the kind of question which its practitioners are most concerned to ask. His history of the first years of the Cambridge University Press is, in general, a work of scholarship of the highest order which, with its unequalled wealth of information, raises our knowledge of early printing to a new level.

Fredson Bowers ('Today's Shakespeare Texts, and Tomorrow's', *Studies in Bibliography*, XIX, 1966, 39–65) emphasizes the need for an old-spelling edition of Shakespeare, and gives a survey of the many problems involved. He holds that 'the basic all-purpose investigation must be into the specific habits of the compositors who set Shakespeare texts' (p. 59).

Arthur Brown ('The Great Variety of Readers', *Shakespeare Survey 18*, 1965, pp. 11–21) indicates 'the main lines of development in the publication of Shakespeare's plays'.

[1] *The Cambridge University Press, 1696–1712* (2 vols., Cambridge, 1966).

[2] *An Early Printing House at Work: Some Notes for Bibliographers* (Wellington, 1965), p. 9. This essay was given as a lecture at the University of Illinois and the University of California (Los Angeles) in May 1963 (see footnote).

Nevill Coghill ('Two Small Points in *Measure for Measure*', *Review of English Studies*, n.s., XVI, November 1965, 393–5) suggests that the line 'After him, fellows; bring him to the block', IV, iii, 61, is spoken by the Provost, and not, as in F, by the Duke: 'the speech-heading has slipped a line, and this could easily be due either to a compositor's mistake at the turn of the page, or to an imperfect alignment of speech-headings in the copy before him'.

T. H. Howard-Hill ('Ralph Crane's Parentheses', *Notes and Queries*, n.s., XII, September 1965, 334–40) discusses the use of parentheses by the scribe who is thought to have written the manuscripts which served as copy for several F texts. In 'Knight, Crane, and the Copy for the Folio *Winter's Tale*' (*Notes and Queries*, n.s., XIII, April 1966, 139–40) he argues that the evidence from colons in stage-directions supports the view that Crane was responsible for the transcript used as copy for *The Winter's Tale*. He also holds that the unusually large number of parentheses strengthens the case for attributing the copy to Crane.

Charlton Hinman (introduction to *Richard the Second, 1597*, Shakespeare Quarto Facsimiles no. 13, Oxford, 1966) finds that 'except for its initial quire A and its final half-sheet K, the book was set throughout, not by successive pages but by formes' (pp. x–xi). In his introduction to the facsimile of *1 Henry IV* (no. 14 in the same series), he confirms that Q1 was printed directly from Q0 (p. viii). The copy for Q0 may have been 'rather a scribal transcript of foul papers than these papers themselves' (p. ix).

E. A. J. Honigmann ('Spelling Tests and the First Quarto of *King Lear*', *The Library*, 5th ser., XX, December 1965, 310–15) argues from a wider range of tests than those used by Philip Williams 'that Compositor B probably only set Acts I–III'. He points out that spelling analysis should aim at providing the fullest possible information about *all* spellings in a text (p. 310).

Honigmann ('The Text of *Richard III*', *Theatre Research*, VII, nos. 1 and 2, 1965, 48–55) holds that the reliance of editors on F, and prejudice against Q, 'while perhaps sound as a general policy, has gone too far' (p. 48).

MacD. P. Jackson ('*Henry V*, III, vi, 181: an Emendation', *Notes and Queries*, n.s., XIII, April 1966, 133–4) argues that the F line 'And on to morrow bid them march away.' should be repunctuated to read: 'And on to-morrow. Bid them march! Away!'

J. C. Maxwell ('*Love's Labour's Lost*, IV, iii, 313–14', *Notes and Queries*, n.s., XIII, April 1966, 128) suggests that 'Do we not with our selues see learning there?' rather than the Q 'Do we not likewise see our learning there?' should be taken 'as Shakespeare's final version of his first draft, though, since the whole passage was then completely rewritten, it is not a restoration of any great moment'.

M. Mincoff ('The Composition of *Henry VI, Part I*', *Shakespeare Quarterly*, XVI, Autumn 1965, 279–87) finds that 'there are three distinct styles apparent in the play, two of which are fairly clearly Shakespeare's, though of different periods. The third may also be his, but, if so, from a period so early that we have nothing with which to compare it. And the remaining scenes, representing over 1000 lines and well over a third of the play, offer very little foothold for inquiry' (pp. 285–6).

Kenneth Muir ('The Duke's Soliloquies in *Measure for Measure*', *Notes and Queries*, n.s., XIII, April 1966, 135–6) agrees with those critics who hold that IV, i, 60–5 originally formed part of the earlier soliloquy, III, ii, 178–82, and 'were transferred to the later scene to cover up the unheard soliloquy between Isabella and Mariana'. But the Duke must have been given something to say at this point. Muir suggests that the missing lines are to be found in the Duke's soliloquy at the end of Act III, where their relevance is not apparent. They would, however, 'be perfectly appropriate to IV, i, since this is the subject of the unheard conversation between the two women' (p. 136). The change was made because 'the audience may have been puzzled by the identity of the woman who listens to the song at the beginning of IV, i', and the transference of the Duke's soliloquy in IV, i to the end of Act III 'ensured that the audience would be reminded of Mariana's existence immediately before her appearance'.

J. H. P. Pafford ('The Methuen Facsimile, 1910, of the First Folio, 1623', *Notes and Queries*, n.s., XIII, April 1966, 126–7) shows that 'the copy, or at any rate the main copy' used for this facsimile was the First Folio now in the Library of the Guildhall, London, E.C.2.

James O. Wood ('"Finde out Moon-shine, Finde out Moone-shine"', *Notes and Queries*, n.s., XIII, April 1966, 128–30) argues that we should reject Rowe's emendation 'New bent' in *A Midsummer Night's Dream*, I, i, 10 and retain the Q 'Now bent', since what is referred to in I, i, 1–11 is a full rather than a new moon.

© J. K. WALTON 1967

INDEX

Akrigg, G. P. V., 158
Alanus, 26 n.
Alekseev, M. P., 159
Alexander, Peter, 160–1, 175, 176
Alexander, Sir William, 18
Anatol, Constantin, 126
Anderson, John, 111
Anikst, A., 127
Apius and Virginia, 19–20, 24, 120 n.
Archer, William, 77
Arden of Feversham, 130
Aretino, 166
Arghezi, Tudor, 125, 127
Aristotle, 4, 26 n.
   Poetics, 33, 34
Armstrong, E. A., 87
Armstrong, William A., 24 n., 72 n., 73 n., 162
Arthos, John, 156–7
Autran, Paulo, 123

Bacon, Francis, 52, 163
   Advancement of Learning, The, 27, 28, 31
Bailey, Helen Phelps, 164
Baker, Anthony, 163
Baker, Howard, 17, 19, 20, 24 n.
Baldwin, T. W., 21, 25 n., 165
Baldwin, William, 26 n.
Bale, Bishop, 25 n., 162
Băleanu, Andrei, 131 n.
Bandeira, Manuel, 123
Bandello, Matteo, 96, 98, 99, 100, 101, 103
Barber, Charles, 144
Barber, C. L., 153
Barish, Jonas, 155
Barker, H. A., 108, 111 n.
Barrault, Jean-Louis, 121
Barroll, J. Leeds, 148, 162–3
Barthelemy, Nicholas, *Christus Xylonicus*, 25 n.
Barton, John, 134, 135
Batteux, Abbé, 34, 35
Baxter, John S., 152
Beaumont, Francis, 1, 7
   Knight of the Burning Pestle, The, 95, 103 n.
   See also Fletcher, John
Beckerman, Bernard, 170
Beeching, H. C., 172
Belleforest, François de, 98, 103
Bentley, G. E., 81 n., 160
Berlioz, 164
Berman, Ronald, 155, 163
Bernhard, Sarah, 121
Bernheimer, Richard, 167

Berry, Francis, 49 n., 158–9
Berry, Herbert, 168
Bertram, Paul, 175
Bethell, S. L., 73 n.
Bevington, D. M., 23, 26 n.
Biggins, Dennis, 150
Bishop, Sir Henry, 107
Bland, D. S., 164
Blecua, J., 98, 105 n.
Blumenthal, Pinchas, 153
Boaistuau, 96, 98, 99, 100, 101, 103
Boethius, 26 n.
Boileau, Nicolas, 7
Boklund, Gunnar, 148
Bolton, Edmund, 28
Bonjour, Adrien, 154
Botbol, Albert, 130
Bowdler, Henrietta Maria, 163
Bowdler, Thomas, 163
Bowers, Fredson, 173, 174, 177
Bradbrook, M. C., 73 n.
Bradley, A. C., 14, 76, 160
Brazil, Shakespeare in, 121–4
Brecht, Bertolt, 117, 118, 120 n.
Bridges-Adams, 77
Brook, Peter, 130
Brooke, Arthur, 18, 96, 99, 100, 101, 104 n.
   Tragical History of Romeus and Juliet, 97, 98
Brooke, Nicholas, 155
Brooks, Harold, 152
Brown, Arthur, 177
Brown, J. R., 49 n., 73 n., 134, 170
Bruno, Giordano, 167
Bullough, Geoffrey, 104 n., 162, 164–5
Burford, T., 111 n.
Burgess, Anthony, 160
Butler, Francelia, 150, 155

Cain, H. Edward, 82 n.
Calderwood, James L., 153
Căliman, Călin, 131 n.
Cambyses, 18, 19, 24, 25 n.
Camden, William, 28
Campbell, Lily B., 147
Capon, William, 107
Caputi, Anthony, 151
Cardoso, Sergio, 122, 123
Carnovsky, Morris, 73 n.
Carrero, Tonia, 123
Carroll, John, 107
Carson, David L., 151
Cartier, Jacqueline, 130

INDEX

INDEX

INDEX

INDEX

INDEX

INDEX